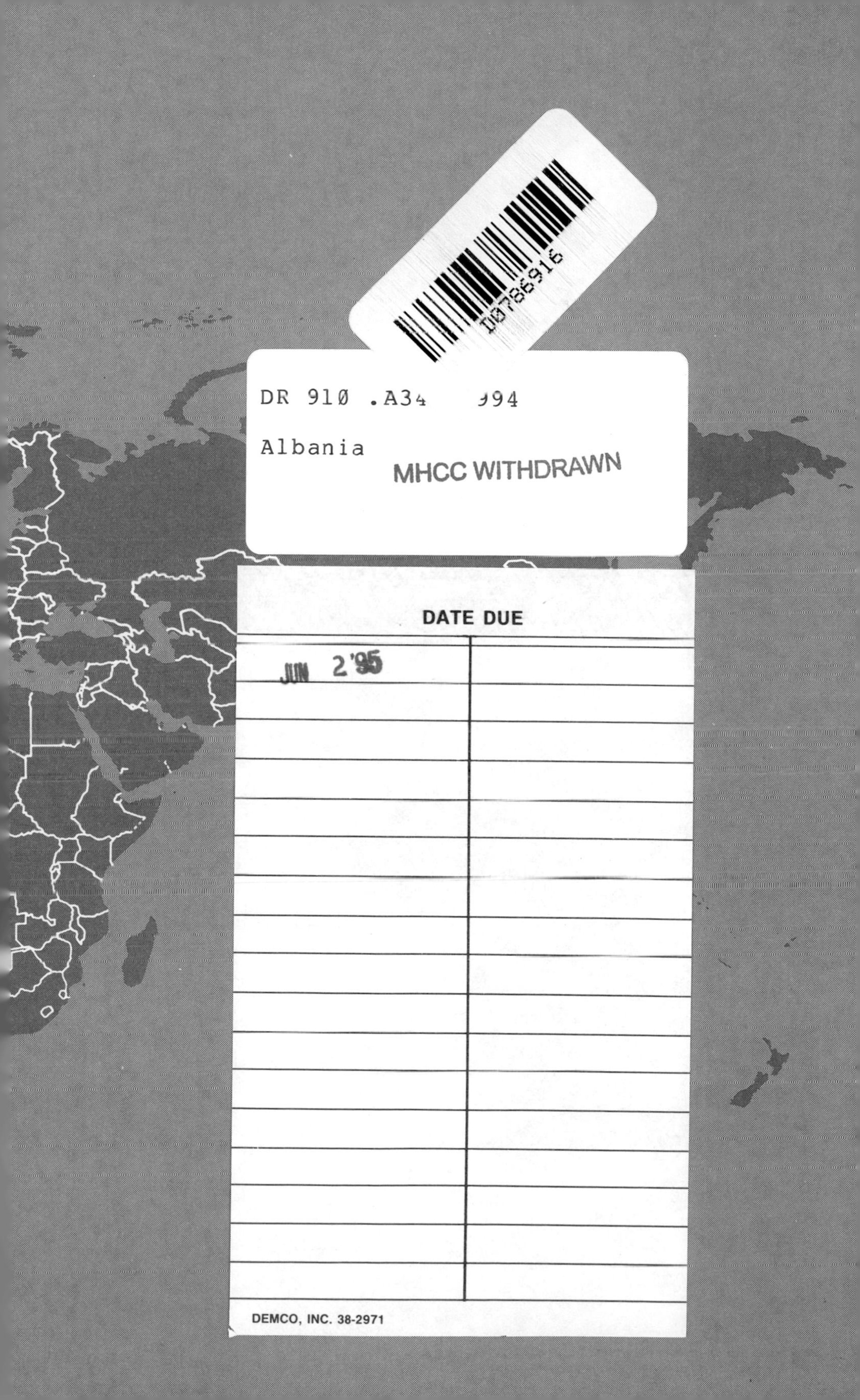

Albania
a country study

Federal Research Division
Library of Congress
Edited by
Raymond Zickel and
Walter R. Iwaskiw
Research Completed
April 1992

On the cover: Clock tower, mosque of Ethem Bey in central Tiranë

Second Edition, First Printing, 1994.

Library of Congress Cataloging-in-Publication Data

Albania : a country study / Federal Research Division, Library of Congress ; edited by Raymond E. Zickel and Walter R. Iwaskiw. — 2nd ed.
p. cm. — (Area handbook series, ISSN 1057-5294) (DA Pam ; 550-98)
"Research completed April 1992."
"Supersedes the 1970 edition of Area handbook for Albania, coauthored by Eugene K. Keefe et al."—T.p. verso.
Includes bibliographical references (pp. 251-262) and index.
ISBN 0-8444-0792-5
1. Albania. I. Zickel, Raymond E., 1934- . II. Iwaskiw, Walter R., 1958- . III. Library of Congress. Federal Research Division. IV. Area handbook for Albania. V. Series. VI. Series: DA Pam ; 550-98.
DR910.A347 1994 93-42885
949.65—dc20 CIP

Headquarters, Department of the Army
DA Pam 550-98

For sale by the Superintendent of Documents, U.S. Government Printing Office
Washington, D.C. 20402

Foreword

This volume is one in a continuing series of books prepared by the Federal Research Division of the Library of Congress under the Country Studies/Area Handbook Program sponsored by the Department of the Army. The last page of this book lists the other published studies.

Most books in the series deal with a particular foreign country, describing and analyzing its political, economic, social, and national security systems and institutions, and examining the interrelationships of those systems and the ways they are shaped by cultural factors. Each study is written by a multidisciplinary team of social scientists. The authors seek to provide a basic understanding of the observed society, striving for a dynamic rather than a static portrayal. Particular attention is devoted to the people who make up the society, their origins, dominant beliefs and values, their common interests and the issues on which they are divided, the nature and extent of their involvement with national institutions, and their attitudes toward each other and toward their social system and political order.

The books represent the analysis of the authors and should not be construed as an expression of an official United States government position, policy, or decision. The authors have sought to adhere to accepted standards of scholarly objectivity. Corrections, additions, and suggestions for changes from readers will be welcomed for use in future editions.

Louis R. Mortimer
Chief
Federal Research Division
Library of Congress
Washington, D.C. 20540

Acknowledgments

The authors acknowledge the numerous individuals who contributed to the preparation of this edition of *Albania: A Country Study*. The work of Eugene K. Keefe, Sarah J. Elpern, William Giloane, James M. Moore, Jr., Stephen Peters, and Eston T. White, the co-authors of the previous edition who completed their research in 1970, is greatly appreciated as both substantive and useful. Special thanks go to Charles Sudetic for expending his time and energy to take the many interesting photographs from which those in the book were selected.

The authors also gratefully acknowledge Ralph K. Benesch for his oversight of the Country Studies—Area Handbook Program for the Department of the Army and Sandra W. Meditz of the Federal Research Division for her guidance and suggestions. Special thanks also go to the following individuals: Marilyn L. Majeska for reviewing editing and managing production; Andrea T. Merrill for editorial assistance; Teresa E. Kamp for cover and chapter illustrations; David P. Cabitto for graphics and map support; Harriet R. Blood, together with the firm of Greenhorne and O'Mara, for preparation of the maps; Pirkko M. Johnes for researching and writing the Country Profile; and Helen Fedor for preparing photograph captions.

Special thanks are also owed to Evan A. Raynes and Vincent Ercolano, who edited the chapters, and to Barbara Edgerton and Izella Watson, who did the word processing. Catherine Schwartzstein performed the final prepublication editorial review. Joan C. Cook compiled the index, and Linda Peterson of the Library of Congress Printing and Processing Section prepared the camera-ready copy, under the supervision of Peggy Pixley.

Contents

List of Figures

Preface

Preparation of this edition of *Albania: A Country Study* began as popular revolutions were drastically altering the political and economic systems of the communist countries of Eastern Europe. In Albania extreme isolation and Stalinist policies slowed, but could not stop, the revolution that striking workers and irate citizens directed against the regime. In early 1992, the Albanian people forced the communist government's fall, ushering in a long-term transition from totalitarianism toward democracy and from a centralized command economy to one based on a private market.

The uncertainty of both the process and the outcome of the transition make descriptions of the changing structures of government, economy, and society somewhat tentative in nature. The authors have attempted to describe the existing, but possibly transitional structures, using scholarly materials, which even from Western sources are very limited. Such descriptions can form a sound basis for readers to understand the ongoing events and assess change in Albania. The most useful sources are cited by the authors at the end of each chapter. Full references to these and other sources are listed in the Bibliography. A Country Profile and a Chronology are also included in the book as reference aids.

Transliteration of Albanian personal names and terms generally follows the Library of Congress transliteration system. Transliteration of place-names, however, follows the system developed by the United States Board on Geographic Names. In the ecclesiastical context, preference is given to the generic term *Orthodox,* rather than *Eastern Orthodox*. The term *Greek Orthodox* (like *Serbian Orthodox* or *Albanian Orthodox)* is used to designate ethnic affiliation, not historical background. Measurements are given in the metric system; a conversion table is provided to assist readers unfamiliar with that system (see table 1, Appendix).

The body of the text reflects information available as of April 1992. Certain other portions of the text, however, have been updated: the Introduction discusses significant events that have occurred since the information cutoff date; the Chronology and the Country Profile include updated information as available; and the Bibliography lists recently published sources thought to be particularly helpful to the reader.

Table A. Chronology of Important Events

Period	Description
ca.1000 B.C.	Illyrians, descendants of ancient Indo-European peoples, settle in western part of the Balkan Peninsula.
358 B.C.	Illyrians defeated by Philip II of Macedonia.
312 B.C.	King Glaucius of Illyria expels Greeks from Durrës.
229 B.C. and 219 B.C.	Roman soldiers overrun Illyrian settlements in Neretva River valley.
165 B.C.	Roman forces capture Illyria's King Gentius at Shkodër.
FIRST CENTURY A.D.	Christianity comes to Illyrian populated areas.
A.D. 9	Romans, under Emperor Tiberius, subjugate Illyrians and divide present-day Albania between Dalmatia, Epirus, and Macedonia.
A.D. 395	Roman Empire's division into eastern and western parts leaves the lands that now comprise Albania administratively under the Eastern Empire but ecclesiastically under Rome.
FOURTH CENTURY–SEVENTH CENTURY	Goths, Huns, Avars, Serbs, Croats, and Bulgars successively invade Illyrian lands in present-day Albania.
732	Illyrian people subordinated to the patriarchate of Constantinople by the Byzantine emperor, Leo the Isaurian.
1054	Christianity divides into Catholic and Orthodox churches, leaving Christians in southern Albania under ecumenical patriarch of Constantinople and those in northern Albania under pope in Rome.
1081	Albania and Albanians mentioned, for the first time in a historical record, by Byzantine emperor.
TWELFTH CENTURY	Serbs occupy parts of northern and eastern Albania.
1204	Venice wins control over most of Albania, but Byzantines regain control of southern portion and establish Despotate of Epirus.
1272	Forces of the King of Naples occupy Durrës and establish an Albanian kingdom.
1385	Albanian ruler of Durrës invites Ottoman forces to intervene against a rival; subsequently, Albanian clans pay tribute and swear fealty to Ottomans.

Table A.—Continued

Period	Description
1389	At Kosovo Polje, Albanians join Serbian-led Balkan army that is crushed by Ottoman forces; coordinated resistance to Ottoman westward progress evaporates.
1403	Gjergj Kastrioti born, later becomes Albanian national hero known as Skanderbeg.
1443	After losing a battle near Nis, Skanderbeg defects from Ottoman Empire, reembraces Roman Catholicism, and begins holy war against the Ottomans.
1444	Skanderbeg proclaimed chief of Albanian resistance.
1449	Albanians, under Skanderbeg, rout Ottoman forces under Sultan Murad II.
1468	Skanderbeg dies.
1478	Krujë falls to Ottoman Turks; Shkodër falls a year later. Subsequently, many Albanians flee to southern Italy, Greece, Egypt, and elsewhere; many remaining are forced to convert to Islam.
EARLY SEVENTEENTH CENTURY	Some Albanians who convert to Islam find careers in Ottoman Empire's government and military service.
SEVENTEENTH CENTURY-EIGHTEENTH CENTURY	About two-thirds of Albanians convert to Islam.
1785	Kara Mahmud Bushati, chief of Albanian tribe based in Shkodër, attacks Montenegrin territory; subsequently named governor of Shkodër by Ottoman authorities.
NINETEENTH AND TWENTIETH CENTURIES	
1822	Albanian leader Ali Pasha of Tepelenë assassinated by Ottoman agents for promoting an autonomous state.
1830	1,000 Albanian leaders invited to meet with Ottoman general who kills about half of them.
1835	Ottoman Sublime Porte divides Albanian-populated lands into *vilayets* of Janina and Rumelia with Ottoman administrators.
1861	First school known to use Albanian language in modern times opens in Shkodër.

Table A.—Continued

Period		Description
1877–78		Russia's defeat of Ottoman Empire seriously weakens Ottoman power over Albanian-populated areas.
1878		Treaty of San Stefano, signed after the Russo-Turkish War, assigned Albanian-populated lands to Bulgaria, Montenegro, and Serbia; but Austria-Hungary and Britain block the treaty's implementation. Albanian leaders meet in Prizren, Kosovo, to form the Prizren League, initially advocating a unified Albania under Ottoman suzerainty. Congress of Berlin overturns the Treaty of San Stefano but places some Albanian lands under Montenegrin and Serbian rule. The Prizren League begins to organize resistance to the Treaty of Berlin's provisions that affect Albanians.
1879		Society for Printing of Albanian Writings, composed of Roman Catholic, Muslim, and Orthodox Albanians, founded in Constantinople.
1881		Ottoman forces crush Albanian resistance fighters at Prizren. Prizren League's leaders and families arrested and deported.
1897		Ottoman authorities disband a reactivated Prizren League, execute its leader later, then ban Albanian language books.
1906		Albanians begin joining the Committee of Union and Progress (Young Turks), which formed in Constantinople, hoping to gain autonomy for their nation within the Ottoman Empire.
1908		Albanian intellectuals meet in Bitola and choose the Latin alphabet as standard script rather than Arabic or Cyrillic.
1912	May	Albanians rise against the Ottoman authorities and seize Skopje.
	October	First Balkan War begins, and Albanian leaders affirm Albania as an independent state.
	November	Muslim and Christian delegates at Vlorë declare Albania independent and establish a provisional government.
	December	Ambassadorial conference opens in London and discusses Albania's fate.
1913	May	Treaty of London ends First Balkan War. Second Balkan War begins.

Table A.—Continued

Period		Description
	August	Treaty of Bucharest ends Second Balkan War. Great Powers recognize an independent Albanian state ruled by a constitutional monarchy.
1914	March	Prince Wilhelm, German army captain, installed as head of the new Albanian state by the International Control Commission, arrives in Albania.
	September	New Albanian state collapses following outbreak of World War I; Prince Wilhelm is stripped of authority and departs from Albania.
1918	November	World War I ends, with Italian army occupying most of Albania and Serbian, Greek, and French force occupying remainder. Italian and Yugoslav powers begin struggle for dominance over Albanians.
	December	Albanian leaders meet at Durrës to discuss presentation of Albania's interests at the Paris Peace Conference.
1919	January	Serbs attack Albania's inhabited cities. Albanians adopt guerrilla warfare.
	June	Albania denied official representation at the Paris Peace Conference; British, French, and Greek negotiators later decide to divide Albania among Greece, Italy, and Yugoslavia.
1920	January	Albanian leaders meeting at Lushnjë reject the partitioning of Albania by the Treaty of Paris, warn that Albanians will take up arms in defense of their territory, and create a bicameral parliament.
	February	Albanian government moves to Tiranë, which becomes the capital.
	September	Albania forces Italy to withdraw its troops and abandon territorial claims to almost all Albanian territory.
	December	Albania admitted to League of Nations as sovereign and independent state.
1921	November	Yugoslav troops invade Albanian territories they had not previously occupied; League of Nations commission forces Yugoslav withdrawal and reaffirms Albania's 1913 borders.
	December	Popular Party, headed by Xhafer Ypi, forms government with Ahmed Zogu, the future King Zog, as internal affairs minister.
1922	August	Ecumenical patriarch in Constantinople recognizes the Autocephalous Albanian Orthodox Church.

Table A.—Continued

Period		Description
	September	Zogu assumes position of prime minister of government; opposition to him becomes formidable.
1923		Albania's Sunni Muslims break last ties with Constantinople and pledge primary allegiance to native country.
1924	March	Zogu's party wins elections for National Assembly, but Zogu steps down after financial scandal and an assassination attempt.
	July	A peasant-backed insurgency wins control of Tiranë; Fan S. Noli becomes prime minister; Zogu flees to Yugoslavia.
	December	Zogu, backed by Yugoslav army, returns to power and begins to smother parliamentary democracy; Noli flees to Italy.
1925	May	Italy, under Mussolini, begins penetration of Albanian public and economic life.
1926	November	Italy and Albania sign First Treaty of Tiranë, which guarantees Zogu's political position and Albania's boundaries.
1928	August	Zogu pressures the parliament to dissolve itself; a new constituent assembly declares Albania a kingdom and Zogu becomes Zog I, "King of the Albanians."
1931		Zog, standing up to Italians, refuses to renew the First Treaty of Tiranë; Italians continue political and economic pressure.
1934		After Albania signs trade agreements with Greece and Yugoslavia, Italy suspends economic support, then attempts to threaten Albania.
1935		Mussolini presents a gift of 3,000,000 gold francs to Albania; other economic aid follows.
1939	April	Mussolini's troops invade and occupy Albania; Albanian parliament votes to unite country with Italy; Zog flees to Greece; Italy's King Victor Emmanual III assumes Albanian crown.
1940	October	Italian army attacks Greece through Albania.
1941	April	Germany, with support of Italy and other allies defeat Greece and Yugoslavia.

Table A.—Continued

Period		Description
	October	Josip Broz Tito, Yugoslav communist leader, directs organizing of Albanian communists.
	November	Albanian Communist Party founded; Enver Hoxha becomes first secretary.
1942	September	Communist party organizes the National Liberation Movement, a popular front resistance organization.
	October	Noncommunist nationalist groups form to resist the Italian occupation.
1943	August	Italy's surrender to Allied forces weakens Italian hold on Albania; Albanian resistance fighters overwhelm five Italian divisions.
	September	German forces invade and occupy Albania.
1944	January	Communist partisans, supplied with British weapons, gain control of southern Albania.
	May	Communists meet to organize an Albanian government; Hoxha becomes chairman of executive committee and supreme commander of the Army of National Liberation.
	July	Communist forces enter central and northern Albania.
	October	Communists establish provisional government with Hoxha as prime minister.
	November	Germans withdraw from Tiranë, communists move into the capital.
	December	Communist provisional government adopts laws allowing state regulation of commercial enterprises, foreign and domestic trade.
1945	January	Communist provisional government agrees to restore Kosovo to Yugoslavia as an autonomous region; tribunals begin to condemn thousands of "war criminals" and "enemies of the people" to death or to prison. Communist regime begins to nationalize industry, transportation, forests, pastures.
	April	Yugoslavia recognizes communist government in Albania.
	August	Sweeping agricultural reforms begin; about half of arable land eventually redistributed to peasants from large landowners; most church properties nationalized. United Nations Relief and Rehabilitation Administration begins sending supplies to Albania.

Table A.—Continued

Period		Description
	November	Soviet Union recognizes provisional government; Britain and United States make full diplomatic recognition conditional.
	December	In elections for the People's Assembly only candidates from the Democratic Front are on ballot.
1946	January	People's Assembly proclaims Albania a "people's republic"; purges of noncommunists from positions of power in government begin.
	Spring	People's Assembly adopts new constitution, Hoxha becomes prime minister, foreign minister, defense minister, and commander in chief; Soviet-style central planning begins.
	July	Treaty of friendship and cooperation signed with Yugoslavia; Yugoslav advisers and grain begin pouring into Albania.
	October	British destroyers hit mines off Albania's coast; United Nations (UN) and the International Court of Justice subsequently condemn Albania.
	November	Albania breaks diplomatic relations with the United States after latter withdraws its informal mission.
1947	April	Economic Planning Commission draws up first economic plan that establishes production targets for mining, manufacturing and agricultural enterprises.
	May	UN commission concludes that Albania, together with Bulgaria and Yugoslavia, supports communist guerrillas in Greece; Yugoslav leaders launch verbal offensive against anti-Yugoslav Albanian communists, including Hoxha; pro-Yugoslav faction begins to wield power.
	July	Albania refuses participation in the Marshall Plan of the United States.
1948	February–March	Albanian Communist Party leaders vote to merge Albanian and Yugoslav economies and militaries.
	June	Cominform expels Yugoslavia; Albanian leaders launch anti-Yugoslav propaganda campaign, cut economic ties, and force Yugoslav advisers to leave; Stalin becomes national hero in Albania.
	September	Hoxha begins purging high-ranking party members accused of "Titoism"; treaty of friendship with Yugoslavia abrogated by Albania; Soviet Union begins giving economic aid to Albania and Soviet advisers replace ousted Yugoslavs.

Table A.—Continued

Period		Description
	November	First Party Congress changes name of Albanian Communist Party to Albanian Party of Labor.
1949	January	Regime issues *Decree on Religious Communities.*
	February	Albania joins Council for Mutual Economic Assistance (Comecon); all foreign trade conducted with member countries.
	December	Pro-Tito Albanian communists purged.
1950		Britain and United States begin inserting anticommunist Albanian guerrilla units into Albania; all are unsuccessful.
	July	A new constitution is approved by People's Assembly. Hoxha becomes minister of defense and foreign minister.
1951	February	Albania and Soviet Union sign agreement on mutual economic assistance.
1954	July	Hoxha relinquishes post of prime minister to Mehmet Shehu but retains primary power as party leader.
1955	May	Albania becomes a founding member of the Warsaw Pact.
1956	February	After Nikita Khrushchev's "secret speech" exposes Stalin's crimes, Hoxha defends Stalin; close relations with Soviet Union become strained.
1959		Large amounts of economic aid from Soviet Union, East European countries, and China begin pouring into Albania.
	May	Khrushchev visits Albania.
1960	June	Albania sides with China in Sino-Soviet ideological dispute; consequently, Soviet economic support to Albania is curtailed and Chinese aid is increased.
	November	Hoxha rails against Khrushchev and supports China during an international communist conference in Moscow.
1961	February	Hoxha harangues against the Soviet Union and Yugoslavia at Albania's Fourth Party Congress.
	December	Soviet Union breaks diplomatic relations; other East European countries severely reduce contacts but do not break relations; Albania looks toward China for support.

Table A.—Continued

Period		Description
1962		Albanian regime introduces austerity program in attempt to compensate for withdrawal of Soviet economic support; China incapable of delivering sufficient aid; Albania becomes China's spokesman at UN.
1964		Hoxha hails Khrushchev's removal as leader of the Soviet Union; diplomatic relations fail to improve.
1966	February	Hoxha initiates Cultural and Ideological Revolution.
	March	Albanian Party of Labor "open letter" to the people establishes egalitarian wage and job structure for all workers.
1967		Hoxha regime conducts violent campaign to extinguish religious life in Albania; by year's end over two thousand religious buildings were closed or converted to other uses.
1968	August	Albania condemns Soviet-led invasion of Czechoslovakia; subsequently, Albania withdraws from Warsaw Pact.
1976	September	Hoxha begins criticizing new Chinese regime after Mao's death.
	December	A new constitution promulgated superceeding the 1950 version; Albania becomes a people's socialist republic.
1977		Top military officials purged after "Chinese conspiracy" is uncovered.
1978	July	China terminates all economic and military aid to Albania.
1980		Hoxha selects Ramiz Alia as the next party head, bypassing Shehu.
1981	December	Shehu, after rebuke by Politburo, dies, possibly murdered on Hoxha's orders.
1982	November	Alia becomes chairman of Presidium of the People's Assembly.
1983		Hoxha begins semiretirement; Alia starts administering Albania.
1985	April	Hoxha dies.
1986	November	Alia featured as party's and country's undisputed leader at Ninth Party Congress.
1987	August	Greece ends state of war that existed since World War II.

Table A.—Continued

Period		Description
	November	Albania and Greece sign a series of long-term agreements.
1989	September	Alia, addressing the Eighth Plenum of the Central Committee, signals that radical changes to the economic system are necessary.
1990	January	Ninth Plenum of the Central Committee; demonstrations at Shkodër force authorities to declare state of emergency.
	April	Alia declares willingness to establish diplomatic relations with the Soviet Union and the United States.
	May	The Secretary General of the UN visits Albania.
	May	Regime announces desire to join the Conference on Security and Cooperation in Europe. People's Assembly passes laws liberalizing criminal code, reforming court system, lifting some restrictions on freedom of worship, and guaranteeing the right to travel abroad.
	Summer	Unemployment throughout the economy increases as a result of government's reform measures; drought reduces electric-power production, forcing plant shutdowns.
	July	Young people demonstrate against regime in Tiranë, and 5,000 citizens seek refuge in foreign embassies; Central Committee plenum makes significant changes in leadership of party and state. Soviet Union and Albania sign protocol normalizing relations.
	August	Government abandons its monopoly on foreign commerce and begins to open Albania to foreign trade.
	September	Alia addresses the UN General Assembly in New York.
	October	Tiranë hosts the Balkan Foreign Ministers' Conference, the first international political meeting in Albania since the end of World War II. Ismail Kadare, Albania's most prominent writer, defects to France.
	December	University students demonstrate in streets and call for dictatorship to end; Alia meets with students; Thirteenth Plenum of the Central Committee of the APL authorizes a multiparty system; Albanian Democratic Party, first opposition party established; regime authorizes political pluralism; draft constitution is published; by year's end, 5,000 Albanian refugees had crossed the mountains into Greece.

Table A.—Continued

Period		Description
1991	January	First opposition newspaper *Rilindja Demokratike* begins publishing. Thousands of Albanians seek refuge in Greece.
	March	Albania and the United States reestablish diplomatic relations after a thirty-five-year break. Thousands more Albanians attempt to gain asylum in Italy.
	March–April	First multiparty elections held since the 1920s; 98.9 percent of voters participate; Albanian Party of Labor wins over 67 percent of vote for People's Assembly seats; Albanian Democratic Party wins about 30 percent.
	April	Communist-dominated People's Assembly reelects Alia to new presidential term. Ministry of Internal Affairs replaced by Ministry of Public Order; Frontier Guards and Directorate of Prison Administration are placed under the Ministry of Defense and the Ministry of Justice, respectively. People's Assembly passes Law on Major Constitutional Provisions providing for fundamental human rights and separation of powers and invalidates 1976 constitution. People's Assembly appoints commission to draft new constitution.
	June	Prime Minister Nano and rest of cabinet resign after trade unions call for general strike to protest worsening economic conditions and killing of opposition demonstrators in Shkodër. Coalition government led by Prime Minister Ylli Bufi takes office; Tenth Party Congress of the Albanian Party of Labor meets and renames party the Socialist Party of Albania (SPA); Albania accepted as a full member of CSCE; United States secretary of state, James A. Baker, visits Albania.
	July	Sigurimi, notorious secret police, is abolished and replaced by National Information Service.
	August	Up to 18,000 Albanians cross the Adriatic Sea to seek asylum in Italy; most are returned. People's Assembly passes law on economic activity that authorizes private ownership of property, privatizing of state property, investment by foreigners, and private employment of workers.
	October	United States Embassy opens in Tiranë. Albania joins International Monetary Fund.
	December	Coalition government dissolves when opposition parties accuse communists of blocking reform and Albanian Democratic Party withdraws its ministers from the cabinet. Prime Minister Bufi resigns and Alia names Vilson Ahmeti as prime minister. Alia sets March 1992 for new elections.

Table A.—Continued

Period		Description
1992	February	Albanian People's Assembly prevents OMONIA, the party representing Greek Albanians, from fielding candidates in the elections planned for March.
	March	Albanian Democratic Party scores decisive election victory over the Socialist Party of Albania in the midst of economic freefall and social chaos.
	April	Sali Berisha, a leader of the Albanian Democratic Party, elected president.
	June	Albania signs Black Sea economic cooperation pact with ten other countries, including six former Soviet republics.
	July	Socialist Party of Albania gains significantly in nationwide local elections.
	September	Former President Alia and eighteen other former communist officials, including Nexhmije Hoxha, arrested and charged with corruption and other offenses.
	December	Albania joins the Organization of the Islamic Conference.
1993	March	Secretary General of the North Atlantic Treaty Organization (NATO) visits Tiranë.
	April	Albania recognizes the former Yugoslav Republic of Macedonia.
	May	President Berisha urges NATO to intervene militarily in Kosovo.
	July	Fatos Nano, chairman of the Socialist Party of Albania and former prime minister, arrested and charged with corruption.
	September	President Berisha and President Momir Bulatovic of Montenegro meet in Tiranë to discuss ways of improving Albanian-Montenegrin relations.
		Socialist Party of Albania loses many votes to Albanian Democratic Party in local elections in Dibrë district.
	October	Greece recalls its ambassador for consultations after series of border incidents and alleged human rights abuses in Albania.
	November	Israel's foreign minister makes first official visit to Tiranë.

Country Profile

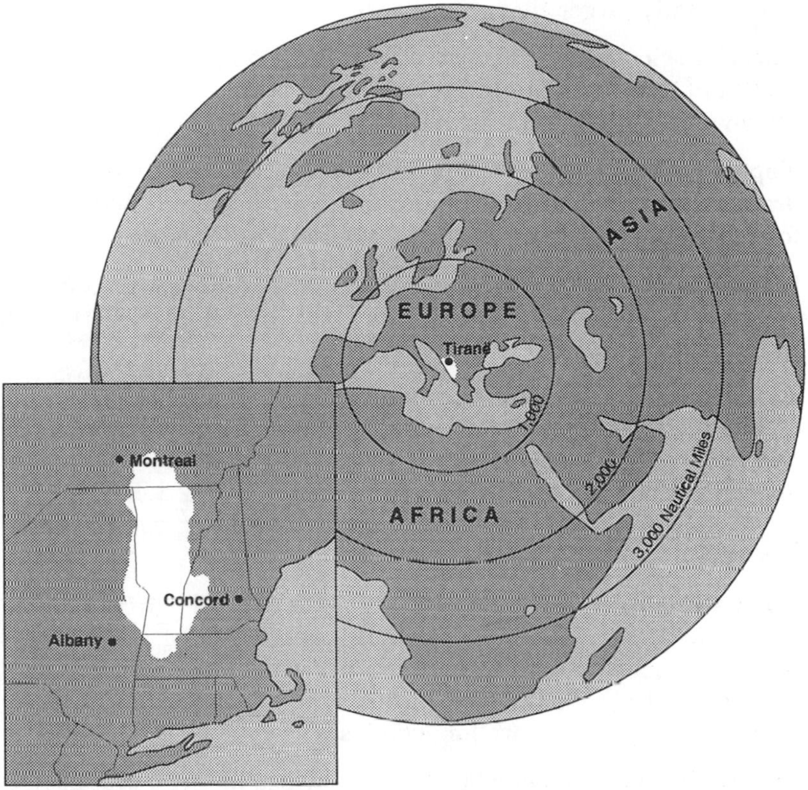

Country

Formal Name: Republic of Albania.

Short Form: Albania.

Term for Citizens: Albanian(s).

Capital: Tiranë.

Date of Independence: November 28, 1912, national holiday celebrated as Liberation Day.

NOTE—The Country Profile contains updated information as available.

Geography

Size: 28,750 square kilometers (land area 27,400 square kilometers); slightly larger than Maryland.

Location: Southeastern coast of Adriatic Sea and eastern part of Strait of Otranto, opposite heel of Italian boot; between approximately 40° and 43° north latitude.

Topography: A little over 20 percent coastal plain, some of it poorly drained. Mostly hills and mountains, often covered with scrub forest. Only navigable river is the Bunë.

Climate: Mild temperate; cool, cloudy, wet winters with January low of 5°C; hot, clear, dry summers with July high of 28°C; interior cooler and wetter.

Boundaries: Land boundaries total 720 kilometers; borders with Greece 282 kilometers; border with former Yugoslav Republic of Macedonia 151 kilometers; border with Serbia 114 kilometers; border with Montengro 173 kilometers; coastline 362 kilometers.

Society

Population: 3,335,000 (July 1991), growth rate 1.8 percent (1991). Birth rate 24 per 1,000 population, death rate 5 per 1,000 population. Total fertility rate 2.9 children per woman. Infant mortality rate 50 deaths per 1,000 live births. Life expectancy at birth 72 years for males, 79 years for females.

Ethnic Groups: Albanian 90 percent, divided into two groups: the Gegs to the north of the Shkumbin River and the Tosks to the south. Greeks probably 8 percent, others (mostly Vlachs, Gypsies, Serbs and Bulgarians) about 2 percent.

Languages: Albanian (Tosk official dialect, Geg also much-used variant), Greek.

Religion: In 1992, estimated 70 percent of people Muslim, 20 percent Orthodox, and 10 percent Roman Catholic. In 1967 all mosques and churches closed and religious observances prohibited; in December 1990, ban on religious observance lifted.

Education: Free at all levels. Eight-grade primary and intermediate levels compulsory beginning at age six. Literacy rate raised from about 20 percent in 1945 to estimated 75 percent in recent years. In 1990, primary school attended by 96 percent of all school-age children, and secondary school by 70 percent. School operations seriously disrupted by breakdown of public order in 1991.

Health and Welfare: All medical services free. Six months of maternity leave at approximately 85 percent salary; noncontributory state social insurance system for all workers, with 70–100 percent of salary during sick leave. Pension about 70 percent of average salary. Retirement age 50–60 for men, 45–55 for women. In early 1990s, health and welfare system adversely affected by economic and social disintegration.

Economy

Salient Features: Until 1991, centrally planned Stalinist economy. Economic reforms crippled by economic and social disintegration in early 1990s. In 1992, new Democratic government announced "shock therapy" program to establish a market economy.

Gross Domestic Product (GDP): L16,234 million in 1990, US$450 per capita, drop of 13.1 percent from previous year; preliminary figures indicated 30 percent drop for 1991.

Gross National Product (GNP): Estimated at US$4.1 billion in 1990; per capita income estimated in range US$600–US$1,250; real growth rate not available.

Government Budget: Revenues US$2.3 billion; expenditures US$2.3 billion (1989). Note: Albania perennially ran substantial trade deficit; government tied imports to exports, so deficit seems to have been greatly reduced if not eliminated.

Labor Force: 1,567,000 (1990); agriculture about 52 percent, industry 22.9 percent (1987). Females made up 48.1 percent of labor force in 1990.

Agriculture: Arable land per capita lowest in Europe. Self-sufficiency in grain production achieved in 1976, according to government figures. A wide variety of temperate-zone crops and livestock raised. Up to 1990, Albania largely self-sufficient in food; thereafter drought and political breakdown necessitated foreign food aid.

Land Use: Arable land 21 percent; permanent crops 4 percent; meadows and pastures 15 percent; forest and woodland 38 percent; other 22 percent.

Industry: Main industries in early 1990s: food products, energy and petroleum, mining and basic metals, textiles and clothing, lumber, cement, engineering, and chemicals.

Natural Resources: Chromium, coal, copper, natural gas, nickel, oil, timber.

Imports: US$255 million (1987 estimate). Major commodities: machinery, machine tools, iron and steel products, textiles, chemicals, and pharmaceuticals.

Exports: US$378 million (1987 estimate). Major commodities: asphalt, bitumen, petroleum products, metals and metallic ores, electricity, oil, vegetables, fruits, tobacco.

Trading Partners: Italy, Yugoslavia, Germany, Greece, East European countries, and China.

Economic aid: In fiscal year 1991, United States government provided US$2.4 million; the European Community (EC) pledged US$9.1 million; and Italy provided US$196 million for emergency food aid, industrial inputs, and education system. In July 1991, EC enrolled Albania in its program for technical assistance to former communist countries.

Currency: Lek (pl., leke); exchange rate in March 1993 L109.62 per US$1.

Fiscal year: calendar year.

Transportation and Communications

Roads: Between 16,000 and 21,000 kilometers of road network suitable for motor traffic; 6,700 kilometers of main roads. In the mountainous north, communications still mostly by pack ponies or donkeys. Private cars not permitted until second half of 1990; bicycles and mules widely used.

Railroads: Total of 543 kilometers, all single track, 509 kilometers in 1.435-meter standard gauge; thirty-four kilometers in narrow gauge. Work on Yugoslav section of fifty-kilometer line between Shkodër and Titograd completed in late 1985; line opened to freight traffic in September 1986.

Aviation: Scheduled flights from Rinas Airport, twenty-eight kilometers from Tiranë to many major European cities. No regular internal air service.

Shipping: In 1986 Albania had twenty merchant ships, with total displacement of about 56,000 gross tons. Main ports: Durrës, Vlorë, Sarandë and Shëngjin. Completion of the new port near Vlorë by early 1990s will allow cargo-handling capacity of 4 million tons per year.

Politics and Government

Political Parties: Albanian Party of Labor (APL), the communist party, became Socialist Party of Albania in 1991. Other parties allowed to form December 1990, including Albanian Democratic Party, Republican Party, Ecology Party, OMONIA (Unity—Greek minority party).

Government: Until April 1991, single-chamber People's Assembly with 250 deputies met only few days each year; decisions made by Presidium of the People's Assembly, whose president head of state, and Council of Ministers; from April 1991, interim constitution provided for president who could not hold other offices concurrently; People's Assembly with at least 140 members legislative organ; Council of Ministers top executive organ.

Ministries: As of August 1993: agriculture; construction, housing, and land; culture, youth, and sports; defense; economy and finance; education; foreign affairs; health, and environment; industry, mining, and energy; justice; labor, emigration, social assistance, and political prisoners; public order; tourism; trade and foreign economic relations; and transport and communications.

Administrative Divisions: Country divided into twenty-six districts, each under People's Council elected every three years.

Judicial System: Supreme Court, elected by People's Assembly, also district and regional courts.

Flag: Black, two-headed eagle centered on red field.

National Security

Armed Forces: In 1991 People's Army included ground forces, air and air defense forces, and naval forces and comprised about 48,000 active-duty and 155,000 reserve personnel.

Ground Forces: Numbered about 35,000, including 20,000 conscripts. Organized along Soviet lines into four infantry brigades, one tank brigade, three artillery regiments, and six coastal artillery battalions. Tanks numbered about 190 and were old, Soviet-type T-34 and T-54s. Artillery mixture of outdated Soviet and Chinese origin equipment and consisted of towed artillery, mortars, multiple rocket launchers, and antitank guns. Infantry brigades operated 130 armored personnel carriers.

Air and Air Defense Forces: About 11,000 members, majority of whose officers assigned to air defense units, which also had about

1,400 conscripts assigned. Combat aircraft, supplied by China in the 1960s and early 1990s, numbered less than 100. Air Forces organized into three squadrons of fighter-bombers, three squadrons of fighters, two squadrons of transports, and two squadrons of unarmed helicopters. Air Defense Forces manned about twenty-two Soviet-made SA-2s at four sites.

Naval Forces: About 2,000 members, of which 1,000 conscripts, organized into two coastal defense brigades. Thirty-seven patrol and coastal combatants, most of which torpedo craft of Chinese origin. Two Soviet-made Whiskey-class submarines. One mine-warfare craft of Soviet origin.

Defense Budget: In 1991 about L1 billion or about 5 percent of gross national product and 10 percent of total government spending.

Internal Security Forces: In 1989 about 5,000 uniformed internal security troops, organized into five regiments of mechanized infantry, and another 5,000 plain-clothed officers. In July 1991 reorganized by People's Assembly.

Frontier Guards: About 7,000 members organized into several battalion-sized units.

Introduction

ALBANIA, PROCLAIMED A "PEOPLE'S REPUBLIC" in 1946, was for more than forty years one of the most obscure and reclusive countries in the world. A totalitarian communist regime, led by party founder and first secretary Enver Hoxha from 1944 until his death in 1985, maintained strict control over every facet of the country's internal affairs, while implementing a staunchly idiosyncratic foreign policy. After World War II, Hoxha and his protégés imposed a Stalinist economic system, and turned alternately to Yugoslavia, the Soviet Union, and China for assistance, before denouncing each of these communist countries as "bourgeois" or "revisionist" and embarking on a course of economic self-reliance. Notwithstanding some notable accomplishments in education, health care, and other areas, Hoxha's policies of centralization, isolation, and repression stifled and demoralized the population, hindered economic development, and relegated Albania to a position of technological backwardness unparalleled in Europe.

Ramiz Alia, Hoxha's handpicked successor, introduced a modicum of pragmatism to policy making, but his ambiguous stance toward reform did little to ameliorate a growing social and economic crisis. Like President Mikhail S. Gorbachev's policy of *perestroika* in the Soviet Union, Alia's efforts at reform were prompted, and tempered, by a commitment to preserving the system that had facilitated his accession to power. In both countries, however, the departure from traditional hard-line policies sufficed merely to unshackle the forces that would accelerate the collapse of the old system.

In December 1990, swayed by large-scale student demonstrations, strikes, and the exodus of thousands of Albanians to Italy and Greece, and fearing the prospect of a violent overthrow, Alia yielded to the popular demand for political pluralism and a multiparty system. The newly created Albanian Democratic Party (ADP), the country's first opposition party since World War II, quickly became a major political force, capturing nearly one-third of the seats in the People's Assembly in the spring 1991 multiparty election. And several months later, as the economy continued to deteriorate, the ADP participated in a "government of national salvation" with the communist Albanian Party of Labor (APL), subsequently renamed the Socialist Party of Albania (SPA). The fragile coalition government led by Prime Minister Ylli Bufi fell apart when the ADP decided to pull out in December. An interim government of nonparty members and specialists headed by Vilson Ahmeti struggled on until the ADP scored a decisive election victory on March 22, 1992, amidst economic free-fall and social chaos, receiving about 62 percent of the vote to the SPA's 26 percent. Alia resigned as president shortly afterward, paving the way for the ADP to take over the government. On April 9, Sali Berisha, a cardiologist by training and a dynamic ADP leader who had figured prominently in the struggle for political pluralism, was elected by the People's Assembly to the post of president. The first post-communist government, headed by ADP founding member Aleksander Meksi, was appointed four days later. This "cabinet of hope," as it was popularly dubbed, consisted mainly of young ADP activists, intellectuals without prior government experience. Unlike their communist predecessors, most of whom were of southern Albanian origin, the ministers hailed from various parts of the country.

The new government made remarkable progress in restoring law and order, reforming the economy, and raising the population's standard of living. It privatized small businesses, closed down unprofitable industrial facilities, distributed about 90 percent of the land previously held by collective farms to private farmers, began to privatize housing, improved the supply of food and basic consumer goods, reduced the rate of inflation, stabilized the lek (Albania's currency unit), cut the budget deficit, and increased the volume of exports. However, more than one year after the Democrats came to power, Albania's economic plight was far from over. Its 400,000 newly registered private farmers had yet to assume full ownership rights over their land, there was insufficient investment in private agriculture, and shortages of tractors and other farming equipment continued to impede agricultural production. Approximately forty percent of the nonagricultural labor force was unemployed, corruption pervaded the state bureaucracy, and the country remained dependent on foreign food aid. In addition, partly because of the general political instability in the Balkans, particularly in the former Yugoslavia (see Glossary), direct investment from abroad was not forthcoming. Although President Berisha's "shock therapy" received the imprimatur of the International Monetary Fund (IMF—see Glossary), it drew sharp criticism from the SPA, which had been resuscitated by significant gains in the July 1992 local elections. The SPA argued that the reforms should have been implemented gradually, that many more jobs had been eliminated than created, and that at least some of the old state-run factories should have been kept open.

In March 1993, SPA chairman Fatos Nano called on the entire cabinet to resign, accusing it of incompetence. On April 6, President Berisha, citing a need to "correct weaknesses and shortcomings" in the government's reform efforts, replaced the ministers of agriculture, internal affairs, education, and tourism (although ADP chairman Eduard Selami denied that these changes had been made in response to the opposition's demands). The new appointees included individuals with greater professional expertise and two political independents. The outgoing ministers of agriculture and internal affairs assumed other government posts. Despite the Socialist challenge, opposition from right-wing extremists, and some manifestations of discord within the ADP, the Democratic government remained in a strong position in late 1993.

In foreign policy, the unresolved question of the status of Kosovo, a formerly autonomous province of Serbia, predominated. Although in September 1991 Kosovo's underground parliament proclaimed this enclave with its large majority of ethnic Albanians a "sovereign and independent state," Albania was the only country that had officially recognized Kosovo's independence from Serbia. The Serbian government carried out a policy of systematic segregation and repression in Kosovo that some Western observers have compared with South Africa's apartheid system. Concerned that Serbia's ethnic cleansing campaigns would spread from Bosnia and Hercegovina to Kosovo and that Albania could be dragged into the ensuing confrontation (potentially a general Balkan war), President Berisha forged closer relations with other Islamic countries, particularly Turkey. In December 1992, Albania joined the Organization of the Islamic Conference (OIC), a move denounced by the SPA as a detriment to the country's reintegration with Europe. But Berisha also sought ties to the North Atlantic Treaty Organization (NATO) and urged repeatedly that NATO forces be deployed in Kosovo. In March 1993, NATO secretary general Manfred Wörner visited Tiranë, and later that month Albanian defense minister Safet Zhulali participated in a meeting of the North Atlantic Cooperation Council in Brussels. Wörner offered various forms of technical assistance to the Albanian armed forces, although membership in NATO itself was withheld.

In April 1993, Albania granted recognition to the former Yugoslav Republic of Macedonia. Important factors in relations between the two countries were the human rights of the Albanian minority in Macedonia, estimated to amount to between a fifth and a third of the population, and possible Albanian irredentism.

Relations benefited from the inclusion of ethnic Albanians in the Macedonian government. Good relations were maintained with Slovenia, Croatia, Italy, Bulgaria, and Romania as well, and steps were taken to improve relations with the neighboring Republic of Montenegro, also home to a large minority Albanian community. In September, Montenegro's president, Momir Bulatovic, met with President Berisha in Tiranë for the highest level talks between the two countries in a half-century. Attempts to expand cooperation and exchanges with Montenegro, however, were hampered by a United Nations embargo against the rump Yugoslavia.

Relations with Greece, Albania's ancient southern neighbor (which, for religious and historical reasons, was expected to side with Serbia in the event of war in Kosovo), deteriorated rapidly in the early 1990s. The tension stemmed primarily from two issues: the influx of hundreds of thousands of illegal aliens, mostly economic immigrants, from Albania to Greece, and the treatment of ethnic Greeks in Albania. Greco-Albanian relations worsened markedly when the Albanian parliament voted in February 1992 to prevent OMONIA (Unity), the political party representing Greek Albanians, from fielding candidates in the March 1992 election. A compromise was reached, permitting OMONIA's members to register under the name of the Union for Human Rights and to have their representatives included among the candidates, but mutual recriminations persisted. Another major setback occurred in June 1993 when Albania expelled a Greek Orthodox priest for allegedly fomenting unrest among ethnic Greeks in southern Albania, and Greece retaliated by deporting 25,000 Albanian illegal immigrants. Several weeks later Greece's prime minister, Constantinos Mitsotakis, demanded "the same rights for the Greek community living in Albania as those that the Albanian government demands for the Albanian communities in the former Yugoslavia." A potential problem was posed also by the status of "Northern Epirus," the Greek-populated region in southern Albania on which Greece had made territorial claims in the past. The regional instability created by such ethnic tensions, combined with continued economic deprivation, threatened Albania's transition to democracy.

January 1, 1994 | Walter R. Iwaskiw

Chapter 1. Historical Setting

Skanderbeg, Albanian national hero of the fifteenth century

"THE ALBANIAN PEOPLE have hacked their way through history, sword in hand," proclaims the preamble to Albania's 1976 Stalinist constitution. These words were penned by the most dominant figure in Albania's modern history, the Orwellian postwar despot, Enver Hoxha. The fact that Hoxha enshrined them in Albania's supreme law is indicative of how he—like his mentor, the Soviet dictator Joseph Stalin—exploited his people's collective memory to enhance the might of the communist system, which he manipulated for over four decades. Supported by a group of sycophantic intellectuals, Hoxha repeatedly transformed friends into hated foes in his determination to shape events. Similarly, he rewrote Albania's history so that national heroes were recast, sometimes overnight, as villains. Hoxha appealed to the Albanians' xenophobia and their defensive nationalism to parry criticism and threats to communist central control and his regime and to justify its brutal, arbitrary rule and economic and social folly. Only Hoxha's death, the timely downfall of communism in Eastern Europe at the end of the 1980s, and the collapse of the nation's economy were enough to break his spell and propel Albania fitfully toward change.

The Albanians are probably an ethnic outcropping of the Illyrians, an ancient Balkan people who intermingled and made war with the Greeks, Thracians, and Macedonians before succumbing to Roman rule around the time of Christ. Eastern and Western powers, secular and religious, battled for centuries after the fall of Rome to control the lands that constitute modern-day Albania. All the Illyrian tribes except the Albanians disappeared during the Dark Ages under the waves of migrating barbarians. A forbidding mountain homeland and resilient tribal society enabled the Albanians to survive into modern times with their identity and their Indo-European language intact.

In the fourteenth and fifteenth centuries, the Ottoman Turks swept into the western Balkans. After a quixotic defense mounted by the Albanians' greatest hero, Skanderbeg, the Albanians succumbed to the Turkish sultan's forces. During five centuries of Ottoman rule, about two-thirds of the Albanian population, including its most powerful feudal landowners, converted to Islam. Many Albanians won fame and fortune as soldiers, administrators, and merchants in far-flung parts of the empire. As the centuries passed, however, Ottoman rulers lost the capacity to command the loyalty of local pashas, who governed districts on the empire's fringes. Soon pressures created by emerging national movements among the empire's farrago of peoples threatened to shatter the empire itself. The Ottoman rulers of the nineteenth century struggled in vain to shore up central authority, introducing reforms aimed at harnessing unruly pashas and checking the spread of nationalist ideas.

Albanian nationalism stirred for the first time in the late nineteenth century when it appeared that Serbia, Montenegro, Bulgaria, and Greece would snatch up the Ottoman Empire's Albanian-populated lands. In 1878 Albanian leaders organized the Prizren League, which pressed for autonomy within the empire. After decades of unrest and the Ottoman Empire's defeat in the First Balkan War in 1912–13, Albanian leaders declared Albania an independent state, and Europe's Great Powers carved out an independent Albania after the Second Balkan War of 1913.

With the complete collapse of the Ottoman and Austro-Hungarian empires after World War I, the Albanians looked to Italy for protection against predators. After 1925, however, Mussolini sought to dominate Albania. In 1928 Albania became a kingdom under Zog I, the conservative Muslim clan chief and former prime minister, but Zog failed to stave off Italian ascendancy in Albanian internal affairs. In 1939 Mussolini's troops occupied Albania, overthrew Zog, and annexed the country. Albanian communists and nationalists fought each other as well as the occupying Italian and German forces during World War II, and with Yugoslav and Allied assistance the communists triumphed.

After the war, communist strongmen Enver Hoxha and Mehmet Shehu eliminated their rivals inside the communist party and liquidated anticommunist opposition. Concentrating primarily on maintaining their grip on power, they reorganized the country's economy along strict Stalinist lines, turning first to Yugoslavia, then to the Soviet Union, and later to China for support. In pursuit of their goals, the communists repressed the Albanian people, subjecting them to isolation, propaganda, and brutal police measures. When China opened up to the West in the 1970s, Albania's rulers turned away from Beijing and implemented a policy of strict autarky, or self-sufficiency, that brought their nation economic ruin.

The Ancient Illyrians

Mystery enshrouds the exact origins of today's Albanians. Most historians of the Balkans believe that the Albanian people are in large part descendants of the ancient Illyrians, who, like other Balkan peoples, were subdivided into tribes and clans. The name Albania is derived from the name of an Illyrian tribe called the Arber, or Arbereshë, and later Albanoi, that lived near Durrës.

The Illyrians were Indo-European tribesmen who appeared in the western part of the Balkan Peninsula about 1000 B.C., a period coinciding with the end of the Bronze Age and the beginning of the Iron Age. They inhabited much of the area for at least the next millennium. Archaeologists associate the Illyrians with the Hallstatt culture, an Iron Age people noted for production of iron and bronze swords with winged-shaped handles and for domestication of horses. The Illyrians occupied lands extending from the Danube, Sava, and Morava rivers to the Adriatic Sea and the Sar Mountains. At various times, groups of Illyrians migrated over land and sea into Italy.

The Illyrians carried on commerce and warfare with their neighbors. The ancient Macedonians probably had some Illyrian roots, but their ruling class adopted Greek cultural characteristics. The Illyrians also mingled with the Thracians, another ancient people with adjoining lands on the east. In the south and along the Adriatic Sea coast, the Illyrians were heavily influenced by the Greeks, who founded trading colonies there. The present-day city of Durrës (Dyrrachium) evolved from a Greek colony known as Epidamnos, which was founded at the end of the seventh century B.C. Another famous Greek colony, Apollonia, arose between Durrës and the port city of Vlorë.

The Illyrians produced and traded cattle, horses, agricultural goods, and wares fashioned from locally mined copper and iron. Feuds and warfare were constant facts of life for the Illyrian tribes, and Illyrian pirates plagued shipping on the Adriatic Sea. Councils of elders chose the chieftains who headed each of the numerous Illyrian tribes. From time to time, local chieftains extended their rule over other tribes and formed short-lived kingdoms. During the fifth century B.C., a well-developed Illyrian population center existed as far north as the upper Sava River valley in what is now Slovenia. Illyrian friezes discovered near the present-day Slovenian city of Ljubljana depict ritual sacrifices, feasts, battles, sporting events, and other activities.

The Illyrian kingdom of Bardhyllus became a formidable local power in the fourth century B.C. In 358 B.C., however, Macedonia's Philip II, father of Alexander the Great, defeated the Illyrians and assumed control of their territory as far as Lake Ohrid (see fig. 1). Alexander himself routed the forces of the Illyrian chieftain Clitus in 335 B.C., and Illyrian tribal leaders and soldiers accompanied Alexander on his conquest of Persia. After Alexander's death in 323 B.C., independent Illyrian kingdoms again arose. In 312 B.C., King Glaucius expelled the Greeks from Durrës. By the end of the third century, an Illyrian kingdom based near what is

Source: Based on information from R. Ernest Dupuy and Trevor N. Dupuy, *The Encyclopedia of Military History*, New York, 1970, 95; Hermann Kinder and Werner Hilgemann, *The Anchor Atlas of World History*, 1, New York, 1974, 90, 94; and *Encyclopaedia Britannica*, 15, New York, 1975, 1092.

Figure 2. Illyria under Roman Rule, First Century B.C.

now the Albanian city of Shkodër controlled parts of northern Albania, Montenegro, and Hercegovina. Under Queen Teuta, Illyrians attacked Roman merchant vessels plying the Adriatic Sea and gave Rome an excuse to invade the Balkans.

In the Illyrian Wars of 229 and 219 B.C., Rome overran the Illyrian settlements in the Neretva River valley. The Romans made new gains in 168 B.C., and Roman forces captured Illyria's King Gentius at Shkodër, which they called Scodra, and brought him to Rome in 165 B.C. A century later, Julius Caesar and his rival Pompey fought their decisive battle near Durrës. In A.D. 9, during the reign of Emperor Tiberius, Rome finally subjugated recalcitrant Illyrian tribes in the western Balkans. The Romans divided the lands that make up present-day Albania among the provinces of Macedonia, Dalmatia, and Epirus (see fig. 2).

For about four centuries, Roman rule brought the Illyrian-populated lands economic and cultural advancement and ended most of the clashes among local tribes. The Illyrian mountain clansmen retained local authority but pledged allegiance to the emperor and acknowledged the authority of his envoys. During a yearly holiday honoring the Caesars, the Illyrian mountaineers swore loyalty to the emperor and reaffirmed their political rights. A form of this tradition, known as the *kuvend,* has survived to the present day in northern Albania.

The Romans established numerous military camps and colonies and completely latinized the coastal cities. They also oversaw the construction of aqueducts and roads, including the Via Egnatia, a famous military highway and trade route that led from Durrës through the Shkumbin River valley to Macedonia and Byzantium (later Constantinople—see Glossary). Copper, asphalt, and silver were extracted from the mountains. The main exports were wine, cheese, and oil, as well as fish from Lake Scutari and Lake Ohrid. Imports included tools, metalware, luxury goods, and other manufactured articles. Apollonia became a cultural center, and Julius Caesar himself sent his nephew, later the Emperor Augustus, to study there.

Illyrians distinguished themselves as warriors in the Roman legions and made up a significant portion of the Praetorian Guard. Several of the Roman emperors were of Illyrian origin, including Diocletian (r. 284–305), who saved the empire from disintegration by introducing institutional reforms; and Constantine the Great (r. 324–37), who accepted Christianity and transferred the empire's capital from Rome to Byzantium, which he called Constantinople. Emperor Justinian (r. 527–65)—who codified Roman law, built the most famous Byzantine church, the Hagia Sofia, and reextended the empire's control over lost territories—was probably also an Illyrian.

Christianity came to the Illyrian-populated lands in the first century A.D. Saint Paul wrote that he preached in the Roman province of Illyricum, and legend holds that he visited Durrës. When the Roman Empire was divided into eastern and western halves in A.D. 395, the lands that now make up Albania were administered by the Eastern Empire but were ecclesiastically dependent on Rome. In A.D. 732, however, a Byzantine emperor, Leo the Isaurian, subordinated the area to the patriarchate of Constantinople. For centuries thereafter, the Albanian lands were an arena for the ecclesiastical struggle between Rome and Constantinople. Most Albanians living in the mountainous north became Roman Catholic, whereas in the southern and central regions the majority became Orthodox.

The Barbarian Invasions and the Middle Ages

The fall of the Roman Empire and the age of great migrations brought radical changes to the Balkan Peninsula and the Illyrian people. Barbarian tribesmen overran many rich Roman cities, destroying the existing social and economic order and leaving the great Roman aqueducts, coliseums, temples, and roads in ruins. The Illyrians gradually disappeared as a distinct people from the Balkans, replaced by the Bulgars, Serbs, Croats, and Albanians. In the late Middle Ages, new waves of invaders swept over the Albanian-populated lands. Thanks to their protective mountains, close-knit tribal society, and sheer pertinacity, however, the Albanian people developed a distinctive identity and language.

In the fourth century, barbarian tribes began to prey upon the Roman Empire, and the fortunes of the Illyrian-populated lands sagged. The Germanic Goths and Asiatic Huns were the first to arrive, invading in mid-century; the Avars attacked in A.D. 570; and the Slavic Serbs and Croats overran Illyrian-populated areas in the early seventh century. About fifty years later, the Bulgars conquered much of the Balkan Peninsula and extended their domain to the lowlands of what is now central Albania. Many Illyrians fled from coastal areas to the mountains, exchanging a sedentary peasant existence for the itinerant life of the herdsman. Other Illyrians intermarried with the conquerors and eventually assimilated. In general, the invaders destroyed or weakened Roman and Byzantine cultural centers in the lands that would become Albania.

Again during the late medieval period, invaders ravaged the Illyrian-inhabited regions of the Balkans. Norman, Venetian, and Byzantine fleets attacked by sea. Bulgar, Serb, and Byzantine forces came overland and held the region in their grip for years. Clashes between rival clans and intrusions by the Serbs produced hardship that triggered an exodus from the region southward into Greece, including Thessaly, the Peloponnese, and the Aegean Islands. The invaders assimilated much of the Illyrian population, but the Illyrians living in lands that comprise modern-day Albania and parts of Yugoslavia (see Glossary) and Greece were never completely absorbed or even controlled.

The first historical mention of Albania and the Albanians as such appears in an account of the resistance by a Byzantine emperor, Alexius I Comnenus, to an offensive, in 1081, into Albanian-populated lands. The offense was waged by Vatican-backed Normans from southern Italy.

The Serbs occupied parts of northern and eastern Albania toward the end of the twelfth century. In 1204, after Western crusaders had sacked Constantinople, Venice won nominal control over Albania and the Epirus region of northern Greece and took possession of Durrës. A prince from the overthrown Byzantine ruling family, Michael Comnenus, made alliances with Albanian chiefs and drove the Venetians from lands that now make up southern Albania and northern Greece. In 1204 he set up an independent principality, the Despotate of Epirus, with Janina (now Ioannina in northwest Greece) as its capital. In 1272 the king of Naples, Charles I of Anjou, occupied Durrës and formed an Albanian kingdom that would last for a century. Internal power struggles further weakened the Byzantine Empire in the fourteenth century, enabling the Serbs' most powerful medieval ruler, Stefan Dusan, to establish a short-lived empire that included all of Albania except Durrës.

The Albanian Lands under Ottoman Domination, 1385–1876

The expanding Ottoman Empire overpowered the Balkan Peninsula in the fourteenth and fifteenth centuries. At first, the feuding Albanian clans proved no match for the armies of the sultan (see Glossary). In the fifteenth century, however, Skanderbeg united the Albanian tribes in a defensive alliance that held up the Ottoman advance for more than two decades. His family's banner, bearing a black two-headed eagle on a red field, became the flag under which the Albanian national movement rallied centuries later.

Five centuries of Ottoman rule left the Albanian people fractured along religious, regional, and tribal lines. The first Albanians to convert to Islam were young boys forcibly conscripted into the sultan's military and administration. In the early seventeenth century, however, Albanians converted to Islam in great numbers. Within a century, the Albanian Islamic community was split between Sunni (see Glossary) Muslims and adherents to the Bektashi (see Glossary) sect. The Albanian people also became divided into two distinct tribal and dialectal groupings, the Gegs and Tosks. In the rugged northern mountains, Geg shepherds lived in a tribal society often completely independent of Ottoman rule. In the south, peasant Muslim and Orthodox Tosks worked the land for Muslim beys, provincial rulers who frequently revolted against the sultan's authority. In the nineteenth century, the Ottoman sultans tried in vain to shore up their collapsing empire by introducing a series of reforms aimed at reining in recalcitrant local officials and dousing the fires of nationalism among its myriad peoples. The power of nationalism, however, proved too strong to counteract.

The Ottoman Conquest of Albania

The Ottoman Turks expanded their empire from Anatolia to

the Balkans in the fourteenth century. They crossed the Bosporus in 1352, and in 1389 they crushed a Serb-led army that included Albanian forces at Kosovo Polje, located in the southern part of present-day Yugoslavia. Europe gained a brief respite from Ottoman pressure in 1402 when the Mongol leader, Tamerlane, attacked Anatolia from the east, killed the Turks' absolute ruler, the sultan, and sparked a civil war. When order was restored, the Ottomans renewed their westward progress. In 1453 Sultan Mehmed II's forces overran Constantinople and killed the last Byzantine emperor.

The division of the Albanian-populated lands into small, quarreling fiefdoms ruled by independent feudal lords and tribal chiefs made them easy prey for the Ottoman armies. In 1385 the Albanian ruler of Durrës, Karl Thopia, appealed to the sultan for support against his rivals, the Balsha family. An Ottoman force quickly marched into Albania along the Via Egnatia and routed the Balshas. The principal Albanian clans soon swore fealty to the Turks. Sultan Murad II launched the major Ottoman onslaught in the Balkans in 1423, and the Turks took Janina in 1431 and Arta, on the Ionian coast, in 1449. The Turks allowed conquered Albanian clan chiefs to maintain their positions and property, but they had to pay tribute, send their sons to the Turkish court as hostages, and provide the Ottoman army with auxiliary troops.

The Albanians' resistance to the Turks in the mid-fifteenth century won them acclaim all over Europe. Gjon Kastrioti of Krujë was one of the Albanian clan leaders who submitted to Turkish suzerainty. He was compelled to send his four sons to the Ottoman capital to be trained for military service. The youngest, Gjergj Kastrioti (1403–68), who would become the Albanians' greatest national hero, captured the sultan's attention. Renamed Iskander when he converted to Islam, the young man participated in military expeditions to Asia Minor and Europe. When appointed to administer a Balkan district, Iskander became known as Skanderbeg. After Ottoman forces under Skanderbeg's command suffered defeat in a battle near Nis, in present-day Serbia, in 1443, the Albanian rushed to Krujë and tricked a Turkish pasha into surrendering to him the Kastrioti family fortress. Skanderbeg then reembraced Roman Catholicism and declared a holy war against the Turks.

On March 1, 1444, Albanian chieftains gathered in the cathedral of Lezhë with the prince of Montenegro and delegates from Venice and proclaimed Skanderbeg commander of the Albanian resistance. All of Albania, including most of Epirus, accepted his leadership against the Ottoman Turks, but local leaders kept control of their

Equestrian statue of Skanderbeg on Skanderbeg Square in central Tiranë
Courtesy Charles Sudetic

own districts. Under a red flag bearing Skanderbeg's heraldic emblem, an Albanian force of about 30,000 men held off brutal Ottoman campaigns against their lands for twenty-four years. Twice the Albanians overcame sieges of Krujë. In 1449 the Albanians routed Sultan Murad II himself. Later, they repulsed attacks led by Sultan Mehmed II. In 1461 Skanderbeg went to the aid of his suzerain, King Alfonso I of Naples, against the kings of Sicily. The government under Skanderbeg was unstable, however, and at times local Albanian rulers cooperated with the Ottoman Turks against him. When Skanderbeg died at Lezhë, the sultan reportedly cried out, "Asia and Europe are mine at last. Woe to Christendom! She has lost her sword and shield."

With support from Naples and the Vatican, resistance to the Ottoman Empire continued mostly in Albania's highlands, where the chieftains even opposed the construction of roads out of fear that they would bring Ottoman soldiers and tax collectors. The Albanians' fractured leadership, however, failed to halt the Ottoman onslaught. Krujë fell to the Ottoman Turks in 1478; Shkodër succumbed in 1479 after a fifteen-month siege; and the Venetians evacuated Durrës in 1501. The defeats triggered a great Albanian exodus to southern Italy, especially to the kingdom of Naples, as well as to Sicily, Greece, Romania, and Egypt. Most of the Albanian refugees belonged to the Orthodox Church. Some of the émigrés to Italy converted to Roman Catholicism, and the rest established a Uniate Church (see Glossary). The Albanians of Italy significantly influenced the Albanian national movement in future centuries, and Albanian Franciscan priests, most of whom were descended from émigrés to Italy, played a significant role in the preservation of Catholicism in Albania's northern regions.

Albanians under Ottoman Rule

The Ottoman sultan considered himself God's agent on earth, the leader of a religious—not a national—state whose purpose was to defend and propagate Islam. Non-Muslims paid extra taxes and held an inferior status, but they could retain their old religion and a large measure of local autonomy. By converting to Islam, individuals among the conquered could elevate themselves to the privileged stratum of society. In the early years of the empire, all Ottoman high officials were the sultan's bondsmen, the children of Christian subjects chosen in childhood for their promise, converted to Islam, and educated to serve. Some were selected from prisoners of war, others sent as gifts, and still others obtained through *devshirme,* the tribute of children levied in the Ottoman Empire's Balkan lands. Many of the best fighters in the sultan's elite guard, the janissaries (see Glossary), were conscripted as young boys from Christian Albanian families, and high-ranking Ottoman officials often had Albanian bodyguards.

In the early seventeenth century, many Albanian converts to Islam migrated elsewhere within the Ottoman Empire and found careers in the Ottoman military and government. Some attained powerful positions in the Ottoman administration. About thirty Albanians rose to the position of grand vizier, chief deputy to the sultan himself. In the second half of the seventeenth century, the Albanian Köprülü family provided four grand viziers, who fought against corruption, temporarily shored up eroding central government control over rapacious local beys, and won several military victories.

The Ottoman Turks divided the Albanian-inhabited lands among a number of districts, or *vilayets*. The Ottoman authorities did not initially stress conversion to Islam. In the seventeenth and eighteenth centuries, however, economic pressures and coercion produced the conversion of about two-thirds of the empire's Albanians.

The Ottoman Turks first focused their conversion campaigns on the Roman Catholic Albanians of the north and then on the Orthodox population of the south. The authorities increased taxes, especially poll taxes, to make conversion economically attractive. During and after a Christian counteroffensive against the Ottoman Empire from 1687 to 1690, when Albanian Catholics revolted against their Muslim overlords, the Ottoman pasha of Pec, a town in the south of present-day Yugoslavia, retaliated by forcing entire Albanian villages to accept Islam. Albanian beys then moved from the northern mountains to the fertile lands of Kosovo, which had been abandoned by thousands of Orthodox Serbs fearing reprisals for their collaboration with the Christian forces.

Most of the conversions to Islam took place in the lowlands of the Shkumbin River valley, where the Ottoman Turks could easily apply pressure because of the area's accessibility. Many Albanians, however, converted in name only and secretly continued to practice Christianity. Often one branch of a family became Muslim while another remained Christian, and many times these families celebrated their respective religious holidays together. As early as the eighteenth century, a mystic Islamic sect, the Bektashi dervishes, spread into the empire's Albanian-populated lands. Probably founded in the late thirteenth century in Anatolia, Bektashism became the janissaries' official faith in the late sixteenth century. The Bektashi sect contains features of the Turks' pre-Islamic religion and emphasizes man as an individual. Women, unveiled, participate in Bektashi ceremonies on an equal basis, and the celebrants use wine despite the ban on alcohol in the Quran. The Bektashis became the largest religious group in southern Albania after the sultan disbanded the janissaries in 1826. Bektashi leaders played key roles in the Albanian nationalist movement of the late nineteenth century and were to a great degree responsible for the Albanians' traditional tolerance of religious differences.

During the centuries of Ottoman rule, the Albanian lands remained one of Europe's most backward areas. In the mountains north of the Shkumbin River, Geg herders maintained their self-governing society comprised of clans. An association of clans was called a *bajrak* (see Glossary). Taxes on the northern tribes were difficult if not impossible for the Ottomans to collect because of the rough terrain and fierceness of the Albanian highlanders. Some mountain tribes succeeded in defending their independence through the centuries of Ottoman rule, engaging in intermittent guerrilla warfare with the Ottoman Turks, who never deemed it worthwhile to subjugate them. Until recent times, Geg clan chiefs, or *bajraktars,* exercised patriarchal powers, arranged marriages, mediated quarrels, and meted out punishments. The tribesmen of the northern Albanian mountains recognized no law but the Code of Lek, a collection of tribal laws transcribed in the fourteenth century by a Roman Catholic priest. The code regulates a variety of subjects, including blood vengeance. Even today, many Albanian highlanders regard the canon as the supreme law of the land.

South of the Shkumbin River, the mostly peasant Tosks lived in compact villages under elected rulers. Some Tosks living in settlements high in the mountains maintained their independence and often escaped payment of taxes. The Tosks of the lowlands, however, were easy for the Ottoman authorities to control. The Albanian tribal system disappeared there, and the Ottomans imposed a system of military fiefs under which the sultan granted soldiers and cavalrymen temporary landholdings, or *timars,* in exchange for military service. By the eighteenth century, many military fiefs had effectively become the hereditary landholdings of economically and politically powerful families who squeezed wealth from their hard-strapped Christian and Muslim tenant farmers. The beys, like the clan chiefs of the northern mountains, became virtually independent rulers in their own provinces, had their own military contingents, and often waged war against each other to increase their landholdings and power. The Sublime Porte (see Glossary) attempted to press a divide-and-rule policy to keep the local beys from uniting and posing a threat to Ottoman rule itself, but with little success.

Local Albanian Leaders in the Early Nineteenth Century

The weakening of Ottoman central authority and the *timar* system brought anarchy to the Albanian-populated lands. In the late eighteenth century, two Albanian centers of power emerged: Shkodër, under the Bushati family; and Janina, under Ali Pasha of Tepelenë. When it suited their goals, both places cooperated with the Sublime Porte, and when it was expedient to defy the central government, each acted independently.

The Bushati family dominated the Shkodër region through a network of alliances with various highland tribes. Kara Mahmud Bushati attempted to establish an autonomous principality and expand the lands under his control by playing off Austria and Russia against the Sublime Porte. In 1785 Kara Mahmud's forces attacked Montenegrin territory, and Austria offered to recognize him as the ruler of all Albania if he would ally himself with Vienna against the Sublime Porte. Seizing an opportunity, Kara Mahmud sent the sultan the heads of an Austrian delegation in 1788, and the Ottomans appointed him governor of Shkodër. When he attempted to wrest land from Montenegro in 1796, however, he was defeated and beheaded. Kara Mahmud's brother, Ibrahim, cooperated with the Sublime Porte until his death in 1810, but his successor, Mustafa Pasha Bushati, proved to be recalcitrant despite participation in Ottoman military campaigns against Greek revolutionaries and rebel pashas. He cooperated with the mountain tribes and brought a large area under his control.

Ali Pasha (1741–1822), the Lion of Janina, was born to a powerful clan from Tepelenë and spent much of his youth as a bandit. He rose to become governor of the Ottoman province of Rumelia, which included Albania, Macedonia, and Thrace, before establishing himself in Janina. Like Kara Mahmud Bushati, Ali Pasha wanted to create an autonomous state under his rule. When Ali Pasha forged links with the Greek revolutionaries, Sultan Mahmud II decided to destroy him. The sultan first discharged the Albanian from his official posts and recalled him to Constantinople. Ali Pasha refused and put up a formidable resistance that Britain's Lord Byron immortalized in poems and letters. In January 1822, however, Ottoman agents assassinated Ali Pasha and sent his head to Constantinople. Nevertheless, it took eight more years before the Sublime Porte would move against Mustafa Pasha Bushati. The sultan sent Reshid Pasha, an Ottoman general, to Bitola (then called Monastir, in Macedonia), where he invited 1,000 Muslim Albanian leaders to meet him; in August 1830 Reshid Pasha had about 500 of the Albanian leaders killed. He then turned on Mustafa Pasha, who surrendered and spent the rest of his life as an official in Constantinople.

After crushing the Bushatis and Ali Pasha, the Sublime Porte introduced a series of reforms, known as the *tanzimat,* which were aimed at strengthening the empire by reining in fractious pashas. The government organized a recruitment program for the military and opened Turkish-language schools to propagate Islam and instill loyalty to the empire. The *timars* officially became large individual landholdings, especially in the lowlands. In 1835 the Sublime Porte divided the Albanian-populated lands into the *vilayets* of Janina and Rumelia and dispatched officials from Constantinople to administer them. After 1865 the central authorities redivided the Albanian lands among the *vilayets* of Shkodër, Janina, Bitola, and Kosovo. The reforms angered the highland Albanian chieftains, who found their privileges reduced with no apparent compensation, and the authorities eventually abandoned efforts to control the chieftains. Ottoman troops crushed local rebellions in the lowlands, however, and conditions there remained bleak. Large numbers of Tosks emigrated to join sizable Albanian émigré communities in Romania, Egypt, Bulgaria, Constantinople, southern Italy, and later the United States. As a result of contacts maintained between the Tosks and their relatives living or returning from abroad, foreign ideas began to seep into Albania.

National Awakening and the Birth of Albania, 1876–1918

By the 1870s, the Sublime Porte's reforms aimed at checking the Ottoman Empire's disintegration had clearly failed. The image of the "Turkish yoke" had become fixed in the nationalist mythologies and psyches of the empire's Balkan peoples, and their march toward independence quickened. The Albanians, because of the preponderance of Muslims who had links with Islam and internal social divisions, were the last of the Balkan peoples to develop a national consciousness. That consciousness was triggered by fears that the Ottoman Empire would lose its Albanian-populated lands to the emerging Balkan states—Serbia, Montenegro, Bulgaria, and Greece. In 1878 Albanian leaders formed the Prizren League, which pressed for territorial autonomy; and after decades of unrest a major uprising exploded in the Albanian-populated Ottoman territories in 1912, on the eve of the First Balkan War. When Serbia, Montenegro, and Greece laid claim to Albanian lands during the war, the Albanians declared independence. The European

Great Powers endorsed an independent Albania in 1913, after the Second Balkan War. The young state, however, collapsed within weeks of the outbreak of World War I.

The Rise of Albanian Nationalism

The 1877–78 Russo-Turkish War dealt a decisive blow to Ottoman power in the Balkan Peninsula, leaving the empire with only a precarious hold on Macedonia and the Albanian-populated lands. The Albanians' fear that the lands they inhabited would be partitioned among Montenegro, Serbia, Bulgaria, and Greece fueled the rise of Albanian nationalism. The first postwar treaty, the abortive Treaty of San Stefano (see Glossary) signed on March 3, 1878, assigned Albanian-populated lands to Serbia, Montenegro, and Bulgaria. Austria-Hungary and Britain blocked the arrangement because it awarded Russia a predominant position in the Balkans and thereby upset the European balance of power. A peace conference to settle the dispute was held later in the year in Berlin.

The Treaty of San Stefano triggered profound anxiety among the Albanians meanwhile, and it spurred their leaders to organize a defense of the lands they inhabited. In the spring of 1878, influential Albanians in Constantinople—including Abdyl Frasheri, the Albanian national movement's leading figure during its early years—organized a secret committee to direct the Albanians' resistance. In May the group called for a general meeting of representatives from all the Albanian-populated lands. On June 10, 1878, about eighty delegates, mostly Muslim religious leaders, clan chiefs, and other influential people from the four Albanian-populated Ottoman *vilayets,* met in the Kosovo town of Prizren. The delegates set up a standing organization, the Prizren League, under the direction of a central committee that had the power to impose taxes and raise an army. The Prizren League worked to gain autonomy for the Albanians and to thwart implementation of the Treaty of San Stefano, but not to create an independent Albania.

At first the Ottoman authorities supported the Prizren League, but the Sublime Porte pressed the delegates to declare themselves to be first and foremost Ottomans rather than Albanians. Some delegates supported this position and advocated emphasizing Muslim solidarity and the defense of Muslim lands, including present-day Bosnia and Hercegovina. Other representatives, under Frasheri's leadership, focused on working toward Albanian autonomy and creating a sense of Albanian identity that would cut across religious and tribal lines. Because conservative Muslims constituted a majority of the representatives, the Prizren League supported maintenance of Ottoman suzerainty.

In July 1878, the league sent a memorandum to the Great Powers at the Congress of Berlin, which had been called to settle the unresolved problems of the Russo-Turkish War. The memorandum demanded that all Albanians be united in a single Ottoman province that would be governed from Bitola by a Turkish governor, who would be advised by an Albanian committee elected by universal suffrage.

The Congress of Berlin ignored the league's memorandum, and Germany's Otto von Bismarck even proclaimed that an Albanian nation did not exist. The congress ceded to Montenegro the cities of Bar and Podgorica and areas around the mountain villages of Gusinje and Plav, which Albanian leaders considered Albanian territory. Serbia also won Albanian-inhabited lands. The Albanians, the vast majority loyal to the empire, vehemently opposed the territorial losses. Albanians also feared the possible loss of Epirus to Greece. The Prizren League organized armed resistance efforts in Gusinje, Plav, Shkodër, Prizren, Prevesa, and Janina. A border tribesman at the time described the frontier as "floating on blood."

In August 1878, the Congress of Berlin ordered a commission to trace a border between the Ottoman Empire and Montenegro. The congress also directed Greece and the Ottoman Empire to negotiate a solution to their border dispute. The Great Powers expected the Ottomans to ensure that the Albanians would respect the new borders; they ignored the fact that the sultan's military forces were too weak to enforce any settlement and that the Ottomans could only benefit by the Albanians' resistance. The Sublime Porte, in fact, armed the Albanians and allowed them to levy taxes, and when the Ottoman army withdrew from areas awarded to Montenegro under the Treaty of Berlin, Roman Catholic Albanian tribesmen simply took control. The Albanians' successful resistance to the treaty forced the Great Powers to alter the border, returning Gusinje and Plav to the Ottoman Empire and granting Montenegro the mostly Muslim Albanian-populated coastal town of Ulcinj. But the Albanians there refused to surrender as well. Finally, the Great Powers blockaded Ulcinj by sea and pressured the Ottoman authorities to bring the Albanians under control. The Great Powers decided in 1881 to cede Greece only Thessaly and the small Albanian-populated district of Arta.

Faced with growing international pressure to "pacify" the refractory Albanians, the sultan dispatched a large army under Dervish Turgut Pasha to suppress the Prizren League and deliver Ulcinj to Montenegro. Albanians loyal to the empire supported the Sublime Porte's military intervention. In April 1881, Dervish Pasha's 10,000 men captured Prizren and later crushed the resistance at

Ulcinj. The Prizren League's leaders and their families were arrested and deported. Frasheri, who originally received a death sentence, was imprisoned until 1885 and exiled until his death seven years later. In the three years it survived, the Prizren League effectively made the Great Powers aware of the Albanian people and their national interests. Montenegro and Greece received much less Albanian-populated territory than they would have won without the league's resistance.

Formidable barriers frustrated Albanian leaders' efforts to instill in their people an Albanian rather than an Ottoman identity. Divided into four *vilayets,* Albanians had no common geographical or political nerve center. The Albanians' religious differences forced nationalist leaders to give the national movement a purely secular character that alienated religious leaders. The most significant factor uniting the Albanians, their spoken language, lacked a standard literary form and even a standard alphabet. Each of the three available choices, the Latin, Cyrillic, and Arabic scripts, implied different political and religious orientations opposed by one or another element of the population. In 1878 there were no Albanian-language schools in the most developed of the Albanian-inhabited areas—Gjirokastër, Berat, and Vlorë—where schools conducted classes either in Turkish or in Greek (see Education: Pre-Communist Era, ch. 2).

In the late nineteenth century, Albanian intellectuals began devising a single, standard Albanian literary language and making demands that it be used in schools. In Constantinople in 1879, Sami Frasheri founded a cultural and educational organization, the Society for the Printing of Albanian Writings, whose membership comprised Muslim, Catholic, and Orthodox Albanians. Naim Frasheri, the most-renowned Albanian poet, joined the society and wrote and edited textbooks. Albanian émigrés in Bulgaria, Egypt, Italy, Romania, and the United States supported the society's work. Others opposed it. The Greeks, who dominated the education of Orthodox Albanians, joined the Turks in suppressing the Albanians' culture, especially Albanian-language education. In 1886 the ecumenical patriarch of Constantinople threatened to excommunicate anyone found reading or writing Albanian, and priests taught that God would not understand prayers uttered in Albanian.

The Ottoman Empire continued to crumble after the Congress of Berlin. The empire's financial troubles prevented Sultan Abdül Hamid II from reforming his military, and he resorted to repression to maintain order. The authorities strove without success to control the political situation in the empire's Albanian-populated lands, arresting suspected nationalist activists. When the sultan refused Albanian demands for unification of the four Albanian-populated *vilayets,* Albanian leaders reorganized the Prizren League and incited uprisings that brought the Albanian lands, especially Kosovo, to near anarchy. The imperial authorities again disbanded the Prizren League in 1897, executed its president in 1902, and banned Albanian-language books and correspondence. In Macedonia, where Bulgarian-, Greek-, and Serbian-backed terrorists were fighting Ottoman authorities and one another for control, Muslim Albanians suffered attacks, and Albanian guerrilla groups retaliated. In 1906 Albanian leaders meeting in Bitola established the secret Committee for the Liberation of Albania. A year later, Albanian guerrillas assassinated the Greek Orthodox metropolitan of Korçë.

In 1906 opposition groups in the Ottoman Empire emerged, one of which evolved into the Committee of Union and Progress, more commonly known as the Young Turks, which proposed restoring constitutional government in Constantinople, by revolution if necessary. In July 1908, a month after a Young Turk rebellion in Macedonia supported by an Albanian uprising in Kosovo and Macedonia escalated into widespread insurrection and mutiny within the imperial army, Sultan Abdül Hamid II agreed to demands by the Young Turks to restore constitutional rule. Many Albanians participated in the Young Turks uprising, hoping that it would gain their people autonomy within the empire. The Young Turks lifted the Ottoman ban on Albanian-language schools and on writing the Albanian language. As a consequence, Albanian intellectuals meeting in Bitola in 1908 chose the Latin alphabet as a standard script. The Young Turks, however, were set on maintaining the empire and not interested in making concessions to the myriad nationalist groups within its borders. After securing the abdication of Abdül Hamid II in April 1909, the new authorities levied taxes, outlawed guerrilla groups and nationalist societies, and attempted to extend Constantinople's control over the northern Albanian mountainmen. In addition, the Young Turks legalized the bastinado, or beating with a stick, even for misdemeanors, banned the carrying of rifles, and denied the existence of an Albanian nationality. The new government also appealed for Islamic solidarity to break the Albanians' unity and used the Muslim clergy to try to impose the Arabic alphabet.

The Albanians refused to submit to the Young Turks' campaign to "Ottomanize" them by force. New Albanian uprisings began in Kosovo and the northern mountains in early April 1910. Ottoman forces quashed these rebellions after three months, outlawed Albanian organizations, disarmed entire regions, and closed down schools and publications. Montenegro, preparing to grab Albanian-populated lands for itself, supported a 1911 uprising by the mountain tribes against the Young Turks regime; the uprising grew into a widespread revolt. Unable to control the Albanians by force, the Ottoman government granted concessions on schools, military recruitment, and taxation and sanctioned the use of the Latin script for the Albanian language. The government refused, however, to unite the four Albanian-inhabited *vilayets*.

The Balkan Wars and Creation of Independent Albania

In May 1912, the Albanians once more rose against the Ottoman Empire and took the Macedonian capitol, Skopje, by August. Stunned, the Young Turks regime acceded to some of the rebels' demands. The First Balkan War, however, erupted before a final settlement could be worked out. Most Albanians remained neutral during the war, during which the Balkan allies—the Serbs, Bulgarians, and Greeks—quickly drove the Turks to the walls of Constantinople. The Montenegrins surrounded Shkodër with the help of northern Albanian tribes anxious to fight the Ottoman Turks. Serb forces took much of northern Albania, and the Greeks captured Janina and parts of southern Albania.

An assembly of eighty-three Muslim and Christian leaders meeting in Vlorë in November 1912 declared Albania an independent country and set up a provisional government. However, in its concluding Treaty of London of May 1913, an ambassadorial conference decided the major questions concerning the Albanians after the First Balkan War. One of Serbia's primary war aims was to gain an Adriatic port, preferably Durrës. Austria-Hungary and Italy opposed giving Serbia an Adriatic outlet, which they feared would become a Russian port. They instead supported the creation of an autonomous Albania. Russia backed Serbia's and Montenegro's claims to Albanian-inhabited lands. Britain and Germany remained neutral. Chaired by Britain's foreign secretary, Sir Edward Grey, the ambassadors' conference initially decided to create an autonomous Albania under continued Ottoman rule, but with the protection of the Great Powers. This solution, as detailed in the Treaty of London, was abandoned in the summer of 1913 when it became obvious that the Ottoman Empire would, in the Second Balkan War, lose Macedonia and hence its overland connection with the Albanian-inhabited lands.

In July 1913, the Great Powers opted to recognize an independent, neutral Albanian state ruled by a constitutional monarchy and under the protection of the Great Powers. The August 1913

Treaty of Bucharest established that independent Albania was a country with about 28,000 square kilometers of territory and a population of 800,000. Montenegro, whose tribesmen had resorted to terror, mass murder, and forced conversion in territories it coveted, had to surrender Shkodër. Serbia reluctantly succumbed to an ultimatum from Austria-Hungary, Germany, and Italy to withdraw from northern Albania. The treaty, however, left large areas, notably Kosovo and western Macedonia, with majority Albanian populations outside the new state and failed to solve the region's nationality problems.

Territorial disputes have divided the Albanians and Serbs since the Middle Ages, but none more so than the clash over the Kosovo region. Serbs consider Kosovo their Holy Land. They argue that their ancestors settled in the region during the seventh century, that medieval Serbian kings were crowned there, and that in the mid-fourteenth century the Serbs' greatest medieval ruler, Stefan Dusan, established the seat of his empire for a time near Prizren. More important, numerous Serbian Orthodox shrines, including the patriarchate of the Serbian Orthodox Church, are located in Kosovo. The key event in the Serbs' national mythology, the defeat of their forces by the Ottoman Turks, took place at Kosovo Polje in 1389. For their part, the Albanians claim the land based on the argument that they are the descendants of the ancient Illyrians, the indigenous people of the region, and have been there since before the first Serb ever set foot in the Balkans. Although the Albanians have not left architectural remains similar to the Serbs' religious shrines, the Albanians point to the fact that Prizren was the seat of their first nationalist organization, the Prizren League, and call the region the cradle of their national awakening. Finally, Albanians claim Kosovo based on the fact that their kinsmen have constituted the vast majority of Kosovo's population since at least the eighteenth century.

When the Great Powers recognized an independent Albania, they also established the International Control Commission, which endeavored to exert and expand its authority and elbow out the Vlorë provisional government and the rival government of Esad Pasha Toptani, who enjoyed the support of large landowners in central Albania and boasted a formidable militia. The control commission drafted a constitution that provided for a National Assembly of elected local representatives, the heads of the Albanians' major religious groups, ten persons nominated by the prince, and other noteworthy persons. The Great Powers chose Prince Wilhelm of Wied, a thirty-five-year-old German army captain, to head the new state. In March 1914, he moved into a Durrës building hastily converted into a palace.

After independence local power struggles, foreign provocations, miserable economic conditions, and modest attempts at social and religious reform fueled Albanian uprisings aimed at the prince and the control commission. Ottoman propaganda, which appealed to uneducated peasants loyal to Islam and Islamic spiritual leaders, attacked the Albanian regime as a puppet of the large landowners and Europe's Christian powers. Greece, unhappy that the Great Powers did not award it southern Albania, also encouraged uprisings against the Albanian government, and armed Greek bands carried out atrocities against Albanian villagers. Italy plotted with Esad Pasha to overthrow the new prince. Montenegro and Serbia plotted with the northern tribesmen. For their part, the Great Powers gave Prince Wilhelm, who was unversed in Albanian affairs, intrigue, or diplomacy, little moral or material backing. A general insurrection in the summer of 1914 stripped the prince of control except in Durrës and Vlorë.

World War I and Its Effects on Albania

Political chaos engulfed Albania after the outbreak of World War I. Surrounded by insurgents in Durrës, Prince Wilhelm departed the country in September 1914, just six months after arriving, and subsequently joined the German army and served on the Eastern Front. The Albanian people split along religious and tribal lines after the prince's departure. Muslims demanded a Muslim prince and looked to Turkey as the protector of the privileges they had enjoyed. Other Albanians became little more than agents of Italy and Serbia. Still others, including many beys and clan chiefs, recognized no superior authority. In late 1914, Greece occupied southern Albania, including Korçë and Gjirokastër. Italy occupied Vlorë, and Serbia and Montenegro occupied parts of northern Albania until a Central Powers offensive scattered the Serbian army, which was evacuated by the French to Thessaloniki. Austro-Hungarian and Bulgarian forces then occupied about two-thirds of the country.

Under the secret Treaty of London signed in April 1915, the Triple Entente powers promised Italy that it would gain Vlorë and nearby lands and a protectorate over Albania in exchange for entering the war against Austria-Hungary. Serbia and Montenegro were promised much of northern Albania, and Greece was promised much of the country's southern half. The treaty left a tiny Albanian state that would be represented by Italy in its relations with the other major powers. In September 1918, Entente forces broke through the Central Powers' lines north of Thessaloniki, and within days Austro-Hungarian forces began to withdraw from Albania. When the war ended on November 11, 1918, Italy's army had occupied most of Albania; Serbia held much of the country's northern mountains; Greece occupied a sliver of land within Albania's 1913 borders; and French forces occupied Korçë and Shkodër as well as other regions with sizable Albanian populations, such as Kosovo, which were later handed over to Serbia.

Interwar Albania, 1918–41

Albania achieved real statehood after World War I, in part because of the diplomatic intercession of the United States. The country suffered from a debilitating lack of economic and social development, however, and its first years of independence were fraught with political instability. Unable to survive in a predatory world without a foreign protector, Albania became the object of tensions between Italy and the Kingdom of the Serbs, Croats, and Slovenes (Yugoslavia), which were both bent on controlling the country. With the kingdom's military assistance, Ahmed Bey Zogu, the son of a clan chieftain, emerged victorious from an internal political power struggle in late 1924. Zogu, however, quickly turned his back on Belgrade and looked to Mussolini's Italy for patronage. In 1928 Zogu coaxed the country's parliament to declare Albania a kingdom and name him king. King Zog remained a hidebound conservative, and Albania was the only Balkan state where the government did not see fit to introduce a comprehensive land reform between the two world wars. Mussolini's forces finally overthrew Zog when they occupied Albania in 1939.

Albania's Reemergence after World War I

Albania's political confusion continued in the wake of World War I. The country lacked a single recognized government, and Albanians feared, with justification, that Greece, Yugoslavia, and Italy would succeed in extinguishing Albania's independence and carve up the country. Italian forces controlled Albanian political activity in the areas they occupied. The Serbs, who largely dictated Yugoslavia's foreign policy after World War I, strove to take over northern Albania, and the Greeks sought to control southern Albania. A delegation sent by a postwar Albanian National Assembly that met at Durrës in December 1918 defended Albanian interests at the Paris Peace Conference, but the conference denied Albania official representation. The National Assembly, anxious to keep Albania intact, expressed willingness to accept Italian protection and even an Italian prince as a ruler so long as it would mean Albania did not lose territory.

In January 1919, the Serbs attacked the Albanian inhabitants of Gusinje and Plav with regular troops and artillery after the Albanians had appealed to Britain for protection. The Serb forces massacred some of the Albanians and forced about 35,000 people to flee to the Shkodër area. In Kosovo the Serbs subjected the Albanians to brutalities, stripped them of territory under the guise of land reform, and rewarded Serb colonists with homesteads. In response, Albanians continued guerrilla warfare in both Serbia and Montenegro.

At the Paris Peace Conference in January 1920, negotiators from France, Britain, and Greece agreed to divide Albania among Yugoslavia, Italy, and Greece as a diplomatic expedient aimed at finding a compromise solution to the territorial conflict between Italy and Yugoslavia. The deal was done behind the Albanians' backs and in the absence of a United States negotiator.

Members of a second Albanian National Assembly held at Lushnjë in January 1920 rejected the partition plan and warned that Albanians would take up arms to defend their country's independence and territorial integrity. The Lushnjë National Assembly appointed a four-man regency to rule the country. A bicameral parliament was also created, appointing members of its own ranks to an upper chamber, the Senate. An elected lower chamber, the Chamber of Deputies, had one deputy for every 12,000 people in Albania and one for the Albanian community in the United States. In February 1920, the government moved to Tiranë, which became Albania's capital.

One month later, in March 1920, President Woodrow Wilson intervened to block the Paris agreement. The United States underscored its support for Albania's independence by recognizing an official Albanian representative to Washington, and in December the League of Nations recognized Albania's sovereignty by admitting it as a full member. The country's borders, however, remained unsettled.

Albania's new government campaigned to end Italy's occupation of the country and encouraged peasants to harass Italian forces. In September 1920, after a siege of Italian-occupied Vlorë by Albanian forces, Rome abandoned its claims on Albania under the 1915 Treaty of London and withdrew its forces from all of Albania except Sazan Island at the mouth of Vlorë Bay. Yugoslavia, however, pursued a predatory policy toward Albania, and after Albanian tribesmen clashed with Serb forces occupying the northern part of the country, Yugoslav troops took to burning villages and killing and expelling civilians. Belgrade then recruited a disgruntled Geg clan chief, Gjon Markagjoni, who led his Roman

Catholic Mirditë tribesmen in a rebellion against the regency and parliament. Markagjoni proclaimed the founding of an independent "Mirditë Republic" based in Prizren, which had fallen into Serbian hands during the First Balkan War. Finally, in November 1921, Yugoslav troops invaded Albanian territory beyond the areas they were already occupying. Outraged at the Yugoslav attack and Belgrade's lies, the League of Nations dispatched a commission composed of representatives of Britain, France, Italy, and Japan that reaffirmed Albania's 1913 borders. Yugoslavia complained bitterly but had no choice but to withdraw its troops. The so-called Mirditë Republic disappeared.

Social and Economic Conditions after World War I

Extraordinarily undeveloped, the Albania that emerged after World War I was home to something less than a million people divided into three major religious groups and two distinct classes: those people who owned land and claimed semifeudal privileges and those who did not. The landowners had always held the principal ruling posts in the country's central and southern regions, but many of them were steeped in the same Oriental conservatism that had brought decay to the Ottoman Empire. The landowning elite expected that they would continue to enjoy precedence. The country's peasants, however, were beginning to dispute the landed aristocracy's control. Muslims made up the majority of the landowning class as well as most of the pool of Ottoman-trained administrators and officials. Thus Muslims filled most of the country's administrative posts.

In northern Albania, the government directly controlled only Shkodër and its environs. The highland clans were suspicious of a constitutional government legislating in the interests of the country as a whole, and the Roman Catholic Church became the principal link between Tiranë and the tribesmen. In many instances, administrative communications were addressed to priests for circulation among their parishioners.

Poor and remote, Albania remained decades behind other Balkan countries in educational and social development. Illiteracy plagued almost the entire population. About 90 percent of the country's peasants practiced subsistence agriculture, using ancient methods and tools, such as wooden plows. Much of the country's richest farmland lay under water in malaria-infested coastal marshlands. Albania lacked a banking system, a railroad, a modern port, an efficient military, a university, and a modern press. The Albanians had Europe's highest birthrate and infant mortality rate, and life expectancy for men was about thirty-eight years. In the post

World War I period, the American Red Cross opened schools and hospitals at Durrës and Tiranë, and one Red Cross worker founded an Albanian chapter of the Boy Scouts that all boys between twelve and eighteen years old were subsequently required by law to join. Although hundreds of schools opened across the country, in 1938 only 36 percent of Albanian children of school age were receiving education of any kind.

Despite the meager educational opportunities, literature flourished in Albania between the two world wars. A Franciscan priest, Gjergj Fishta, Albania's greatest poet, dominated the literary scene with his poems on the Albanians' perseverance during their quest for freedom.

Independence also brought changes to religious life in Albania. The ecumenical patriarch of Constantinople recognized the autocephaly of the Albanian Orthodox Church after a meeting of the country's Albanian Orthodox congregations in Berat in August 1922. The most energetic reformers in Albania came from the Orthodox, who wanted to see Albania move quickly away from its Muslim, Turkish past, during which Christians made up the underclass. Albania's conservative Sunni Muslim community broke its last ties with Constantinople in 1923, formally declaring that there had been no caliph (see Glossary) since the Prophet Muhammad himself and that Muslim Albanians pledged primary allegiance to their native country. The Muslims also banned polygyny and allowed women to choose whether or not to wear a veil.

Government and Politics

Albania's first political parties emerged only after World War I. Even more than in other parts of the Balkans, political parties were impermanent gatherings centered on prominent persons who created temporary alliances to achieve their personal aims. The major conservative party, the Progressive Party, attracted some northern clan chiefs and prominent Muslim landholders of southern Albania whose main platform was firm opposition to any agricultural reform program that would transfer their lands to the peasantry. The country's biggest landowner, Shefqet Bey Verlaci, led the Progressive Party. The Popular Party's ranks included the reform-minded Orthodox bishop of Durrës, Fan S. Noli, who was imbued with Western ideas at his alma mater, Harvard University, and had even translated Shakespeare and Ibsen into Albanian. The Popular Party also included Ahmed Zogu, the twenty-four-year-old son of the chief of the Mati, a central Albanian Muslim tribe. The future King Zog drew his support from some northern clans and kept an armed gang in his service, but many Geg clan leaders refused to support either main party.

Interwar Albanian governments appeared and disappeared in rapid succession. Between July and December 1921 alone, the premiership changed hands five times. The Popular Party's head, Xhafer Ypi, formed a government in December 1921, with Noli as foreign minister and Zogu as internal affairs minister. Noli, however, resigned soon after Zogu, in an attempt to disarm the lowland Albanians, resorted to repression, despite the fact that bearing arms was a traditional custom. When the government's enemies attacked Tiranë in early 1922, Zogu stayed in the capital and, with the help of the British ambassador, repulsed the assault. He took over the premiership later in the year and turned his back on the Popular Party by announcing his engagement to the daughter of the Progressive Party leader, Shefqet Beg Verlaci.

Zogu's protégés organized themselves into the Government Party. Noli and other Western-oriented leaders formed the Opposition Party of Democrats, which attracted Zogu's many personal enemies, ideological opponents, and people left unrewarded by his political machine. Ideologically, the Democrats included a broad sweep of people who advocated everything from conservative Islam to Noli's dreams of rapid modernization. Opposition to Zogu was formidable. Orthodox peasants in Albania's southern lowlands loathed Zogu because he supported the Muslim landowners' efforts to block land reform; Shkodër's citizens felt shortchanged because their city did not become Albania's capital; and nationalists were dissatisfied because Zogu's government did not press Albania's claims to Kosovo or speak up more energetically for the rights of the ethnic Albanian minorities in present-day Yugoslavia and Greece.

Zogu's party handily won elections for a National Assembly in early 1924. Zogu soon stepped aside, however, handing over the premiership to Verlaci in the wake of a financial scandal and an assassination attempt by a young radical that left Zogu wounded. The opposition withdrew from the assembly after the leader of a radical youth organization, Avni Rustemi, was murdered in the street outside the parliament building. Noli's supporters blamed the murder on Zogu's Mati clansmen, who continued to practice blood vengeance. After the walkout, discontent mounted, and by July 1924 a peasant-backed insurgency had won control of Tiranë. Noli became prime minister, and Zogu fled to Yugoslavia.

Fan Noli, an idealist, rejected demands for new elections on the grounds that Albania needed a "paternal" government. In a manifesto describing his government's program, Noli called for abolishing feudalism, resisting Italian domination, and establishing a Western-style constitutional government. Scaling back the bureaucracy, strengthening local government, assisting peasants, throwing Albania open to foreign investment, and improving the country's bleak transportation, public health, and education facilities filled out the Noli government's overly ambitious agenda. Noli, however, encountered resistance to his program from people who had helped him oust Zogu, and he never attracted the foreign aid necessary to carry out his reform plans. Concerned over potential Italian domination, Noli criticized the League of Nations for failing to settle the threat facing Albania on its land borders.

Under Fan Noli, the government set up a special tribunal that passed death sentences, in absentia, on Zogu, Verlaci, and others and confiscated their property. In Yugoslavia Zogu recruited a mercenary army, and Belgrade furnished the Albanian leader with weapons, about 1,000 Yugoslav army regulars, and refugee troops from the Russian Civil War to mount an invasion that the Serbs hoped would bring them disputed areas along the border. After Noli's regime decided to establish diplomatic relations with the Soviet Union, a bitter enemy of the Serbian ruling family, Belgrade began making wild allegations that the Albanian regime was about to embrace Bolshevism. On December 13, 1924, Zogu's Yugoslav-backed army crossed into Albanian territory. By Christmas Eve, Zogu had reclaimed the capital, and Noli and his government had fled to Italy.

Zogu quickly smothered Albania's experiment in parliamentary democracy. Looking after the interests of the large landowners, clan chiefs, and others with a vested interest in maintaining the old order, he undertook no serious reform measures. The parliament quickly adopted a new constitution, proclaimed Albania a republic, and granted Zogu dictatorial powers that allowed him to appoint and dismiss ministers, veto legislation, and name all major administrative personnel and a third of the Senate. On January 31, Zogu was elected president for a seven-year term. Opposition parties and civil liberties disappeared, opponents of the regime were murdered, and the press suffered strict censorship. Zogu ruled Albania using four military governors responsible to him alone. He appointed clan chieftains as reserve army officers, who were kept on call to protect the regime against domestic or foreign threats.

Italian Penetration

Belgrade, in return for aiding Zogu's invasion, expected repayment in the form of territory and influence in Tiranë. It is certain that Zogu promised Belgrade frontier concessions before the invasion, but once in power the Albanian leader continued to press Albania's own territorial claims. On July 30, 1925, the two nations signed an agreement returning the town of Saint Naum on Lake Ohrid and other disputed borderlands to Yugoslavia. The larger country, however, never reaped the dividends it hoped for when it invested in Zogu. He shunned Belgrade and turned Albania toward Italy for protection.

Advocates of territorial expansion in Italy gathered strength in October 1922 when Benito Mussolini took power in Rome. His fascist supporters undertook an unabashed program aimed at establishing a new Roman empire in the Mediterranean region that would rival Britain and France. Mussolini saw Albania as a foothold in the Balkans, and after the war the Great Powers in effect recognized an Italian protectorate over Albania.

In May 1925, Italy began a penetration into Albania's national life that would culminate fourteen years later in its occupation and annexation of Albania. The first major step was an agreement between Rome and Tiranë that allowed Italy to exploit Albania's mineral resources. Soon Albania's parliament agreed to allow the Italians to found the Albanian National Bank, which acted as the Albanian treasury even though its main office was in Rome and Italian banks effectively controlled it. The Albanians also awarded Italian shipping companies a monopoly on freight and passenger transport to and from Albania.

In late 1925, the Italian-backed Society for the Economic Development of Albania began to lend the Albanian government funds at high interest rates for transportation, agriculture, and public-works projects, including Zogu's palace. In the end, the loans turned out to be subsidies.

In mid-1926 Italy set to work to extend its political influence in Albania, asking Tiranë to recognize Rome's special interest in Albania and accept Italian instructors in the army and police. Zogu resisted until an uprising in the northern mountains pressured the Albanian leader to conclude the First Treaty of Tiranë with the Italians in November 1926. In the treaty, both states agreed not to conclude any agreements with any other states prejudicial to their mutual interests. The agreement, in effect, guaranteed Zogu's political position in Albania as well as the country's boundaries. In November 1927, Albania and Italy entered into a defensive alliance, the Second Treaty of Tiranë, which brought an Italian general and about forty officers to train the Albanian army. Italian military experts soon began instructing paramilitary youth groups. Tiranë also allowed the Italian navy access to the port of Vlorë, and the Albanians received large deliveries of armaments from Italy.

Zog's Kingdom

In 1928 Zogu secured the parliament's consent to its own dissolution. A new constituent assembly amended the constitution, making Albania a kingdom and transforming Zogu into Zog I, "King of the Albanians." International recognition arrived forthwith, but many Albanians regarded their country's nascent dynasty as a tragic farce. The new constitution abolished the Senate, creating a unicameral National Assembly, but King Zog retained the dictatorial powers he had enjoyed as President Zogu. Soon after his coronation, Zog broke off his engagement to Shefqet Bey Verlaci's daughter, and Verlaci withdrew his support for the king and began plotting against him. Zog had accumulated a great number of enemies over the years, and the Albanian tradition of blood vengeance required them to try to kill him. Zog surrounded himself with guards and rarely appeared in public. The king's loyalists disarmed all of Albania's tribes except for his own Mati tribesmen and their allies, the Dibra. Nevertheless, on a visit to Vienna in 1931, Zog and his bodyguards fought a gun battle with would-be assassins on the Opera House steps.

Zog remained sensitive to steadily mounting disillusion with Italy's domination of Albania. The Albanian army, though always less than 15,000-strong, sapped the country's funds, and the Italians' monopoly on training the armed forces rankled public opinion. As a counterweight, Zog kept British officers in the Gendarmerie despite strong Italian pressure to remove them. In 1931 Zog openly stood up to the Italians, refusing to renew the 1926 First Treaty of Tiranë. In 1932 and 1933, Albania could not make the interest payments on its loans from the Society for the Economic Development of Albania. In response, Rome turned up the pressure, demanding that Tiranë name Italians to direct the Gendarmerie; join Italy in a customs union; grant Italy control of the country's sugar, telegraph, and electrical monopolies; teach the Italian language in all Albanian schools; and admit Italian colonists. Zog refused. Instead, he ordered the national budget slashed by 30 percent, dismissed the Italian military advisers, and nationalized Italian-run Roman Catholic schools in the northern part of the country.

By June 1934, Albania had signed trade agreements with Yugoslavia and Greece, and Mussolini had suspended all payments to Tiranë. An Italian attempt to intimidate the Albanians by sending a fleet of warships to Albania failed because the Albanians only allowed the forces to land unarmed. Mussolini then attempted to buy off the Albanians. In 1935 he presented the Albanian government 3 million gold francs as a gift.

Zog's success in defeating two local rebellions convinced Mussolini that the Italians had to reach a new agreement with the Albanian king. A government of young men led by Mehdi Frasheri, an enlightened Bektashi administrator, won a commitment from Italy to fulfill financial promises that Mussolini had made to Albania and to grant new loans for harbor improvements at Durrës and other projects that would keep the Albanian government afloat. Soon Italians began taking positions in Albania's civil service, and Italian settlers were allowed into the country.

Through all the turmoil of the interwar years, Albania remained Europe's most economically backward nation. Peasant farmers accounted for the vast majority of the Albanian population. Albania had practically had no industry, and the country's potential for hydroelectric power was virtually untapped. Oil represented the country's main extractable resource. A pipeline between the Kuçovë oil field and the port at Vlorë expedited shipments of crude petroleum to Italy's refineries after the Italians took over the oil-drilling concessions of all other foreign companies in 1939. Albania also possessed bitumen, lignite, iron, chromite, copper, bauxite, manganese, and some gold. Shkodër had a cement factory; Korçë, a brewery; and Durrës and Shkodër, cigarette factories that used locally grown tobacco.

During much of the interwar period, Italians held most of the technical jobs in the Albanian economy. Albania's main exports were petroleum, animal skins, cheese, livestock, and eggs, and prime imports were grain and other foodstuffs, metal products, and machinery. In 1939 the value of Albania's imports outstripped that of its exports by about four times. About 70 percent of Albania's exports went to Italy. Italian factories furnished about 40 percent of Albania's imports, and the Italian government paid for the rest.

Italian Occupation

As Germany annexed Austria and moved against Czechoslovakia, Italy saw itself becoming a second-rate member of the Axis. After Hitler invaded Czechoslovakia without notifying Mussolini in advance, the Italian dictator decided in early 1939 to proceed with his own annexation of Albania. Italy's King Victor Emmanuel III criticized the plan to take Albania as an unnecessary risk.

Rome, however, delivered Tiranë an ultimatum on March 25, 1939, demanding that it accede to Italy's occupation of Albania. Zog refused to accept money in exchange for countenancing a full Italian takeover and colonization of Albania, and on April 7, 1939, Mussolini's troops invaded Albania. Despite some stubborn resistance, especially at Durrës, the Italians made short work of the Albanians. Unwilling to become an Italian puppet, King Zog, his wife Queen Geraldine Apponyi, and their infant son Skander fled to Greece and eventually to London. On April 12, the Albanian parliament voted to unite the country with Italy. Victor Emmanuel III took the Albanian crown, and the Italians set up a fascist government under Shefqet Verlaci and soon absorbed Albania's military and diplomatic service into Italy's.

After the German army had defeated Poland, Denmark, and France, a still-jealous Mussolini decided to use Albania as a springboard to invade Greece. The Italians launched their attack on October 28, 1940, and at a meeting of the two fascist dictators in Florence, Mussolini stunned Hitler with his announcement of the Italian invasion. Mussolini counted on a quick victory, but Greek resistance fighters halted the Italian army in its tracks and soon advanced into Albania. The Greeks took Korçë and Gjirokastër and threatened to drive the Italians from the port city of Vlorë. The chauvinism of the Greek troops fighting in Albania cooled the Albanians' enthusiasm for fighting the Italians, and Mussolini's forces soon established a stable front in central Albania. In April 1941, Germany and its allies crushed both Greece and Yugoslavia, and a month later the Axis gave Albania control of Kosovo. Thus Albanian nationalists ironically witnessed the realization of their dreams of uniting most of the Albanian-populated lands during the Axis occupation of their country.

World War II and the Rise of Communism, 1941–44

Between 1941 and 1944, communist partisans and nationalist guerrillas fought Italian and German occupation forces, and more often each other, in a brutal struggle to take control of Albania. Backed by Yugoslavia's communists and armed with British and United States weaponry, Albania's partisans defeated the nationalists in a civil war fought between Italy's capitulation in September 1943 and the withdrawal of German forces from Albania in late 1944. Military victory, and not the lure of Marxism, brought the Albanian communists from behind the scenes to center stage in Albania's political drama. Although Albanian writers never tired of pointing out that the communists had "liberated" Albania without a single Soviet soldier setting foot on its territory, they often neglected to mention that the communist forces in Albania were organized by the Yugoslavs and armed by the West or that the Axis retreat from Albania was in response to military defeats outside the country.

The Communist and Nationalist Resistance

Faced with an illiterate, agrarian, and mostly Muslim society monitored by Zog's security police, Albania's communist movement attracted few adherents in the interwar period. In fact, the country had no full-fledged communist party before World War II. After Fan Noli fled in 1924 to Italy and later the United States, several of his leftist protégés migrated to Moscow, where they affiliated themselves with the Balkan Confederation of Communist Parties and through it the Communist International (Comintern), the Soviet-sponsored association of international communist parties. In 1930 the Comintern dispatched Ali Kelmendi to Albania to organize communist cells. But Albania had no working class for the communists to exploit, and Marxism appealed to only a minute number of quarrelsome, Western-educated, mostly Tosk, intellectuals and to landless peasants, miners, and other persons discontented with Albania's obsolete social and economic structures. Forced to flee Albania, Kelmendi fought in the Garibaldi International Brigade during the Spanish Civil War and later moved to France, where together with other communists, including a student named Enver Hoxha, he published a newspaper. Paris became the Albanian communists' hub until Nazi deportations depleted their ranks after the fall of France in 1940.

Enver Hoxha and another veteran of the Spanish Civil War, Mehmet Shehu, eventually rose to become the most powerful figures in Albania during the decades after the war. The dominant figure in modern Albanian history, Enver Hoxha rose from obscurity to lead his people for a longer time than any other ruler. Born in 1908 to a Muslim Tosk landowner from Gjirokastër who returned to Albania after working in the United States, Hoxha attended the country's best college-preparatory school, the National Lycée in Korçë. In 1930 he attended the university in Montpelier, France, but lost an Albanian state scholarship for neglecting his studies. Hoxha subsequently moved to Paris and Brussels. After returning to Albania in 1936 without earning a degree, he taught French for years at his former lycée and participated in a communist cell in Korçë. When the war erupted, Hoxha joined the Albanian partisans. Shehu, also a Muslim Tosk, studied at Tiranë's American Vocational School. He went on to a military college in Naples but was expelled for left-wing political activity. In Spain Shehu fought in the Garibaldi International Brigade. After internment in France, he returned to Albania in 1942 and fought with the partisans, gaining a reputation for brutality.

In October 1941, the leader of Communist Party of the Yugoslavia,

Josip Broz Tito, dispatched agents to Albania to forge the country's disparate, impotent communist factions into a monolithic party organization. Within a month, they had established a Yugoslav-dominated Albanian Communist Party of 130 members under the leadership of Hoxha and an eleven-member Central Committee. The party at first had little mass appeal, and even its youth organization netted few recruits. In mid-1942, however, party leaders increased their popularity by heeding Tito's order to muffle their Marxist-Leninist propaganda and call instead for national liberation. In September 1942, the party organized a popular front organization, the National Liberation Movement (NLM), from a number of resistance groups, including several that were strongly anticommunist. During the war, the NLM's communist-dominated partisans, in the form of the National Liberation Army, did not heed warnings from the Italian occupiers that there would be reprisals for guerrilla attacks. Partisan leaders, on the contrary, counted on using the lust for revenge such reprisals would elicit to win recruits.

A nationalist resistance to the Italian occupiers emerged in October 1942. Ali Klissura and Midhat Frasheri formed the Western-oriented and anticommunist Balli Kombetar (National Union), a movement that recruited supporters from both the large landowners and peasantry. The Balli Kombetar opposed King Zog's return and called for the creation of a republic and the introduction of some economic and social reforms. The Balli Kombetar's leaders acted conservatively, however, fearing that the occupiers would carry out reprisals against innocent peasants or confiscate the landowners' estates. The nationalistic Geg chieftains and the Tosk landowners often came to terms with the Italians, and later the Germans, to prevent the loss of their wealth and power.

With the overthrow of Mussolini's fascist regime and Italy's surrender in 1943, the Italian military and police establishment in Albania buckled. Albanian fighters overwhelmed five Italian divisions, and enthusiastic recruits flocked to the guerrilla forces. The communists took control of most of Albania's southern cities, except Vlorë, which was a Balli Kombetar stronghold, and nationalists attached to the NLM gained control over much of the north. British agents working in Albania during the war fed the Albanian resistance fighters with information that the Allies were planning a major invasion of the Balkans and urged the disparate Albanian groups to unite their efforts. In August 1943, the Allies convinced communist and Balli Kombetar leaders to meet in the village of Mukaj, near Tiranë, and form a Committee for the Salvation of Albania that would coordinate their guerrilla operations. The two groups eventually ended all collaboration, however, over a disagreement on the postwar status of Kosovo. The communists, under Yugoslav tutelage, supported returning the region to Yugoslavia after the war, while the nationalist Balli Kombetar advocated keeping the province. The delegates at Mukaj agreed that a plebiscite should be held in Kosovo to decide the matter; but under Yugoslav pressure, the communists soon reneged on the accord. A month later, the communists attacked Balli Kombetar forces, igniting a civil war that was fought for the next year, mostly in southern Albania.

Germany occupied Albania in September 1943, dropping paratroopers into Tiranë before the Albanian guerrillas could take the capital, and the German army soon drove the guerrillas into the hills and to the south. Berlin subsequently announced it would recognize the independence of a neutral Albania and organized an Albanian government, police, and military. The Germans did not exert heavy-handed control over Albania's administration. Rather, they sought to gain popular support by backing causes popular with Albanians, especially the annexation of Kosovo. Some Balli Kombetar units cooperated with the Germans against the communists, and several Balli Kombetar leaders held positions in the German-sponsored regime. Albanian collaborators, especially the Skanderbeg SS Division, also expelled and killed Serbs living in Kosovo. In December 1943, a third resistance organization, an anticommunist, anti-German royalist group known as Legality, took shape in Albania's northern mountains. Legality, led by Abaz Kupi, largely consisted of Geg guerrillas who withdrew their support for the NLM after the communists renounced Albania's claims on Kosovo.

The Communist Takeover of Albania

The communist partisans regrouped and, thanks to freshly supplied British weapons, gained control of southern Albania in January 1944. In May they called a congress of members of the National Liberation Front (NLF, as the movement was by then called) at Përmet, which chose an Anti-Fascist Council of National Liberation to act as Albania's administration and legislature. Hoxha became the chairman of the council's executive committee and the National Liberation Army's supreme commander. The communist partisans defeated the last Balli Kombetar forces in southern Albania by mid-summer 1944 and encountered only scattered resistance from the Balli Kombetar and Legality when they entered central and northern Albania by the end of July. The British military mission urged the nationalists not to oppose the communists' advance, and the Allies evacuated Kupi to Italy. Before

War memorial in Durrës
Courtesy Fred Conrad

the end of November, the Germans had withdrawn from Tiranë, and the communists, supported by Allied air cover, had no problem taking control of the capital. A provisional government the communists had formed at Berat in October administered Albania with Enver Hoxha as prime minister, and in late 1944 Hoxha dispatched Albanian partisans to help Tito's forces rout Albanian nationalists in Kosovo.

Albania stood in an unenviable position after World War II. Greece and Yugoslavia hungered for Albanian lands they had lost or claimed. The NLF's strong links with Yugoslavia's communists, who also enjoyed British military and diplomatic support, guaranteed that Belgrade would play a key role in Albania's postwar order. The Allies never recognized an Albanian government in exile or King Zog, nor did they ever raise the question of Albania or its borders at any of the major wartime conferences. No reliable statistics on Albania's wartime losses exist, but the United Nations Relief and Rehabilitation Administration reported about 30,000 Albanian war dead, 200 destroyed villages, 18,000 destroyed houses, and about 100,000 people left homeless. Albanian official statistics claim somewhat higher losses.

Communist Albania

Official Albanian writers and artists presented the history of communist Albania as the saga of a backward, besieged people marching toward a Stalinist utopia. The actual story of communist Albania is, however, quintessentially dystopian: a bleak inventory of bloody purges and repression, a case study in betrayal and obsessive xenophobia, and a cacophony of bitter polemics.

After five years of party infighting and extermination campaigns against the country's anticommunist opposition, Enver Hoxha and Mehmet Shehu emerged as the dominant figures in Albania. The duumvirate concentrated primarily on securing and maintaining their power base and secondarily on preserving Albania's independence and reshaping the country according to the procrustean precepts of orthodox Stalinism. In pursuit of these goals, the communist elite co-opted or terrorized the entire Albanian population into blind obedience, herding them into obligatory front organizations, bombarding them with propaganda, and disciplining them with a police force that completely disregarded legal, ethical, religious, or political norms. Hoxha and Shehu dominated Albania and denied the Albanian people the most basic human and civil rights by presenting themselves, as well as the communist party and state security apparatus they controlled, as the vigilant defenders of the country's independence. After Albania's break with Yugoslavia in late 1948, Albania was a client of the Soviet Union. Following the Soviet Union's rapprochement with Tito after Stalin's death, Albania turned away from Moscow and found a new benefactor in China. When China's isolation ended in the 1970s, Albania turned away from its giant Asian patron and adopted a strict policy of autarky that brought the country economic ruin. But through it all, Hoxha engineered an elaborate cult of personality (see Glossary) whose spokesmen elevated his persona to the status of a god-man. When he died in 1985, few Albanian eyes were without tears.

Consolidation of Power and Initial Reforms

A tiny collection of militant communists moved quickly after World War II to subdue all potential political enemies in Albania, break the country's landowners and minuscule middle class, and isolate Albania from the noncommunist world. By early 1945, the communists had liquidated, discredited, or driven into exile most of the country's interwar elite. The internal affairs minister, Koçi Xoxe, a pro-Yugoslav erstwhile tinsmith, presided over the trial and the execution of thousands of opposition politicians, clan chiefs, and members of former Albanian governments, who were condemned as "war criminals." Thousands of their family members were imprisoned for years in work camps and jails and later exiled for decades to state farms built on reclaimed marshlands. The communists' consolidation of control also produced a shift in political power in Albania from the northern Gegs to the southern Tosks. Most communist leaders were middle-class Tosks, and the party drew most of its recruits from Tosk-inhabited areas; the Gegs, with their centuries-old tradition of opposing authority, distrusted the new Albanian rulers and their alien Marxist doctrines.

In December 1945, Albanians elected a new People's Assembly, but only candidates from the Democratic Front (previously the National Liberation Movement, then the National Liberation Front) appeared on the electoral lists, and the communists used propaganda and terror tactics to gag the opposition. Official ballot tallies showed that 92 percent of the electorate voted and that 93 percent of the voters chose the Democratic Front ticket. The assembly convened in January 1946, annulled the monarchy, and transformed Albania into a "people's republic." After months of angry debate, the assembly adopted a constitution that mirrored the Yugoslav and Soviet constitutions. Then in the spring, the assembly members chose a new government. Hoxha, the Albanian Communist Party's first secretary, became prime minister, foreign minister, defense minister, and the army's commander in chief. Xoxe remained both internal affairs minister and the party's organizational secretary. In late 1945 and early 1946, Xoxe and other party hard-liners purged moderates who had pressed for close contacts with the West, a modicum of political pluralism, and a delay in the introduction of strict communist economic measures until Albania's economy had more time to develop. Hoxha remained in control despite the fact that he had once advocated restoring relations with Italy and even allowing Albanians to study in Italy.

The communists also undertook economic measures to expand their power. In December 1944, the provisional government adopted laws allowing the state to regulate foreign and domestic trade, commercial enterprises, and the few industries the country possessed. The laws sanctioned confiscation of property belonging to political exiles and "enemies of the people." The state also expropriated all German- and Italian-owned property, nationalized transportation enterprises, and canceled all concessions granted by previous Albanian governments to foreign companies.

The government took major steps to introduce a Stalinist-style centrally planned economy in 1946. It nationalized all industries, transformed foreign trade into a government monopoly, brought almost all domestic trade under state control, and banned land sales and transfers. Planners at the newly founded Economic Planning Commission emphasized industrial development, and in 1947 the government introduced the Soviet cost-accounting system.

In August 1945, the provisional government adopted the first sweeping agricultural reforms in Albania's history. The country's 100 largest landowners, who controlled close to a third of Albania's arable land, had frustrated all agricultural reform proposals before the war. The communists' reforms were aimed at squeezing large landowners out of business, winning peasant support, and increasing farm output to avert famine. The government annulled outstanding agricultural debts, granted peasants access to inexpensive water for irrigation, and nationalized forest and pastureland. Under the Agrarian Reform Law, which redistributed about half of Albania's arable land, the government confiscated property belonging to absentee landlords and people not dependent on agriculture for a living. The few peasants with agricultural machinery were permitted to keep up to forty hectares of land; the landholdings of religious institutions and peasants without agricultural machinery were limited to twenty hectares; and landless peasants and peasants with tiny landholdings were given up to five hectares, although they had to pay nominal compensation. Thus tiny farmsteads replaced large private estates across Albania. By mid-1946 Albanian peasants were cultivating more land and producing higher corn and wheat yields than ever before.

Albanian-Yugoslav Tensions

Until Yugoslavia's expulsion from the Cominform (see Glossary) in 1948, Albania acted like a Yugoslav satellite, and Tito aimed to use his choke hold on the Albanian party to incorporate the entire country into Yugoslavia. After Germany's withdrawal from Kosovo in late 1944, Yugoslavia's communist partisans took possession of the province and committed retaliatory massacres against Albanians. Before World War II, the Communist Party of Yugoslavia had supported transferring Kosovo to Albania, but Yugoslavia's postwar communist regime insisted on preserving the country's prewar borders. In repudiating the 1943 Mukaj agreement under pressure from the Yugoslavs, Albania's communists had consented to restore Kosovo to Yugoslavia after the war. In January 1945, the two governments signed a treaty reincorporating Kosovo into Yugoslavia as an autonomous province. Shortly thereafter, Yugoslavia became the first country to recognize Albania's provisional government.

In July 1946, Yugoslavia and Albania signed a treaty of friendship and cooperation that was quickly followed by a series of technical and economic agreements laying the groundwork for integrating the Albanian and Yugoslav economies. The pacts provided for coordinating the economic plans of both states, standardizing their monetary systems, and creating a common pricing system and a customs union. So close was the Yugoslav-Albanian relationship that Serbo-Croatian became a required subject in Albanian high schools. Yugoslavia signed a similar friendship treaty with Bulgaria, and Marshal Tito and Bulgaria's Georgi Dimitrov talked of plans to establish a Balkan federation to include Albania, Yugoslavia, and Bulgaria. Yugoslav advisers poured into Albania's government offices and its army headquarters. Tiranë was desperate for outside aid, and about 20,000 tons of Yugoslav grain helped stave off famine. Albania also received US$26.3 million from the United Nations Relief and Rehabilitation Administration immediately after the war but had to rely on Yugoslavia for investment and development aid.

The Yugoslav government clearly regarded investment in Albania as investment in the future of Yugoslavia itself. Joint Albanian-Yugoslav companies were created for mining, railroad construction, the production of petroleum and electricity, and international trade. Yugoslav investments led to the construction of a sugar refinery in Korçë, a food-processing plant in Elbasan, a hemp factory at Rrogozhine, a fish cannery in Vlorë, and a printing press, telephone exchange, and textile mill in Tiranë. The Yugoslavs also bolstered the Albanian economy by paying three times the world price for Albanian copper and other materials.

Relations between Albania and Yugoslavia declined, however, when the Albanians began complaining that the Yugoslavs were paying too little for Albanian raw materials and exploiting Albania through the joint stock companies. In addition, the Albanians sought investment funds to develop light industries and an oil refinery, while the Yugoslavs wanted the Albanians to concentrate on agriculture and raw-material extraction. The head of Albania's Economic Planning Commission and one of Hoxha's allies, Nako Spiru, became the leading critic of Yugoslavia's efforts to exert economic control over Albania. Tito distrusted Hoxha and the other intellectuals in the Albanian party and, through Xoxe and his loyalists, attempted to unseat them.

In 1947 Yugoslavia's leaders engineered an all-out offensive against anti-Yugoslav Albanian communists, including Hoxha and Spiru. In May Tiranë announced the arrest, trial, and conviction of nine People's Assembly members, all known for opposing Yugoslavia, on charges of antistate activities. A month later, the Communist Party of Yugoslavia's Central Committee accused Hoxha of following "independent" policies and turning the Albanian people against Yugoslavia. Apparently attempting to buy support inside the Albanian Communist Party, Belgrade extended Tiranë

US$40 million worth of credits, an amount equal to 58 percent of Albania's 1947 state budget. A year later, Yugoslavia's credits accounted for nearly half of the state budget. Relations worsened in the fall, however, when Spiru's commission developed an economic plan that stressed self-sufficiency, light industry, and agriculture. The Yugoslavs complained bitterly, and when Spiru came under criticism and failed to win support from anyone in the Albanian party leadership, he committed suicide.

The insignificance of Albania's standing in the communist world was clearly highlighted when the emerging East European nations did not invite the Albanian party to the September 1947 founding meeting of the Cominform. Rather, Yugoslavia represented Albania at Cominform meetings. Although the Soviet Union gave Albania a pledge to build textile and sugar mills and other factories and to provide Albania agricultural and industrial machinery, Stalin told Milovan Djilas, at the time a high-ranking member of Yugoslavia's communist hierarchy, that Yugoslavia should "swallow" Albania.

The pro-Yugoslav faction wielded decisive political power in Albania well into 1948. At a party plenum in February and March, the communist leadership voted to merge the Albanian and Yugoslav economies and militaries. Hoxha, to the core an opportunist, even denounced Spiru for attempting to ruin Albanian-Yugoslav relations. During a party Political Bureau (Politburo) meeting a month later, Xoxe proposed appealing to Belgrade to admit Albania as a seventh Yugoslav republic. When the Cominform expelled Yugoslavia on June 28, however, Albania made a rapid about-face in its policy toward Yugoslavia. The move surely saved Hoxha from a firing squad and as surely doomed Xoxe to one. Three days later, Tiranë gave the Yugoslav advisers in Albania forty-eight hours to leave the country, rescinded all bilateral economic agreements with its neighbor, and launched a virulent anti-Yugoslav propaganda blitz that transformed Stalin into an Albanian national hero, Hoxha into a warrior against foreign aggression, and Tito into an imperialist monster.

Albania entered an orbit around the Soviet Union, and in September 1948 Moscow stepped in to compensate for Albania's loss of Yugoslav aid. The shift proved to be a boon for Albania because Moscow had far more to offer than hard-strapped Belgrade. The fact that the Soviet Union had no common border with Albania also appealed to the Albanian regime because it made it more difficult for Moscow to exert pressure on Tiranë. In November at the First Party Congress of the Albanian Party of Labor (APL), the former Albanian Communist Party renamed at Stalin's suggestion,

Hoxha pinned the blame for the country's woes on Yugoslavia and Xoxe. Hoxha had had Xoxe sacked as internal affairs minister in October, replacing him with Shehu. After a secret trial in May 1949, Xoxe was executed. The subsequent anti-Titoist purges in Albania brought the liquidation of fourteen members of the party's thirty-one-person Central Committee and thirty-two of the 109 People's Assembly deputies. Overall, the party expelled about 25 percent of its membership. Yugoslavia responded with a propaganda counterattack, canceled its treaty of friendship with Albania, and in 1950 withdrew its diplomatic mission from Tiranë.

Deteriorating Relations with the West

Albania's relations with the West soured after the communist regime's refusal to allow free elections in December 1945. Albania restricted the movements of United States and British personnel in the country, charging that they had instigated anticommunist uprisings in the northern mountains. Britain announced in April that it would not send a diplomatic mission to Tiranë, the United States withdrew its mission in November, and both the United States and Britain opposed admitting Albania to the United Nations (UN). The Albanian regime feared that the United States and Britain, which were supporting anticommunist forces in the civil war in Greece, would back Greek demands for territory in southern Albania; and anxieties grew in July when a United States Senate resolution backed the Greek demands.

A major incident between Albania and Britain erupted in 1946 after Tiranë claimed jurisdiction over the channel between the Albanian mainland and the Greek island of Corfu. Britain challenged Albania by sailing four destroyers into the channel. Two of the ships struck mines on October 22, 1946, and forty-four crew members died. Britain complained to the UN and the International Court of Justice, which, in its first case ever, ruled against Tiranë.

After 1946 the United States and Britain began implementing an elaborate covert plan to overthrow Albania's communist regime by backing anticommunist and royalist forces within the country. By 1949 the United States and British intelligence organizations were working with King Zog and the fanatic mountainmen of his personal guard. They recruited Albanian refugees and émigrés from Egypt, Italy, and Greece; trained them in Cyprus, Malta, and the Federal Republic of Germany (West Germany); and infiltrated them into Albania. Guerrilla units entered Albania in 1950 and 1952, but Albanian security forces killed or captured all of them. Kim Philby, a Soviet double agent working as a liaison officer between the British intelligence service and the United States Central

Intelligence Agency, had leaked details of the infiltration plan to Moscow, and the security breach claimed the lives of about 300 infiltrators.

A wave of subversive activity, including the failed infiltration and the March 1951 bombing of the Soviet embassy in Tiranë, encouraged the Albanian regime to implement harsh internal security measures. In September 1952, the assembly enacted a penal code that required the death penalty for anyone over eleven years old found guilty of conspiring against the state, damaging state property, or committing economic sabotage.

Albania and the Soviet Union

Albania became dependent on Soviet aid and know-how after the break with Yugoslavia in 1948. In February 1949, Albania gained membership in the communist bloc's organization for coordinating economic planning, the Council for Mutual Economic Assistance (Comecon). Tiranë soon entered into trade agreements with Poland, Czechoslovakia, Hungary, Romania, and the Soviet Union. Soviet and East European technical advisers took up residence in Albania, and the Soviet Union also sent Albania military advisers and built a submarine installation on Sazan Island. After the Soviet-Yugoslav split, Albania and Bulgaria were the only countries the Soviet Union could use to funnel war matériel to the communists fighting in Greece. What little strategic value Albania offered the Soviet Union, however, gradually shrank as nuclear arms technology developed.

Anxious to pay homage to Stalin, Albania's rulers implemented new elements of the Stalinist economic system. In 1949 Albania adopted the basic elements of the Soviet fiscal system, under which state enterprises paid direct contributions to the treasury from their profits and kept only a share authorized for self-financed investments and other purposes. In 1951 the Albanian government launched its first five-year plan, which emphasized exploiting the country's oil, chromite, copper, nickel, asphalt, and coal resources; expanding electricity production and the power grid; increasing agricultural output; and improving transportation. The government began a program of rapid industrialization after the APL's Second Party Congress and a campaign of forced collectivization of farmland in 1955. At the time, private farms still produced about 87 percent of Albania's agricultural output, but by 1960 the same percentage came from collective or state farms.

Soviet-Albanian relations remained warm during the last years of Stalin's life despite the fact that Albania was an economic liability for the Soviet Union. Albania conducted all its foreign trade with Soviet bloc countries in 1949, 1950, and 1951 and over half its trade with the Soviet Union itself. Together with its satellites, the Soviet Union underwrote shortfalls in Albania's balance of payments with long-term grants (see Dependence on the Soviet Union, 1948–60, ch. 3).

Although far behind Western practice, health care and education improved dramatically for Albania's 1.2 million people in the early 1950s. The number of Albanian doctors increased by a third to about 150 early in the decade (although the doctor-patient ratio remained unacceptable by most standards), and the state opened new medical training facilities. The number of hospital beds rose from 1,765 in 1945 to about 5,500 in 1953. Better health care and living conditions produced an improvement in Albania's dismal infant mortality rate, lowering it from 112.2 deaths per 1,000 live births in 1945 to 99.5 deaths per 1,000 births in 1953 (see Medical Care and Nutrition, ch. 2). The education system, considered a tool for propagating communism and creating the academic and technical cadres necessary for construction of a socialist state and society, also improved dramatically. The number of schools, teachers, and students doubled between 1945 and 1950. Illiteracy declined from perhaps 85 percent in 1946 to 31 percent in 1950. The Soviet Union provided scholarships for Albanian students and supplied specialists and study materials to improve instruction in Albania. The Enver Hoxha University at Tiranë was founded in 1957, and the Albanian Academy of Sciences opened fifteen years later. Despite these advances, however, education in Albania suffered as a result of restrictions on freedom of thought. For example, educational institutions had scant influence on their own curricula, methods of teaching, or administration (see Education under Communist Rule, ch. 2).

Stalin died in March 1953, and apparently fearing that the Soviet ruler's demise might encourage rivals within the Albanian party's ranks, neither Hoxha nor Shehu risked traveling to Moscow to attend his funeral. The Soviet Union's subsequent movement toward rapprochement with the hated Yugoslavs rankled the two Albanian leaders. Tiranë soon came under pressure from Moscow to copy, at least formally, the new Soviet model for a collective leadership. In July 1953, Hoxha handed over the foreign affairs and defense portfolios to loyal followers, but he kept both the top party post and the premiership until 1954, when Shehu became Albania's prime minister. The Soviet Union, responding with an effort to raise the Albanian leaders' morale, elevated diplomatic relations between the two countries to the ambassadorial level.

Despite some initial expressions of enthusiasm, Hoxha and Shehu mistrusted Nikita Khrushchev's programs of "peaceful coexistence" and "different roads to socialism" because they appeared to pose the threat that Yugoslavia might again try to take control of Albania. Hoxha and Shehu were also alarmed at the prospect that Moscow might prefer less dogmatic rulers in Albania. Tiranë and Belgrade renewed diplomatic relations in December 1953, but Hoxha refused Khrushchev's repeated appeals to rehabilitate posthumously the pro-Yugoslav Xoxe as a gesture to Tito. The Albanian duo instead tightened their grip on their country's domestic life and let the propaganda war with the Yugoslavs grind on. In 1955 Albania became a founding member of the Warsaw Treaty Organization (see Glossary), better known as the Warsaw Pact, the only military alliance the nation ever joined. Although the pact represented the first promise Albania had obtained from any of the communist countries to defend its borders, the treaty did nothing to assuage the Albanian leaders' deep mistrust of Yugoslavia.

Hoxha and Shehu tapped the Albanians' deep-seated fear of Yugoslav domination in order to remain in power during the thaw following the Twentieth Party Congress of the Communist party of the Soviet Union in 1956, when Khrushchev denounced Stalin's crimes in his "secret speech." Hoxha defended Stalin and blamed the Titoist heresy for the troubles vexing world communism, including the disturbances in Poland and the rebellion in Hungary in 1956. Hoxha mercilessly purged party moderates with pro-Soviet and pro-Yugoslav leanings, but he toned down his anti-Yugoslav rhetoric after an April 1957 trip to Moscow, where he won cancellation of about US$105 million in outstanding loans and about US$7.8 million in additional food assistance. By 1958, however, Hoxha was again complaining about Tito's "fascism" and "genocide" against Albanians in Kosovo. He also grumbled about a Comecon plan for integrating the East European economies, which called for Albania to produce agricultural goods and minerals instead of emphasizing development of heavy industry. On a twelve-day visit to Albania in 1959, Khrushchev reportedly tried to convince Hoxha and Shehu that their country should aspire to become socialism's "orchard."

Albania and China

Albania played a role in the Sino-Soviet conflict far outweighing both its size and its importance in the communist world. By 1958 Albania stood with China in opposing Moscow on issues of peaceful coexistence, de-Stalinization, and Yugoslavia's "separate road to socialism" through decentralization of economic life. The

Soviet Union, other East European countries, and China all offered Albania large amounts of aid. Soviet leaders also promised to build a large Palace of Culture in Tiranë as a symbol of the Soviet people's "love and friendship" for the Albanians. But despite these gestures, Tiranë was dissatisfied with Moscow's economic policy toward Albania. Hoxha and Shehu apparently decided in May or June 1960 that Albania was assured of Chinese support, and they openly sided with China when sharp polemics erupted between China and the Soviet Union. Ramiz Alia, at the time a candidate-member of the Politburo and Hoxha's adviser on ideological questions, played a prominent role in the rhetorical battle.

The Sino-Soviet split burst into the open in June 1960 at a Romanian Workers' Party congress, at which Khrushchev attempted to secure condemnation of Beijing. Albania's delegation, alone among the European delegations, supported the Chinese. The Soviet Union immediately retaliated by organizing a campaign to oust Hoxha and Shehu in the summer of 1960. Moscow cut grain deliveries to Albania during a drought, and the Soviet embassy in Tiranë overtly encouraged a pro-Soviet faction in the APL to speak out against the party's pro-Chinese stand. Moscow also apparently was involved in a plot within the APL to unseat Hoxha and Shehu by force. But given their tight control of the party machinery, the army, and Shehu's secret police, the Directorate of State Security (Drejtorija e Sigurimit te Shtetit—Sigurimi), the two Albanian leaders easily parried the threat. Five pro-Soviet Albanian leaders were eventually tried and executed. China immediately began making up for the cancellation of Soviet wheat shipments despite a paucity of foreign currency and its own economic hardships.

Albania again sided with China when Hoxha launched an attack on the Soviet Union's leadership of the international communist movement at the November 1960 Moscow conference of the world's eighty-one communist parties. Hoxha inveighed against Khrushchev for encouraging Greek claims to southern Albania, sowing discord within the APL and the army, and using economic blackmail. "Soviet rats were able to eat while the Albanian people were dying of hunger," Hoxha railed, referring to purposely delayed Soviet grain deliveries. Communist leaders loyal to Moscow described Hoxha's performance as "gangsterish" and "infantile," and the speech extinguished any chance of an agreement between Moscow and Tiranë. For the next year, Albania played proxy for China. Pro-Soviet communist parties, reluctant to confront China directly, criticized Beijing by castigating Albania. China, for its part, frequently gave prominence to the Albanians' fulminations against the Soviet Union and Yugoslavia, which Tiranë referred to as a "socialist hell."

Hoxha and Shehu continued their harangue against the Soviet Union and Yugoslavia at the APL's Fourth Party Congress in February 1961. During the congress, the Albanian government announced the broad outlines of the country's Third Five-Year Plan (1961–65), which allocated 54 percent of all investment to industry, thereby rejecting Khrushchev's wish to make Albania primarily an agricultural producer. Moscow responded by canceling aid programs and lines of credit for Albania, but the Chinese again came to the rescue.

After additional sharp exchanges between Soviet and Chinese delegates over Albania at the Communist Party of the Soviet Union's Twenty-Second Party Congress in October 1961, Khrushchev lambasted the Albanians for executing a pregnant, pro-Soviet member of the Albanian party Politburo, and the Soviet Union finally broke diplomatic relations with Albania in December. Moscow then withdrew all Soviet economic advisers and technicians from the country, including those at work on the Palace of Culture, and halted shipments of supplies and spare parts for equipment already in place in Albania. In addition, the Soviet Union continued to dismantle its naval installations on Sazan Island, a process that had begun even before the break in relations.

China again compensated Albania for the loss of Soviet economic support, supplying about 90 percent of the parts, foodstuffs, and other goods the Soviet Union had promised. Beijing lent the Albanians money on more favorable terms than Moscow, and, unlike Soviet advisers, Chinese technicians earned the same low pay as Albanian workers and lived in similar housing. China also presented Albania with a powerful radio transmission station from which Tiranë sang the praises of Stalin, Hoxha, and Mao Zedong for decades. For its part, Albania offered China a beachhead in Europe and acted as China's chief spokesman at the UN. To Albania's dismay, however, Chinese equipment and technicians were not nearly so sophisticated as the Soviet goods and advisers they replaced. Ironically, a language barrier even forced the Chinese and Albanian technicians to communicate in Russian. Albanians no longer took part in Warsaw Pact activities or Comecon agreements. The other East European communist nations, however, did not break diplomatic or trade links with Albania. In 1964 the Albanians went so far as to seize the empty Soviet embassy in Tiranë, and Albanian workers pressed on with construction of the Palace of Culture on their own.

The shift away from the Soviet Union wreaked havoc on Albania's economy. Half of its imports and exports had been geared toward Soviet suppliers and markets, so the souring of Tiranë's relations with Moscow brought Albania's foreign trade to near collapse as China proved incapable of delivering promised machinery and equipment on time. The low productivity, flawed planning, poor workmanship, and inefficient management at Albanian enterprises became clear when Soviet and East European aid and advisers were withdrawn. In 1962 the Albanian government introduced an austerity program, appealing to the people to conserve resources, cut production costs, and abandon unnecessary investment.

In October 1964, Hoxha hailed Khrushchev's fall from power, and the Soviet Union's new leaders made overtures to Tiranë. It soon became clear, however, that the new Soviet leadership had no intention of changing basic policies to suit Albania, and relations failed to improve. Tiranë's propaganda continued for decades to refer to Soviet officials as "treacherous revisionists" and "traitors to communism," and in 1964 Hoxha said that Albania's terms for reconciliation were a Soviet apology to Albania and reparations for damages inflicted on the country. Soviet-Albanian relations dipped to new lows after the Warsaw Pact invasion of Czechoslovakia in 1968, when Albania responded by officially withdrawing from the alliance.

The Cultural and Ideological Revolution

In the mid-1960s, Albania's leaders grew wary of a threat to their power by a burgeoning bureaucracy. Party discipline had eroded. People complained about malfeasance, inflation, and low-quality goods. Writers strayed from the orthodoxy of socialist realism, which demanded that art and literature serve as instruments of government and party policy. As a result, after Mao unleashed the Cultural Revolution in China in 1965, Hoxha launched his own Cultural and Ideological Revolution. The Albanian leader concentrated on reforming the military, government bureaucracy, and the economy as well as on creating new support for his Stalinist system. The regime abolished military ranks, reintroduced political commissars into the military, and renounced professionalism in the army. Railing against a "white-collar mentality," the authorities also slashed the salaries of mid- and high-level officials, ousted administrators and specialists from their desk jobs, and sent such persons to toil in the factories and fields. Six ministries, including the Ministry of Justice, were eliminated. Farm collectivization spread to even the remote mountains. In addition, the government attacked dissident writers and artists, reformed its education system, and generally reinforced Albania's isolation from European culture in an effort to keep out foreign influences.

In 1967 the authorities conducted a violent campaign to extinguish religious life in Albania, claiming that religion had divided the Albanian nation and kept it mired in backwardness. Student agitators combed the countryside, forcing Albanians to quit practicing their faith. Despite complaints, even by APL members, all churches, mosques, monasteries, and other religious institutions had been closed or converted into warehouses, gymnasiums, and workshops by year's end. A special decree abrogated the charters by which the country's main religious communities had operated. The campaign culminated in an announcement that Albania had become the world's first atheistic state, a feat touted as one of Enver Hoxha's greatest achievements (see Hoxha's Antireligious Campaign, ch. 2).

Traditional kinship links in Albania, centered on the patriarchal family, were shattered by the postwar repression of clan leaders, collectivization of agriculture, industrialization, migration from the countryside to urban areas, and suppression of religion. The postwar regime brought a radical change in the status of Albania's women. Considered second-class citizens in traditional Albanian society, women performed most of the work at home and in the fields. Before World War II, about 90 percent of Albania's women were illiterate, and in many areas they were regarded as chattels under ancient tribal laws and customs. During the Cultural and Ideological Revolution, the party encouraged women to take jobs outside the home in an effort to compensate for labor shortages and to overcome their conservatism. Hoxha himself proclaimed that anyone who trampled on the party's edict on women's rights should be "hurled into the fire" (see Social Structure under Communist Rule, ch. 2).

The Break with China and Self-Reliance

Albanian-Chinese relations had stagnated by 1970, and when the Asian superpower began to reemerge from isolation in the early 1970s, Mao and the other Chinese leaders reassessed their commitment to tiny Albania. In response, Tiranë began broadening its contacts with the outside world. Albania opened trade negotiations with France, Italy, and the recently independent Asian and African states, and in 1971 it normalized relations with Yugoslavia and Greece. Albania's leaders abhorred China's renewal of contacts with the United States in the early 1970s, and its press and radio ignored President Richard Nixon's trip to Beijing in 1972. Albania actively worked to reduce its dependence on China by

Albanian painting in the socialist-realist style
Courtesy Charles Sudetic

diversifying trade and improving diplomatic and cultural relations, especially with Western Europe. But Albania shunned the Conference on Security and Cooperation in Europe and was the only European country that refused to take part in the Helsinki Conference of July 1975. Soon after Mao's death in 1976, Hoxha criticized the new leadership as well as Beijing's pragmatic policy toward the United States and Western Europe. The Chinese responded by inviting Tito to visit Beijing in 1977 and ending assistance programs for Albania in 1978.

The break with China left Albania with no foreign protector. Tiranë ignored calls by the United States and the Soviet Union to normalize relations. Instead, Albania expanded diplomatic ties with Western Europe and the developing nations and began stressing the principle of self-reliance as the keystone of the country's strategy for economic development. However, Hoxha's cautious opening toward the outside world had stirred up nascent movements for change inside Albania. As the dictator's health slipped, muted calls arose for the relaxation of party controls and greater openness. In response, Hoxha launched a series of purges that removed the defense minister and many top military officials. A year later, Hoxha purged ministers responsible for the economy and replaced them with younger persons.

As Hoxha's health declined, the dictator began planning for an orderly succession. He worked to institutionalize his policies, hoping to frustrate any attempt his successors might make to venture from the Stalinist path he had blazed for Albania. In December 1976, Albania adopted its second Stalinist constitution of the postwar era. The document "guaranteed" Albanians freedom of speech, the press, organization, association, and assembly but subordinated these rights to the individual's duties to society as a whole. The constitution enshrined in law the idea of autarky and prohibited the government from seeking financial aid or credits or from forming joint companies with partners from capitalist or revisionist communist countries. The constitution's preamble also boasted that the foundations of religious belief in Albania had been abolished.

In 1980 Hoxha turned to Ramiz Alia to succeed him as Albania's communist patriarch, overlooking his long-standing comrade-in-arms, Mehmet Shehu. Hoxha first tried to convince Shehu to step aside voluntarily, but when this move failed Hoxha arranged for all the members of the Politburo to rebuke him for allowing his son to become engaged to the daughter of a former bourgeois family. Shehu allegedly committed suicide on December 18, 1981. It is suspected, however, that Hoxha had him killed. Hoxha, obviously fearing retaliation, purged the members of Shehu's family and his supporters within the police and military. In November 1982, Hoxha announced that Shehu had been a foreign spy working simultaneously for the United States, British, Soviet, and Yugoslav intelligence agencies in planning the assassination of Hoxha himself. "He was buried like a dog," the dictator wrote in the Albanian edition of his book, *The Titoites*.

Hoxha went into semiretirement in early 1983, and Alia assumed responsibility for Albania's administration. Alia traveled extensively around Albania, standing in for Hoxha at major events and delivering addresses laying down new policies and intoning litanies to the enfeebled president. When Hoxha died on April 11, 1985, he left Albania a legacy of repression, technological backwardness, isolation, and fear of the outside world. Alia succeeded to the presidency and became legal secretary of the APL two days later. In due course, he became a dominant figure in the Albanian media, and his slogans appeared painted in crimson letters on signboards across the country. The APL's Ninth Party Congress in November 1986 featured Alia as the party's and the country's undisputed leader.

* * *

Because Albania's fate is so tightly interwoven with developments in the Balkans, it is recommended that readers unfamiliar with the region first examine Barbara Jelavich's two-volume *History of the Balkans,* which provides an excellent overview as well as sections on Albania and the formation of the state. Robert Lee Wolff's *The Balkans in Our Time* is another useful survey of Balkan history. Edith Durham's *High Albania* and her other travelogues on Albania from the early twentieth century read like adventure novels and provide insight into the cultural underpinnings of the nationalism endemic to the Balkans. The best examination of the Albanian nationalist movement in the late nineteenth century and the creation of Albania itself are Stavro Skendi's *The Albanian National Awakening* and Joseph Swire's *Albania: The Rise of a Kingdom.* Anton Logoreci's *The Albanians: Europe's Forgotten Survivors* and Peter R. Prifti's *Socialist Albania since 1944: Domestic and Foreign Developments* are both solidly grounded surveys of Albania and its trials, especially after World War II. Postwar Albania, especially the last years of Enver Hoxha's regime, is well treated in Elez Biberaj's *Albania.* No reader on Albanian affairs, in fact no student of the former communist world, should overlook *With Stalin, The Titoites,* or Enver Hoxha's other official works, which would be right at home shelved beside George Orwell's *Animal Farm* and other works in the genre of dystopian fiction. (For further information and complete citations, see Bibliography.)

Chapter 2. The Society and Its Environment

Albanian family out for a stroll

EUROPE'S LEAST DEVELOPED country, Albania is located along the central west coast of the Balkan Peninsula. Albania's Adriatic and Ionian coasts are adjacent to shipping lanes that have been important since early Greek and Roman times. Tiranë, the capital and largest city, is less than an hour by air from eight other European capitals and barely more than two hours from the most distant of them. Yet, in large part because of its rugged terrain and, in recent times, its Stalinist regime, Albania remained isolated from the rest of Europe until the early 1990s.

Large expanses of mountainous and generally inaccessible terrain provided refuge for the Albanian nation and permitted its distinctive identity to survive throughout the centuries, in spite of successive foreign invasions and long periods of occupation. Kinship and tribal affiliations, a common spoken language, and enduring folk customs provided continuity and a sense of community. Foreign influence was inevitable, however. Additions and modifications to the language were made as a result of Latin, Greek, Slavic, and Turkish contacts. Lacking an organized religion as part of their Illyrian heritage, Albanians adopted the Muslim, Orthodox, and Roman Catholic faiths brought to them by their conquerors.

Following the Italian and German occupations of World War II, Albania was subjected to more than forty-six years of authoritarian rule, from which it was emerging, materially and spiritually impoverished, in 1992. Its churches and mosques had been destroyed, the school system was a shambles, hospitals struggled with extreme shortages of basic medical supplies, and the hungry, dejected people had come to rely entirely on foreign food aid and other forms of assistance. With the collapse of communism, a democratically elected government faced the formidable challenge of ending decades of self-imposed isolation, restoring public order, and improving social conditions for the more than 3.3 million people of Albania.

Physical Environment

National Boundaries

Albania, with a total area of 28,750 square kilometers, is slightly larger than the state of Maryland. It shares a 287-kilometer border with the Yugoslav republics of Montenegro and Serbia to the north, a 151-kilometer border with the former Yugoslav republic of Macedonia to the north and east, and a 282-kilometer border with Greece to the south and southeast. Its coastline is 362 kilometers long. The lowlands of the west face the Adriatic Sea and the strategically important Strait of Otranto, which puts less than 100 kilometers of water between Albania and the heel of the Italian "boot."

The distinct ethnic character of the Albanian people and their isolation within a generally definable area underscored their demands for independence in the early twentieth century. In some places, however, the mingling of different ethnic groups has complicated the determination of national borders. Kosovo, across the northeastern Albanian border, is a Serbian-governed province, although ethnic Albanians make up over 90 percent of its population. Many Albanians still regard Kosovo's status as an issue. Greeks and Albanians live in the mountains on both sides of the southeastern Albanian boundary. Neither Greece nor Albania is satisfied with the division of nations effected by their common border.

With the exception of the coastline, all Albanian borders are artificial. They were established in principle at the 1912–13 conference of ambassadors in London. The country was occupied by Italian, Serbian, Greek, and French forces during World War I, but the 1913 boundaries were essentially reaffirmed by the victorious states in 1921. The original principle was to define the borders in accordance with the best interests of the Albanian people and the nationalities in adjacent areas. The northern and eastern borders were intended, insofar as possible, to separate the Albanians from the Serbs and Montenegrins; the southeast border was to separate Albanians and Greeks; the valuable western Macedonian lake district was to be divided among the three states—Albania, Greece, and Yugoslavia—whose populations shared the area. When there was no compromise involving other factors, borderlines were chosen to make the best possible separation of national groups, connecting the best marked physical features available.

Allowance was made for local economic situations, for example, to prevent separation of a village from its animals' grazing areas or from the markets for its produce. Political pressures also were a factor in the negotiations, but the outcome was subject to approval by powers having relatively abstract interests, most of which involved the balance of power rather than specific economic ambitions.

Division of the lake district among three states required that each of them have a share of the lowlands in the vicinity. Such an artificial distribution, once made, necessarily affected the borderlines to the north and south. The border that runs generally north from the lakes, although it follows the ridges of the eastern highlands, stays sixteen to thirty-two kilometers west of the watershed divide. Because negotiators at the London conference declined to use the watershed divide as the northeast boundary of the new state of Albania, a large Albanian population in Kosovo was incorporated into Serbia.

In Albania's far north and the northeast mountainous sections, the border connects high points and follows mountain ridges through the largely inaccessible North Albanian Alps, known locally as Bjeshkët e Namuna. For the most part, there is no natural boundary from the highlands to the Adriatic, although Lake Scutari and a portion of the Bunë River south of it were used to mark Albania's northwest border. From the lake district south and southwest to the Ionian Sea, the country's southeast border goes against the grain of the land, crossing a number of ridges instead of following them.

Topography

The 70 percent of the country that is mountainous is rugged and often inaccessible. The remainder, an alluvial plain, receives precipitation seasonally, is poorly drained, and is alternately arid or flooded. Much of the plain's soil is of poor quality. Far from offering a relief from the difficult interior terrain, the alluvial plain is often as inhospitable as the mountains. Good soil and dependable precipitation, however, are found in intermontane river basins, in the lake district along the eastern frontier, and in a narrow band of slightly elevated land between the coastal plains and the interior mountains (see fig. 3).

In the far north, the mountains are an extension of the Dinaric Alps and, more specifically, the Montenegrin limestone plateau. Albania's northern mountains are more folded and rugged, however, than most of the plateau. The rivers have deep valleys with steep sides and arable valley floors. Generally unnavigable, the rivers obstruct rather than encourage movement within the alpine region. Roads are few and poor. Lacking internal communications and external contacts, a tribal society flourished in this area for centuries. Only after World War II were serious efforts made to incorporate the people of the region into Albanian national life.

A low coastal belt extends from the northern boundary southward to the vicinity of Vlorë. On average, it extends less than sixteen kilometers inland, but widens to about fifty kilometers in the Elbasan area in central Albania. In its natural state, the coastal belt is characterized by low scrub vegetation, varying from barren to dense. There are large areas of marshlands and other areas of bare, eroded badlands. Where elevations rise slightly and precipitation is regular—in the foothills of the central uplands, for example—the land is highly arable. Marginal land is reclaimed wherever irrigation is possible.

Just east of the lowlands, the central uplands, called Çermenikë by Albanians, are an area of generally moderate elevations, between 305 and 915 meters, with a few points reaching above 1,520 meters. Shifting along the faultline that roughly defines the western edge of the central uplands causes frequent, and occasionally severe, earthquakes.

Although rugged terrain and points of high elevation mark the central uplands, the first major mountain range inland from the Adriatic is an area of predominantly serpentine rock (which derives its name from its dull green color and often spotted appearance), extending nearly the length of the country, from the North Albanian Alps to the Greek border south of Korçë. Within this zone, there are many areas in which sharp limestone and sandstone outcroppings predominate, although the ranges as a whole are characterized by rounded mountains.

The mountains east of the serpentine zone are the highest in Albania, exceeding 2,740 meters in the Mal Korab range. Together with the North Albanian Alps and the serpentine zone, the eastern highlands are the most rugged and inaccessible of any terrain on the Balkan Peninsula.

The three lakes of easternmost Albania—Lake Ohrid, Lake Prespa, and Prespa e Vogël—are remote and picturesque. Much of the terrain in their vicinity is not overly steep, and it supports a larger population than any other inland portion of the country. Albania's eastern border passes through Lake Ohrid; all but a small tip of Prespa e Vogël is in Greece; and the point at which the boundaries of three states meet is in Lake Prespa. Each of the two larger lakes has a total surface areas of about 260 square kilometers, and Prespa e Vogël is about one-fifth as large. The surface elevation is about 695 meters for Lake Ohrid and 855 meters for the other two lakes.

The southern mountain ranges are more accessible than the serpentine zone, the eastern highlands, or the North Albanian Alps. The transition to the lowlands is less abrupt, and the arable valley floors are wider. Limestone, the predominant mineral, is responsible for the cliffs and clear water of the coastline southeast of Vlorë. Erosion of a blend of softer rocks has provided the sediment that has caused wider valleys to form in the southern mountain area than those characteristic of the remainder of the country. This

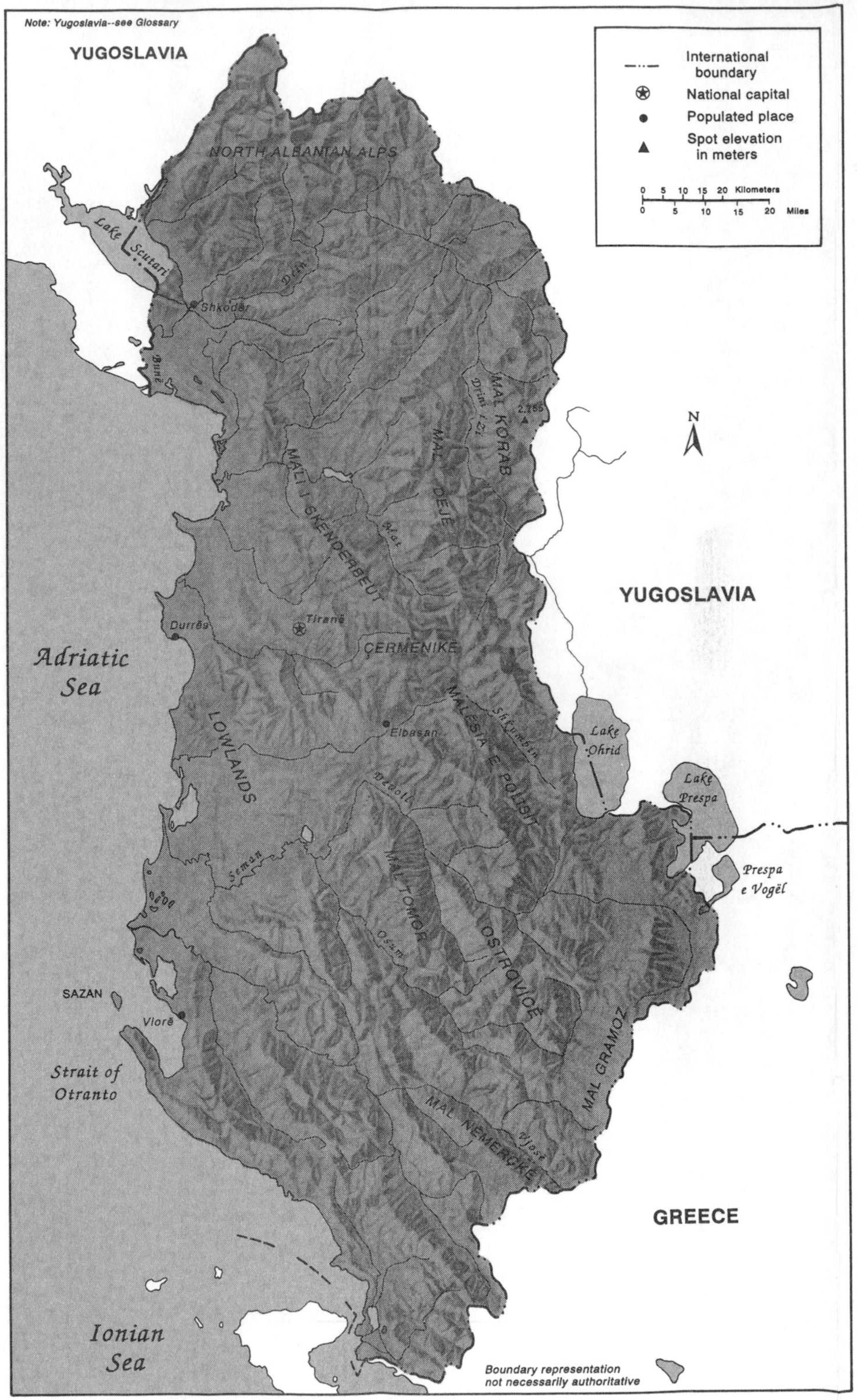

Figure 3. Topography and Drainage

terrain encouraged the development of larger landholding, thus influencing the social structure of southern Albania.

Drainage

Nearly all of the precipitation that falls on Albania drains into the rivers and reaches the coast without even leaving the country. In the north, only one small stream escapes Albania. In the south, an even smaller rivulet drains into Greece. Because the topographical divide is east of the Albanian border with its neighbors, a considerable amount of water from other countries drains through Albania. An extensive portion of the basin of the Drini i Bardhë River, called Beli Drim by Serbs, is in the Kosovo area, across Albania's northeastern border. The three eastern lakes that Albania shares with its neighboring countries, as well as the streams that flow into them, drain into the Drini i Zi. The watershed divide in the south also dips nearly seventy-five kilometers into Greece at one point. Several tributaries of the Vjosë River rise in that area.

With the exception of the Drini i Zi, which flows northward and drains nearly the entire eastern border region before it turns westward to the sea, most of the rivers in northern and central Albania flow fairly directly westward to the sea. In the process, they cut through the ridges rather than flow around them. This apparent geological impossibility occurs because the highlands originally were lifted without much folding. The streams came into existence at that time. The compression and folding of the plateau into ridges occurred later. The folding process was rapid enough in many instances to dam the rivers temporarily. The resulting lakes existed until their downstream channels became wide enough to drain them. This sequence created the many interior basins that are typically a part of the Albanian landform. During the lifetime of the temporary lakes, enough sediment was deposited in them to form the basis for fertile soils. Folding was rarely rapid enough to force the streams into radically different channels.

The precipitous fall from higher elevations and the highly irregular seasonal flow patterns that are characteristic of nearly all streams in the country reduce the economic value of the streams. They erode the mountains and deposit the sediment that created the lowlands and continues to augment them, but the rivers flood when there is local rainfall. When the lands are parched and need irrigation, the rivers usually are dry. Their violence when they are full makes them difficult to control, and they are unnavigable. The Bunë River is an exception. It is dredged between Shkodër and the Adriatic Sea and can be negotiated by small ships. In contrast to their history of holding fast to their courses in the mountains, the rivers constantly change channels on the lower plains, making waste of much of the land they create.

The Drin River is the largest and most constant stream. Fed by melting snows from the northern and eastern mountains and by the more evenly distributed seasonal precipitation of that area, its flow does not have the extreme variations characteristic of nearly all other rivers in the country. Its normal flow varies seasonally by only about one-third. Along its length of about 282 kilometers, it drains nearly 5,957 square kilometers within Albania. As it also collects water from the Adriatic portion of the Kosovo watershed and the three border lakes (Lake Prespa drains to Lake Ohrid via an underground stream), its total basin encompasses about 15,540 square kilometers.

The Seman and Vjosë are the only other rivers that are more than 160 kilometers long and have basins larger than 2,600 square kilometers. These rivers drain the southern regions and, reflecting the seasonal distribution of rainfall, are torrents in winter and nearly dry in the summer in spite of their length. This variable nature also characterizes the many shorter streams. In the summer, most of them carry less than a tenth of their winter averages, if they are not altogether dry.

Although the sediment carried by the mountain torrents continues to be deposited, new deposits delay exploitation. Stream channels rise as silt is deposited in them and eventually become higher than the surrounding terrain. Shifting channels frustrate development in many areas. Old channels become barriers to proper drainage and create swamps or marshlands. In general, it is difficult to build roads or railroads across the lowlands or otherwise use the land.

Irrigation has been accomplished on a small scale by Albanian peasants for many years. Large irrigation projects were not completed, however, until after World War II. Such projects include the Vjosë-Levan-Fier irrigation canal, with an irrigation capacity of 15,000 hectares, and the reservoir at Thanë in Lushnjë District, with an irrigation capacity of 35,100 hectares. In 1986 nearly 400,000 hectares of land, or 56 percent of the total cultivated area, were under irrigation, compared with 29,000 hectares, or 10 percent of the total cultivated area, in 1938.

Climate

With its coastline facing the Adriatic and Ionian seas, its highlands backed upon the elevated Balkan landmass, and the entire country lying at a latitude subject to a variety of weather patterns during the winter and summer seasons, Albania has a high number of climatic regions for so small an area. The coastal lowlands have typically Mediterranean weather; the highlands have a Mediterranean continental climate. In both the lowlands and the interior, the weather varies markedly from north to south.

The lowlands have mild winters, averaging about 7°C. Summer temperatures average 24°C, humidity is high, and the weather tends to be oppressively uncomfortable. In the southern lowlands, temperatures average about five degrees higher throughout the year. The difference is greater than five degrees during the summer and somewhat less during the winter.

Inland temperatures are affected more by differences in elevation than by latitude or any other factor. Low winter temperatures in the mountains are caused by the continental air mass that dominates the weather in Eastern Europe and the Balkans. Northerly and northeasterly winds blow much of the time. Average summer temperatures are lower than in the coastal areas and much lower at higher elevations, but daily fluctuations are greater. Daytime maximum temperatures in the interior basins and river valleys are very high, but the nights are almost always cool.

Average precipitation is heavy, a result of the convergence of the prevailing airflow from the Mediterranean Sea and the continental air mass. Because the convergence usually comes at the point where the terrain rises, the heaviest rain falls in the central uplands. Vertical currents initiated when the Mediterranean air is uplifted also cause frequent thunderstorms. Many of these storms are accompanied by high local winds and torrential downpours.

When the continental air mass is weak, Mediterranean winds drop their moisture farther inland. When there is a dominant continental air mass, cold air spills onto the lowland areas, which occurs most frequently in the winter. Because the season's lower temperatures damage olive trees and citrus fruits, groves and orchards are restricted to sheltered places with southern and western exposures even in areas with high average winter temperatures.

Lowland rainfall averages from 1,000 millimeters to more than 1,500 millimeters annually, with the higher levels in the north. Nearly 95 percent of the rain falls in the winter.

Rainfall in the upland mountain ranges is heavier. Adequate records are not available, and estimates vary widely, but annual averages are probably about 1,800 millimeters and are as high as 2,550 millimeters in some northern areas. The seasonal variation is not quite as great in the coastal area.

The higher inland mountains receive less precipitation than the intermediate uplands. Terrain differences cause wide local variations, but the seasonal distribution is the most consistent of any area.

The Albanian People

Population

The average annual growth rate of the Albanian population for the period 1960-90 was 2.4 percent, or approximately three to four times higher than that of other European countries. Population growth was actively encouraged by the government, which deemed it "essential for the further strengthening and prosperity of socialist society." Albania had a population of 3,335,000 in July 1991, compared with 2,761,000 in mid-1981 and 1,626,000 in 1960. The most sparsely populated Balkan country until 1965, Albania attained a population density of 111 inhabitants per square kilometer in 1989—the highest in the Balkans. The 1991 growth rate was 1.8 percent.

In 1991 Albania had a birth rate of 24 per 1,000, and its death rate had declined from 14 per 1,000 in 1950 to 5 per 1,000. A concomitant of the reduced death rate was an increase in life expectancy. Official Albanian sources indicated that average life expectancy at birth increased from fifty-three years in 1950 to seventy-two years for males and seventy-nine years for females in 1991. The population was among the most youthful in Europe, with an average age of twenty-seven years, and the fertility rate—2.9 children born per woman—was one of Europe's highest.

Albania is the only country in Europe with more males than females. The disparity in the male-to-female ratio, which was 1,055:1,000 in 1970, had increased to the point where males accounted for 51.5 percent of the population in 1990. This discrepancy was attributed in part to a higher mortality rate among female infants, caused by neglect and the traditional deference accorded male progeny. Losses in World War II, estimated by the United Nations at 30,000 persons, or 2.5 percent of the population, apparently had little influence on the ratio of males to females.

Ethnicity

Gegs and Tosks

Among ethnic Albanians are two major subgroups: the Gegs, who generally occupy the area north of the Shkumbin River, and the Tosks, most of whom live south of the river. The Gegs account for slightly more than half of the resident Albanian population. Ethnic Albanians are estimated to account for 90 percent of the population.

The Gegs and Tosks use distinct dialects; there are also linguistic variations within subgroups. Well into the twentieth century, ethnic clans exercised extensive local authority, particularly in the

A beach outside the port town of Durrës
Courtesy Charles Sudetic

north. Some progress was made during the reign of King Zog I (r. 1928–39), however, toward bringing the clans under government control and eliminating blood feuds.

After taking power in 1944, the communist regime imposed controls intended to eliminate clan rule entirely and waged a continuing struggle against customs and attitudes believed to impede the growth of socialism. Blood feuds were repressed. Party and government leaders, in their effort to develop national, social, and cultural solidarity in a communist society, publicly tended to ignore ethnic differences.

Communist leader Enver Hoxha, first secretary of the Albanian Party of Labor and head of state until his death in 1985, came from the south. He received the bulk of his support during World War II from that area and frequently gave preference to persons and customs of Tosk origin. Most party and government executives were Tosk speakers and of Muslim background. The Gegs, who had dominated Albanian politics before 1945, were educationally disadvantaged by the adoption of a "standard literary Albanian language" based on the Tosk dialect.

Because of their greater isolation in the mountainous areas of the north, the Gegs held on to their tribal organization and customs more tenaciously than did the Tosks. As late as the 1920s, approximately 20 percent of male deaths in some areas of northern Albania were attributable to blood feuds. Under the unwritten tribal codes, whose purview included the regulation of feuds, any blow, as well as many offenses committed against women, called for vengeance. Permitting a girl who had been betrothed in infancy to marry another, for example, could set off a blood feud. The *besa,* a pledge to keep one's word as a solemn obligation, was given in various situations and sometimes included promises to postpone quarrels. A man who killed a fellow tribesman was commonly punished by his neighbors, who customarily would burn his house and destroy his property. As fugitives from their own communities, such persons were often given assistance by others.

A man who failed to carry out the prescribed vengeance against a member of another tribe or that individual's relatives was subjected to ridicule. Insult was considered one of the gravest forms of dishonor, and the upholding of one's honor was the primary duty of a Geg. If the individual carried out the required act of vengeance, he was in turn subject to retribution by the victim's relatives. Women were excluded from the feud, and when a man escorted a woman he too was considered inviolable. In other respects, however, a woman's lot in society generally was one of deprivation and subjugation.

The isolation from influences beyond his community and the constant struggle with nature tended to make the male Geg an ascetic. Traditionally his closest bonds were with members of his clan. Obstinate and proud, the Gegs had proved themselves ruthless and cruel fighters. Visitors from outside the clan generally were suspect, but every traveler was by custom accorded hospitality.

Less isolated by geography and enjoying slightly less limited contact with foreign cultures, Tosks generally were more outspoken and imaginative than Gegs. Contacts with invaders and foreign occupiers had left an influence, and before 1939 some Tosks had traveled to foreign countries to earn money to buy land, or to obtain an education. The clan or tribal system, which by the nineteenth century was far less extensive in the south than in the north, began to disappear after independence was achieved in 1912.

Greeks and Other Minorities

The Greek minority, Albania's largest, has deep roots in the country's two southeasternmost districts, Sarandë and Gjirokastër, in an area many Greeks call Northern Epirus (see fig. 1). Estimates of the size of the Greek population in 1989 varied from 59,000, or 1 percent of the total (from the official Albanian census), to 266,800, or 8 percent (from data published by the United States government), to as high as 400,000, or 12 percent (from the "Epirot lobby" of Greeks with family roots in Albania). Greeks were harshly affected by the communist regime's attempts to homogenize the population through restrictions on the religious, cultural, educational, and linguistic rights of minorities. Internal exile and other population movements served as instruments of policy to dilute concentrations of Greeks and to deprive Greeks of their status as a recognized minority. Despite improvements in Greco-Albanian relations during the late 1980s and a significant increase in cross-border visits, reports of persecution, harassment, and discrimination against Greeks, as well as other minorities, persisted.

Smaller ethnic groups, including Bulgarians, Gypsies, Jews, Macedonians, Montenegrins, Serbs, and Vlachs, altogether account for about 2 percent of the total population. Persons of Macedonian and Bulgarian origin live mostly in the border area near Lake Prespa. The Vlachs, akin to modern Romanians, are most numerous in the Pindus Mountains and in the districts of Fier, Korçë, and Vlorë. A few persons of Serbian and Montenegrin derivation reside around the city of Shkodër. There are small Jewish communities in Tiranë, Vlorë, and Korçë, and Gypsies are scattered throughout the country.

Albanians in Kosovo

Large numbers of ethnic Albanians live outside the country, in Italy, Greece, Turkey, the United States, and especially in Yugoslavia or its former republics (see fig. 4). Estimates based on Yugoslav census data indicated that the number of Albanians in Yugoslavia in 1981 totaled more than 1.7 million, or almost 8 percent of the country's total population, of which about 70 percent resided in Kosovo, a province of Serbia; 20 percent in Macedonia; and 9 percent in Montenegro. The predominantly Albanian Kosovo had the highest birthrate in Europe and one of the highest in the world: 29.9 per 1,000 in 1987. Persons under twenty-seven years old accounted for 60 percent of Kosovo's total population, and students—a reservoir of political ferment—over 30 percent. In 1981 only 12 percent of the Albanian population in Kosovo was employed.

Student protests over living conditions in early 1981 led to bloody riots throughout Kosovo, which accelerated the exodus of Serbs and Montenegrins. The number of departures totalled 60,000 between 1981 and 1991. Haunted by the specter of secession, the Serbian government resorted to repressive measures, culminating in the revocation of Kosovo's autonomous status in July 1990. Hundreds of Albanian activists were tried and imprisoned, and

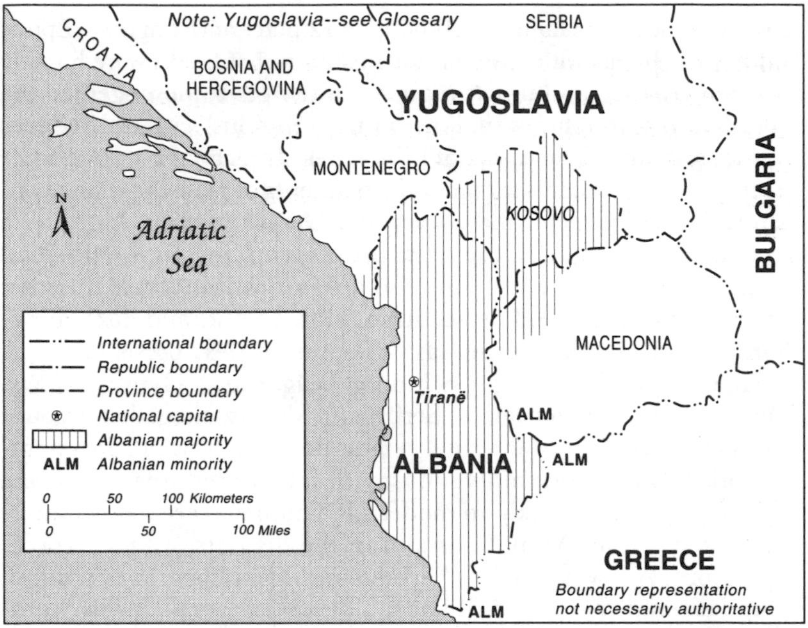

Figure 4. Distribution of Ethnic Albanians on the Balkan Peninsula, 1992

a campaign was launched to entice Serbs to settle in Kosovo. Serbian authorities suspended publication of the Albanian-language daily *Rilindja,* alleging that it had become a "mouthpiece" of Albanian nationalists. A Serbian-language standard curriculum was introduced for all middle and secondary schools. The action led to protests by thousands of students and parents. As a result of the curriculum's implementation, many Albanian-language schools had to be closed. At Kosovo's University of Pristina, student placements were reserved, in disproportion to the population, for ethnic Serbs and Montenegrins—many from outside Kosovo. (Even though a number of these reserved places were not filled in the fall of 1990, Albanian applicants were denied admission to the university.) Discrimination against Albanians seeking employment or housing was rampant.

Languages and Dialects

The Albanian language is spoken by nearly all inhabitants of Albania, as well as by the vast majority of the population of neighboring Kosovo. Greeks, Macedonians, and other ethnic groups in Albania use their ancestral languages, in addition to Albanian, to the extent that this right can be exercised. Ethnic minorities, according to the testimony of many émigrés, were in the past forbidden to speak their own languages in public.

A member of the Indo-European family of languages, modern Albanian is derived from ancient Illyrian and Thracian. Additions and modifications were made as a result of foreign contacts, beginning in the pre-Christian era. The most significant of these changes were the result of Latin influence during the centuries of Roman domination, Italian influences resulting from trade with Venice during the Renaissance, and Italian hegemony over Albania in more recent times. Contributions also were made by the Greeks, Turks, and Slavs. Because the first written documents in Albanian did not appear until the fifteenth century, tracing the early development of the language is difficult.

Beginning in the fifteenth century and continuing over a period of some 450 years, the repressive policies of the Ottoman Empire rulers retarded language development. Writing in Albanian was forbidden, and only the Turkish or Greek languages could be used in schools. Émigré Albanians, particularly those living in Italy, helped keep the written forms of the language alive. Until the nineteenth century, the language was sustained in Turkish-dominated areas largely by verbal communication, including ballads and folk tales.

By the early twentieth century, more than a dozen different alphabets were being used by Albanians. Some were predominantly Latin, Greek, or Turko-Arabic. Many were a mixture of several forms. It was not until 1908 that a standardized orthography was adopted. The Latin-based alphabet of twenty-six letters, approved at that time by a linguistic congress at Monastir (now Bitola, in Macedonia), was made official by a government directive in 1924 and continued to be in use in the early 1990s.

The two principal Albanian dialects are Geg, spoken by about two-thirds of the people, including almost all Albanians in Kosovo, and Tosk, used by the remaining third. Within each dialect, there are subdialects. Despite the variations that have developed in the many isolated communities, Albanians generally communicate well with each other.

During the 1920s and 1930s, the government attempted to establish the dialect of the Elbasan area, which was a mixture of Geg and Tosk, as the official language. The local dialects persisted, however, and writers and even officials continued to use the dialect of their association. After Hoxha acceded to power, the Tosk dialect became the official language of the country. Some scholars saw the imposition of "standard" Albanian as a political scheme to denigrate the Geg dialect and culture.

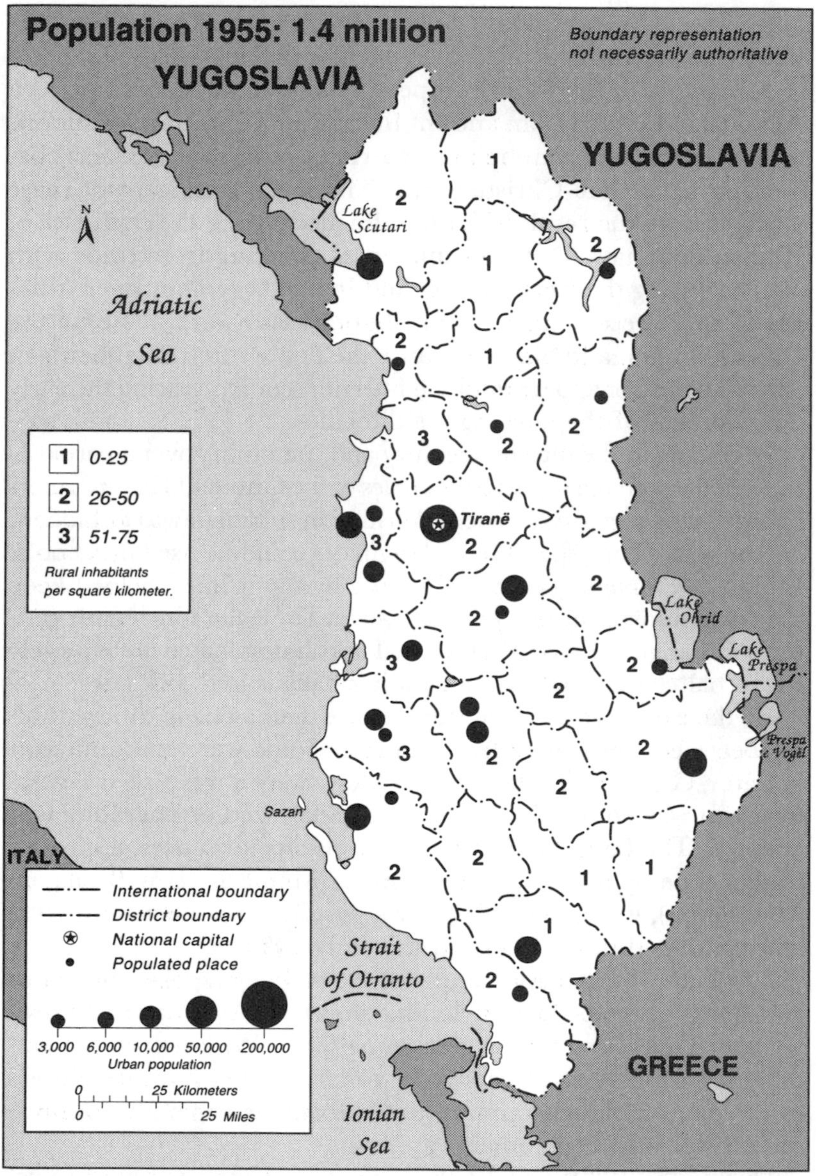

Source: Based on information from Örjan Sjöberg, *Rural Change and Development in Albania*, Boulder, Colorado, 1991, 60–61.

Figure 5. Population Density by District, 1955

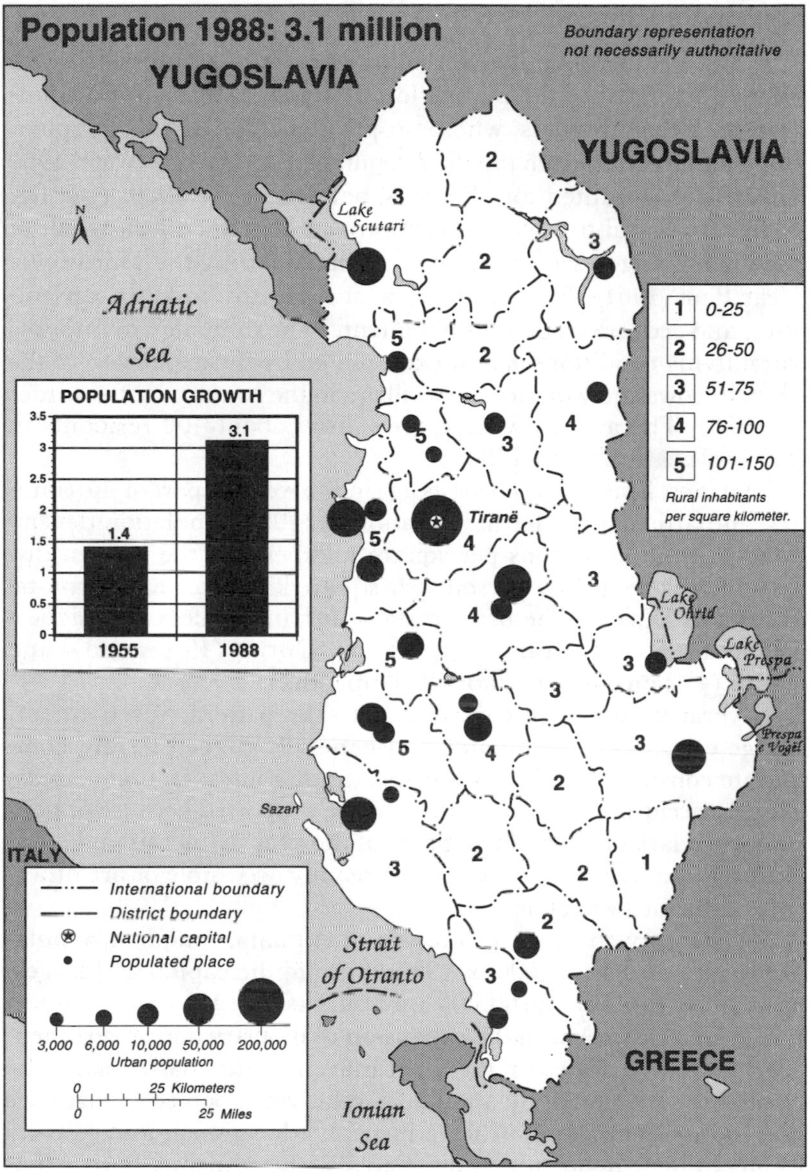

Source: Based on information from Örjan Sjöberg, *Rural Change and Development in Albania*, Boulder, Colorado, 1991, 60–61.

Figure 6. Population Density by District, 1988

Settlement Patterns

In the early 1990s, Albania remained predominantly rural, with about 65 percent of the population living in villages or the countryside. Urban dwellers, whose proportion of the national population had increased from one-fifth to almost one-third between 1950 and 1970, accounted for about 34 percent in the 1980s (see fig. 5; fig. 6). Rural-to-urban migration was contained as a result of the regime's aggressive programs, initiated during the Third Five-Year Plan (1961-65), to restrict urban growth, build up agriculture, and accelerate rural development. (The campaign to improve rural living conditions is best exemplified by the expansion of the electric-power network to every village in the country by the winter of 1970.) The average village grew from about 400 residents in 1955 to nearly 700 in 1980.

The most heavily settled areas are in the western part of the country, in particular the fertile lowlands. In 1987 population density ranged from 30 persons per square kilometer in the eastern district of Kolonjë to 281 persons per square kilometer in the coastal district of Durrës. The proportion of urban dwellers was highest in the districts of Tiranë (67 percent), Durrës (49 percent), and Vlorë (47 percent) (see table 2, Appendix).

Several factors have contributed to the pattern of settlement. Large expanses of mountains and generally rugged terrain complicate construction of land transportation routes. In many areas, large concentrations of people cannot be supported because of poor soil and a lack of water during part of the year. Minerals and other natural resources generally are not readily accessible or are otherwise difficult to exploit.

Of the sixty-six cities and towns in Albania, nine had populations greater than 25,000 in 1987. Tiranë, the capital and largest city, grew from about 60,000 inhabitants in 1945 to 226,000 in 1987, largely because of the expansion of industry and government bureaucracy. Located on the inner margin of the coastal plain, the capital is surrounded by an area of relatively good soil. Tiranë is the country's main political, industrial, educational, and cultural center. Other major towns are Durrës, the principal port, Elbasan, Shkodër, and Vlorë. About 44 percent of all towns had fewer than 5,000 inhabitants in 1987.

Social System

Traditional Social Patterns and Values

The social structure of the country was, until the 1930s, basically tribal in the north and semifeudal in the central and southern regions. The highlanders of the north retained their medieval pattern of life until well into the twentieth century and were considered the last people in Europe to preserve tribal autonomy. In the central and southern regions, increasing contact with the outside world and invasions and occupations by foreign armies gradually weakened tribal society.

Traditionally there have been two major subcultures in the Albanian nation: the Gegs in the north and the Tosks in the south. The Gegs, partly Roman Catholic but mostly Muslim, lived until after World War II in a mountain society characterized by blood feuds and fierce clan and tribal loyalties. The Tosks, whose number included many Muslims as well as Orthodox Christians, were less culturally isolated mainly because of centuries of foreign influence. Because they had came under the rule of the Muslim landed aristocracy, the Tosks had apparently largely lost the spirit of individuality and independence that for centuries characterized the Gegs, especially in the highlands.

Until the end of World War II, society in the north and, to a much lesser extent, in the south, was organized in terms of kinship and descent. The basic unit of society was the extended family, usually composed of a couple, their married sons, the wives and children of the sons, and any unmarried daughters. The extended family formed a single residential and economic entity held together by common ownership of means of production and common interest in the defense of the group. Such families often included scores of persons, and, as late as 1944, some encompassed as many as sixty to seventy persons living in a cluster of huts surrounding the father's house.

Extended families were grouped into clans whose chiefs preserved patriarchal powers over the entire group. The clan chief arranged marriages, assigned tasks, settled disputes, and set the course to be followed concerning essential matters such as blood feuds and politics. Descent was traced from a common ancestor through the male line, and brides usually were chosen from outside the clan. Clans in turn were grouped into tribes.

In the Tosk regions of the south, the extended family was also the most important social unit, although patriarchal authority had been diluted by the feudal conditions usually imposed by the Muslim bey (see Glossary).

Social leadership in the lowlands was concentrated in the hands of the semifeudal local tribal bey and pasha (see Glossary). The region around Tiranë, for example, was controlled by the Zogolli, Toptani, and Vrioni families, all Muslims and all owners of extensive agricultural estates. Ahmed Zogu, subsequently King Zog I, was from the Zogolli family. Originally pashas ranked slightly higher than beys, but differences gradually diminished and just the term *bey* remained in use. In the northern highlands, the *bajraktar* (see Glossary) was the counterpart of the bey and enjoyed similar hereditary rights to titles and positions.

The Geg clans put great importance on marriage traditions. According to custom, a young man always married a young woman from outside his clan but from within his tribe. In some tribes, marriages between Christians and Muslims were tolerated, but as a rule such unions were frowned upon.

A variety of offenses against women could spark blood feuds. Many females were engaged to marry in their infancy by their parents. If later a woman did not wish to marry the man whom the parents had chosen for her and married another, in all likelihood a blood feud would ensue. Among the Tosks, religious beliefs and customs were more important than clan and tribal traditions in the regulation of marriage.

For centuries, the family was the basic unit of the country's social structure. To a great extent, the privacy of the family supplanted that of the state. Children were brought up to respect their elders and, above all, their father, whose word was law within the confines of his family.

Upon the death of the father, family authority devolved upon his oldest son. The females of the household occupied an inferior position; they were confined at home, treated like servants, and not allowed to eat at the same table with the men. When the time came for sons to set up their own households, all parental property was distributed equally among them. Females owned no property and did not have the right to seek divorce. In northern Albania, the ancient Code of Lek permitted the husband "to beat his wife and to bind her in chains if she defies his words and orders."

Geographical conditions affected Tosk social organization. Southern Albania's accessibility led to its coming much more firmly under Ottoman control. In turn, the Ottoman Empire's rule resulted in the breakup of the large, independent, family landholdings and their replacement by extensive estates owned by powerful Muslims, each with his own retinue, fortresses, and large cohort of tenant peasants to work his lands. These landowners' allegiance to the sultans was secured by the granting of administrative positions either at home or elsewhere in the Ottoman Empire.

The consolidation of the large estates was a continuous process. Landowning beys would entrap peasants into their debt and thus establish themselves as semifeudal patrons of formerly independent villagers. In this way, a large Muslim aristocracy developed in the south, while the majority of the Tosk peasants assumed the characteristics of an oppressed social class. As late as the 1930s, two-thirds of the best land in central and southern Albania belonged to large landowners.

The tribal society of the Geg highlanders contrasted sharply with that of the passive, oppressed Tosk peasantry, most of whose members lived on the large estates of the beys and were often represented in the political arena by the beys themselves. The Tosk semifeudal society survived in the south well into the twentieth century. After independence was achieved in 1912, however, a small Tosk middle class began to develop. In the early 1920s, that group, finding common interests with the more enlightened beys, played a major role in attempts to create a modern society. But in 1925 Ahmet Zogu curbed Tosk influence and cemented his power in the tribal north by governing through influential tribal and clan chiefs. To secure the loyalty of these chiefs, he placed them on the government payroll and sent several back to their tribes with the military rank of colonel. In 1928 a new constitution declared Albania a kingdom and Zogu the monarch. King Zog I ruled until the Italian invasion in 1939.

Social Structure under Communist Rule

Albania's general class structure at the time of the communist takeover in 1944 consisted of peasants and workers, who made up the lower class, and a small upper class. Representing over 80 percent of the total population, most peasants lived at no better than subsistence level. Nonagricultural workers numbered about 30,000 persons, most of whom worked in the mines and in the small handicraft industries. The upper class, whose capital was invested mostly in trade, commerce, and the Italian industrial concessions, comprised professional people and intellectuals, merchants with small and medium-sized enterprises, moneylenders, and well-to-do artisans. Industrialists also belonged to the upper class, although generally they owned very small industries and workshops.

The clergy of the major religious denominations did not form a distinct social group. Members of the higher clergy typically were upper-class intellectuals; income from the fairly extensive church estates and state subsidies provided them with a comfortable, but not luxurious living. The rank-and-file clerics, however, were of peasant origin, and most of their parishes were as impoverished as the peasant households they served.

A new social order was legally instituted in Albania with the adoption of the first communist constitution in March 1946, which created a "state of workers and laboring peasants" and abolished all ranks and privileges based on heredity (such as those enjoyed by tribal chiefs and the beys), position, wealth, or cultural standing. According to the constitution, all citizens were equal, regardless of nationality, race, or religion.

Communist spokesmen listed three principal social classes as prevalent in the early years of the regime: the working class, the laboring peasants, and the so-called exploiting class, that is, the landowners in the agricultural economy and the bourgeoisie in trade. The "exploiting class" was liquidated during the early stages of the regime. The bourgeoisie was destroyed by the nationalization of industry, transport, mines, and banks, as well as by the establishment of a state monopoly on foreign commerce and state control over internal trade. The feudal landlords disappeared with the application of the agrarian reforms of 1945–46. These steps were followed by a program of rapid industrialization, whose result was the creation of a substantial working class. A program of agricultural collectivization had as its stated goal the formation of a homogeneous peasant class. Eventually all individual farmers were collectivized, the artisan collectives were converted to state industrial enterprises, the number of private traders was reduced to a minimum, and members of the clergy who avoided imprisonment or execution were sent to work either in industrial plants or agricultural collectives.

Aside from the workers and peasants, the only group to which the Tiranë authorities continued to give special attention was the intelligentsia. Usually termed a layer or stratum of the new social order, the intelligentsia was considered by the communist regime to be a special social group because of the country's need for professional, technical, and cultural talent. To justify this special attention, ideologists often quoted Lenin to the effect that "the intelligentsia will remain a special stratum until the communist society reaches its highest development."

The communist regime, however, transformed the social composition of the intelligentsia. From 1944 to 1948, this transformation involved purging a number of Western-educated intellectuals, whom the regime deemed potentially dangerous, as well as some high-level communist intellectuals who were suspected of having anti-Yugoslav or pro-Western sentiments. The remaining intellectuals were "reeducated" and employed in training new personnel for work in industry, government service, and the party bureaucracy. As a rule, the subsequent generation of intellectuals toed the communist party line. A notable exception was Albania's foremost writer, Ismail Kadare, who managed to walk a tightrope between conformity and dissent until his defection to France in 1990.

The theoretical egalitarian social order had little in common with the real class structure that existed in the country until 1991, when the communist party lost its monopoly on power. In fact, there existed different classes and gradations of rank and privilege, beginning with an upper class composed of the party elite, particularly Political Bureau (Politburo) and Central Committee members. In this category were also leaders of the state and mass organizations, and high-ranking officers of the military and internal security forces. Top party officials and their families received special medical care, exclusive housing in a protected compound in Tiranë, free food and liquor, vacation allowances, entertainment subsidies, and many other perquisites. At government expense, they purchased stylish French and Italian clothing, cosmetics, appliances, and vacation homes. An inquiry conducted by Albania's newly formed coalition government in 1991 concluded that "the former party leadership created for itself every opportunity to acquire privileges and enrich itself while the people were deceived by bogus and cynical propaganda about a struggle against privileges, luxury, and inequality."

Just below the Politburo and the Central Committee were the vast party and government bureaucracies, professional people and intellectuals, and managers of state industrial and agricultural enterprises. The top party elite was distinct from the lower party and state functionaries in terms of privileges, influence, authority, and responsibility. The group of lower party and state officials were bound together by the economic privileges and prestige that went with their positions and membership in, or sympathy for, the Albanian Party of Labor, as the communist party was called from 1948 to 1991. These officials all benefited from their association with the regime and enjoyed educational and economic advantages denied the rest of the population. Below this group were the rank-and-file party members, whose leadership role was constitutionally guaranteed. Aside from the prestige they enjoyed as party members, however, their privileges and economic benefits did not differ much from those of the next lower class in the social structure, the workers.

Constituting an estimated 47 percent of the total population in 1985, the working class (which, according to the official classification, included rural dwellers employed by state farms) was created after the communist seizure of power and composed almost wholly of peasants. Although under constant pressure to increase productivity, exceed production norms, and perform "volunteer" labor, workers were entitled to an annual two-week paid vacation. State-subsidized rest houses for this purpose were established at various locations across the country.

The regime's policy of complete agricultural collectivization deprived peasants of their landholdings, except for tiny personal plots, and required them to work on collective farms. Despite government attempts to equalize the wages of peasants and workers, peasant income remained approximately at subsistence level. One or two members of a peasant family would often engage in rural nonagricultural occupations, such as mining or forestry, that offered superior wages and benefits.

Soon after adoption of the constitution of 1946, new laws were implemented regulating marriage and divorce. Marriages had to be contracted before an official of the local People's Council. After 1967, religious wedding ceremonies were forbidden. The minimum age for marriage was set at sixteen for women and eighteen for men. Because marriage was now supposed to be based on the full equality of both spouses, the concept of the father as head of the family, recognized by precommunist civil law and considered essential to Albanian family life, was officially deprived of legitimacy. A husband and wife now had the legal right to choose their own residence and professions. However, marriage to foreigners was prohibited except with the permission of the government.

The new divorce laws were designed to facilitate proceedings. The separation of spouses was made grounds for divorce, and in such cases a court could grant a divorce without considering related facts or the causes of the separation. Either spouse could ask for a divorce on the basis of incompatibility of character, continued misunderstandings, irreconcilable hostility, or for any other reason that disrupted marital relations to the point where cohabitation had become intolerable. Certain crimes committed by the spouse, especially so-called crimes against the state and crimes involving moral turpitude, were also recognized as grounds for divorce. In divorce cases, custody of children was granted to the parent "with better moral and political conditions for the children's proper education."

About 27,400 marriages were contracted in 1987, about 8.9 per 1,000 inhabitants. There were more than 2,500 divorces in the same year, or about 0.8 per 1,000 inhabitants.

Article 41 of the 1976 constitution guaranteed women equal rights with men "in work, pay, holidays, social security, education, in all sociopolitical activity, as well as in the family." About 33 percent of the party's active members in 1988 were women, as well as over 40 percent of those elected to the people's councils. Nearly one-half of the country's students were women. Statistics showed that women accounted for 47 percent of the work force.

Residential buildings in Tiranë
A construction site in central Tiranë
Courtesy Charles Sudetic

Despite progress during the communist regime, significant inequalities remained. In 1990 only one full member of the ruling Politburo was a woman. In agriculture the predominantly female work force generally had male supervisors. Women were underrepresented in certain professions, particularly engineering. Furthermore, until 1991, abortions were illegal and women were encouraged to have "as many children as possible," in addition to working outside the home. Some traditional practices, such as the presentation of dowries and arranged marriages, reportedly were condoned by the authorities.

Throughout its existence, the communist regime persisted in its campaign against the patriarchal family system. In the mountainous north, where vestiges of traditional tribal structures were particularly prevalent, the local patriarchs were detained and the property of their clans was appropriated. Patriarchalism, according to party propaganda, was the most dangerous internal challenge to Albanian society.

Religion

Before 1944

One of the major legacies of nearly five centuries of Ottoman rule was the conversion of up to 70 percent of the Albanian population to Islam. Therefore, at independence the country emerged as a predominantly Muslim nation, the only Islamic state in Europe. No census taken by the communist regime after it assumed power in 1944 indicated the religious affiliations of the people. It has been estimated that of a total population of 1,180,500 at the end of World War II, about 826,000 were Muslims, 212,500 were Orthodox, and 142,000 were Roman Catholics. The Muslims were divided into two groups: about 600,000 adherents of the Sunni (see Glossary) branch and more than 220,000 followers of a dervish order known as Bektashi (see Glossary), which was an offshoot of the Shia (see Glossary) branch. Bektashism was regarded as a tolerant Muslim sect that also incorporated elements of paganism and Christianity.

Christianity was introduced during Roman rule. After the division of the Roman Empire in 395, Albania became politically a part of the Eastern, or Byzantine, Empire, but remained ecclesiastically dependent on Rome. When the final schism occurred in 1054 between the Roman and Eastern churches, the Christians in southern Albania came under the jurisdiction of the ecumenical patriarch in Constantinople (see Glossary), and those in the north came under the purview of the papacy in Rome. This arrangement

The eighteenth-century mosque of Ethem Bey on Skanderbeg Square in the heart of Tiranë
Courtesy Charles Sudetic

The mosque of Ethem Bey (close-up)
Courtesy Charles Sudetic

prevailed until the Ottoman invasions of the fourteenth century, when the Islamic faith was introduced. The conversion of the people to Islam took many decades.

In the mountainous north, the propagation of Islam was strongly opposed by Roman Catholics. Gradually, however, backwardness, illiteracy, the absence of an educated clergy, and material inducements weakened resistance. Coerced conversions sometimes occurred, especially when foreign Roman Catholic powers, such as the Venetian Republic, were at war with the Ottoman Empire. By the close of the seventeenth century, the Catholics in the north were outnumbered by the Muslims.

After the Ottoman conquest, thousands of Orthodox Christians fled from southern Albania to Sicily and southern Italy, where their descendants, most of whom joined the Uniate Church (see Glossary), still constitute a sizable community. Large-scale forced conversions of the Orthodox Christians who remained in Albania did not occur until the seventeenth century and the Russo-Turkish wars of the eighteenth and nineteenth centuries. Pressure was put on the Orthodox Christians because the Ottoman Turks considered the members of this group sympathetic to Orthodox Russia. The situation of the Orthodox adherents improved temporarily after the Treaty of Kuchuk-Kainarji (1774), in which Russia was recognized as the protector of the Orthodox followers in the Ottoman Empire. The most effective method employed by the Ottoman Turks in their missionary efforts, especially in the central and southern parts of the country, was the creation of a titled Muslim class of pashas and beys who were endowed with both large estates and extensive political and administrative powers. Through their political and economic influence, these nobles controlled the peasants, large numbers of whom were converted to Islam either through coercion or the promise of economic benefits.

In the period from independence to the communist seizure of power, the Muslim noble class constituted Albania's ruling elite, but this group never interfered with religious freedom, which was sanctioned by the various pre-World War II constitutions. These constitutions had stipulated that the country have no official religion, that all religions be respected, and that their freedom of exercise be assured. These provisions reflected the true feelings of the people who, whether Muslim, Orthodox, or Roman Catholic, were generally tolerant in religious matters.

For generations, religious pragmatism was a distinctive trait of the Albanians. Even after accepting Islam, many people privately remained practicing Christians. As late as 1912, in a large number of villages in the Elbasan area, most men had two names, a

Muslim one for public use and a Christian one for private use. Adherence to ancient pagan beliefs also continued well into the twentieth century, particularly in the northern mountain villages, many of which were devoid of churches and mosques. A Roman Catholic intellectual, Vaso Pashko (1825–92), made the trenchant remark, later co-opted by Enver Hoxha, that "the religion of the Albanians is Albanianism."

Hoxha's Antireligious Campaign

A dogmatic Stalinist, Hoxha considered religion a divisive force and undertook an active campaign against religious institutions, despite the virtual absence of religious intolerance in Albanian society. The Agrarian Reform Law of August 1945, for example, nationalized most property of religious institutions, including the estates of monasteries, orders, and dioceses. Many clergy and believers were tried, tortured, and executed. All foreign Roman Catholic priests, monks, and nuns were expelled in 1946.

In January 1949, almost three years after the adoption of the first communist constitution, which guaranteed freedom of religion, the government issued a far-reaching Decree on Religious Communities. The law required that religious communities be sanctioned by the state, that they comply with "the laws of the state, law and order, and good customs," and that they submit all appointments, regulations, and bylaws for approval by the government. Even pastoral letters and parish announcements were subject to the approval of party officials. Religious communities or branches that had their headquarters outside the country, such as the Jesuit and Franciscan orders, were henceforth ordered to terminate their activities in Albania. Religious institutions were forbidden to have anything to do with the education of the young because that had been made the exclusive province of the state. All religious communities were prohibited from owning real estate and from operating philanthropic and welfare institutions and hospitals.

Although there were tactical variations in Hoxha's approach to each of the major denominations, his overarching objective was the eventual destruction of all organized religion in Albania. In the late 1940s and 1950s, the regime achieved control over the Muslim faith by formalizing the split between the Sunni and Bektashi sects, eliminating all leaders who opposed Hoxha's policies, and exploiting those who were more tractable. Steps were also taken to purge all Orthodox clergy who did not yield to the demands of the regime, and to use the church as a means of mobilizing the Orthodox population behind government policies. The Roman Catholic Church, chiefly because it maintained close relations with the Vatican and was more highly organized than the Muslim and Orthodox faiths, became the principal target of persecution. Between 1945 and 1953, the number of priests was reduced drastically and the number of Roman Catholic churches was decreased from 253 to 100. All Catholics were stigmatized as fascists, although only a minority had collaborated with the Italian occupation authorities during World War II.

The campaign against religion peaked in the 1960s. Inspired by China's Cultural Revolution, Hoxha called for an aggressive cultural-educational struggle against "religious superstition" and assigned the antireligious mission to Albania's students. By May 1967, religious institutions had been forced to relinquish all 2,169 churches, mosques, cloisters, and shrines in Albania, many of which were converted into cultural centers for young people. As the literary monthly *Nendori* reported the event, the youth had thus "created the first atheist nation in the world."

The clergy were publicly vilified and humiliated, their vestments taken and desecrated. Many Muslim mullahs and Orthodox priests buckled under and renounced their "parasitic" past. More than 200 clerics of various faiths were imprisoned, others were forced to seek work in either industry or agriculture, and some were executed or starved to death. The cloister of the Franciscan order in Shkodër was set on fire, which resulted in the death of four elderly monks.

All previous decrees that had officially sanctioned the nominal existence of organized religion were annulled in 1967. Subsequently, the 1976 constitution banned all "fascist, religious, warmongerish, antisocialist activity and propaganda," and the penal code of 1977 imposed prison sentences of three to ten years for "religious propaganda and the production, distribution, or storage of religious literature." A new decree that in effect targeted Albanians with Christian names stipulated that citizens whose names did not conform to "the political, ideological, or moral standards of the state" were to change them. It was also decreed that towns and villages with religious names must be renamed. Thus, in the southern areas populated by ethnic Greeks, about ninety towns and places named after Greek Orthodox saints received secular names.

Hoxha's brutal antireligious campaign succeeded in eradicating formal worship, but some Albanians continued to practice their faith clandestinely, risking severe punishment. Individuals caught with Bibles, icons, or other religious objects faced long prison sentences. Parents were afraid to pass on their faith, for fear that their children would tell others. Officials tried to entrap practicing Christians and Muslims during religious fasts, such as Lent and

Ramadan, by distributing dairy products and other forbidden foods in school and at work, and then publicly denouncing those who refused the food. Clergy who conducted secret services were incarcerated; in 1980, a Jesuit priest was sentenced to "life until death" for baptizing his nephew's newborn twins.

The Revival of Religion

In the 1980s, officials grudgingly began to concede that the campaign against religion had not been entirely successful, and indeed probably was counterproductive. A sociological study revealed that over 95 percent of the country's young people were choosing spouses of the same religious background, whereas, prior to the antireligious onslaught, marriages between Muslims and Christians were not uncommon. Albania's government also became more sensitive to the barrage of criticism from the international community. Hoxha's successor, Ramiz Alia, adopted a relatively tolerant stance toward religious practice, referring to it as "a personal and family matter." Émigré clergymen were permitted to reenter the country in 1988 and officiate at religious services. Mother Teresa, an ethnic Albanian, visited Tiranë in 1989, where she was received by the foreign minister and by Hoxha's widow. In December 1990, the ban on religious observance was officially lifted, in time to allow thousands of Christians to attend Christmas services.

Religious leaders estimated that 95 percent of all mosques and churches had been razed or gutted during the years of communist rule. A few had been spared and designated as "cultural monuments." Others, such as the Roman Catholic cathedral in Shkodër, were converted to sports arenas. The status of the clergy was equally appalling; the number of Roman Catholic priests, for example, had declined from 300 in 1944, when the communists took power, to thirty by early 1992. In 1992 plans were under way to restore the houses of worship, seminaries were being reopened, and several Islamic countries had sent teachers to provide religious instruction to young Albanian Muslims who knew virtually nothing about their religion. "Hoxha destroyed the human soul," an official of Albania's new noncommunist government observed, adding, "This will take generations to restore."

Education

Precommunist Era

As late as 1946, about 85 percent of the people were illiterate, principally because schools using the Albanian language had been practically nonexistent in the country before it became independent in 1912. Until the mid-nineteenth century, the Ottoman rulers had prohibited use of the Albanian language in schools. Turkish was spoken in the few schools that served the Muslim population, but these institutions were located mainly in cities and large towns. The schools for Orthodox Christian children were under the supervision of the Constantinople Ecumenical Patriarchate. The teachers at these schools usually were recruited from the Orthodox clergy, and the language of instruction was Greek. The first school known to use Albanian in modern times was a Franciscan seminary that opened in 1861 in Shkodër.

From about 1880 to 1910, several Albanian patriots intent on creating a sense of national consciousness founded elementary schools in a few cities and towns, mostly in the south, but these institutions were closed by the Ottoman authorities. The advent of the Young Turks (see Glossary) movement in 1908 motivated the Albanian patriots to intensify their efforts, and in the same year a group of intellectuals met in Monastir to choose an Albanian alphabet. Books written in Albanian before 1908 had used a mixture of alphabets, consisting mostly of combinations of Latin, Greek, and Turkish-Arabic letters.

The participants in the Monastir meeting developed a unified alphabet based on Latin letters. A number of textbooks soon were written in the new alphabet, and Albanian elementary schools opened in various parts of the country. In 1909, to meet the demand for teachers able to teach in the native tongue, a normal school was established in Elbasan. But in 1910, the Young Turks, fearing the emergence of Albanian nationalism, closed all schools that used Albanian as the language of instruction.

Even after Albania became independent, schools were scarce. The unsettled political conditions caused by the Balkan wars and by World War I hindered the development of a unified education system. The foreign occupying powers, however, opened some schools in their respective areas of control, each power offering instruction in its own language. A few of these schools, especially the Italian and French ones, continued to function after World War I and played a significant role in introducing Western educational methods and principles. Particularly important was the National Lycée of Korçë, in which the language of instruction was French.

Soon after the establishment in 1920 of a national government, which included a ministry of education, the foundation was laid for a national education system. Elementary schools were opened in the cities and some of the larger towns, and the Italian and French schools that had opened during World War I were strengthened. In the meantime, two important American schools were founded:

Unrestored Roman Catholic church converted by the communist regime into an industrial facility and reclaimed in 1991 by local Catholics
Courtesy Charles Sudetic

Priest with previously hidden religious artifacts, Shkodër
Courtesy Fred Conrad

the American Vocational School in Tiranë, established by the American Junior Red Cross in 1921; and the American Agricultural School in Kavajë, sponsored by the Near East Foundation. Several future communist party and government luminaries were educated in the foreign schools: Enver Hoxha graduated from the National Lycée in 1930, and Mehmet Shehu, who would become prime minister, completed studies at the American Vocational School in 1932.

In the 1920s, the period when the foundations of the modern Albanian state were laid, considerable progress was made toward development of a genuinely Albanian education system. In 1933 the Royal Constitution was amended to make the education of citizens an exclusive right of the state. All foreign-language schools, except the American Agricultural School, were either closed or nationalized. This move was intended to stop the rapid spread of schools sponsored directly by the Italian government, especially among Roman Catholics in the north.

The nationalization of schools was followed in 1934 by a far-reaching reorganization of the entire education system. The new system called for compulsory elementary education from the ages of four to fourteen. It also provided for the expansion of secondary schools of various kinds; the establishment of new technical, vocational, and commercial secondary schools; and the acceleration and expansion of teacher training. The obligatory provisions of the 1934 reorganization law were never enforced in rural areas because the peasants needed their children to work in the fields, and because of a lack of schoolhouses, teachers, and means of transportation.

The only minority schools operating in Albania before World War II were those for the Greek minority living in the district of Gjirokastër. These schools too were closed by the constitutional amendment of 1933, but Greece referred the case to the International Permanent Court of Justice, which forced Albania to reopen them.

Pre-World War II Albania had no university-level education and all advanced studies were pursued abroad. Every year the state granted a limited number of scholarships to deserving high school graduates, who otherwise could not afford to continue their education. But the largest number of university students came from well-to-do families and thus were privately financed. The great majority of the students attended Italian universities because of their proximity and because of the special relationship between the Rome and Tiranë governments. The Italian government itself, following a policy of political, economic, military, and cultural penetration

Country grade schools
Courtesy Fred Conrad

of the country, granted a number of scholarships to Albanian students recommended by its legation in Tiranë.

Soon after the Italians occupied Albania in April 1939, the education system came under complete Italian control. Use of the Italian language was made compulsory in all secondary schools, and the fascist ideology and orientation were incorporated into the curricula. After 1941, however, when guerrilla groups began to operate against the Italian forces, the whole education system became paralyzed. Secondary schools became centers of resistance and guerrilla recruitment, and many teachers and students went to the mountains to join resistance groups. By September 1943, when Italy capitulated to the Allies and German troops invaded and occupied Albania, education had come to a complete standstill.

Education under Communist Rule

Upon taking power in late 1944, the communist regime gave high priority to reopening the schools and organizing the whole education system to reflect communist ideology. The regime's objectives for the new school system were to wipe out illiteracy in the country as soon as possible, to struggle against "bourgeois survivals" in the country's culture, to transmit to Albanian youth the ideas and principles of communism as interpreted by the party, and finally to educate the children of all social classes on the basis of these principles. The 1946 communist constitution made it clear that the regime intended to bring all children under the control of the state. All schools were soon placed under state management.

The 1946 Education Reform Law provided specifically that Marxist-Leninist principles would permeate all school texts. This law also made the struggle against illiteracy a primary objective of the new school system. In September 1949, the government promulgated a law requiring all citizens between the ages of twelve and forty who could not read to attend classes in reading and writing. Courses for illiterate peasants were established by the education sections of the people's councils. The political organs of the armed forces provided parallel courses for illiterate military personnel.

In addition to providing for free seven-year obligatory elementary schooling and four-year secondary education, the 1946 law called for the establishment of a network of vocational, trade, and teacher-training schools to prepare personnel, technicians, and skilled workers for various social, cultural, and economic activities. Another education law adopted in 1948 provided for the further expansion of vocational and professional courses to train skilled and semiskilled workers and to increase the theoretical and professional knowledge of the technicians.

In the 1950s, the school system was given a thorough Soviet orientation in terms both of communist ideological propaganda and central government control. Secondary technical schools were established along the same lines. In 1951 three institutes of higher learning were founded: the Higher Pedagogic Institute, the Higher Polytechnical Institute, and the Higher Agricultural Institute, all patterned on Soviet models. Most textbooks, especially those dealing with scientific and technical matters, were translations of Soviet materials. Courses for teacher preparation were established in which the Russian language, Soviet methods of pedagogy and psychology, and Marxist-Leninist dialectics were taught by Soviet instructors. A team of Soviet educators laid the structural, curricular, and ideological foundations of Enver Hoxha University at Tiranë, which was established in 1957.

By 1960 the system of elementary and secondary education had evolved into an eleven-year program encompassing schools of general education and vocational and professional institutes. The schools of general education consisted of primary grades one to four, intermediate grades five to seven, and secondary grades eight to eleven. In October 1960, however, as Soviet-Albanian tensions were reaching the breaking point, the Albanian Party of Labor issued a resolution calling for the reorganization of the whole school system. The resolution's real aim was to purge the schools of Soviet influence and rewrite the textbooks. An additional year was added to the eleven-year general education program, and the whole school system was integrated more closely with industry in order to prepare Albanian youth to replace the Soviet specialists, should the latter be withdrawn, as they eventually were in 1961.

A subsequent reform divided the education system into four general categories: preschool, general eight-year program, secondary education, and higher education. The compulsory eight-year program was designed to provide pupils with the elements of ideological, political, moral, aesthetic, physical, and military education. The new system lowered the entrance age for pupils from seven to six, and no longer separated primary and intermediate schools.

Secondary education began with grade nine (usually at age fourteen), and ended with grade twelve. Secondary schools offered four-year general education programs or four-year vocational and professional programs, including industrial, agricultural, pedagogic, trade, arts, and health tracks, among others. Some programs lasted only two years.

The term of study in the institutes of higher education lasted three to five years, and tuition was also free at this level. Provision was made to expand higher education by increasing the number of full-time students, setting up new branches in places where there were no post-secondary institutes, and organizing specialized courses in which those who had completed higher education would be trained to become highly qualified technical and scientific cadres. All full-time graduate students had to serve a probationary period of nine months in industrial production and three months in military training, in addition to the prescribed military training in school.

Adult education was provided in the same sequence as full-time schooling for younger students, with two exceptions. First, the eight-year general education segment was noncompulsory and was compressed into a six-year program that allowed for completion of the first four grades in two years. Second, those who wanted to proceed to higher institutes after completing secondary school had to devote one year to preparatory study instead of engaging in production work, as full-time students did.

Official statistics indicated that the regime made considerable progress in education. Illiteracy had been virtually eliminated by the late 1980s. From a total enrollment of fewer than 60,000 students at all levels in 1939, the number of people in school had grown to more than 750,000 by 1987; also, there were more than 40,000 teachers in Albania. About 47 percent of all students were female. The proportion of eighth-grade graduates who continued with some type of secondary education increased from 39 percent in 1980 to 73 percent in 1990, with no village reporting a figure lower than 56 percent.

A reorganization plan was announced in 1990 that would extend the compulsory education program from eight to ten years. The following year, however, a major economic and political crisis in Albania, and the ensuing breakdown of public order, plunged the school system into chaos. Widespread vandalism and extreme shortages of textbooks and supplies had a devastating effect on school operations, prompting Italy and other countries to provide material assistance. The minister of education reported in September 1991 that nearly one-third of the 2,500 schools below the university level had been ransacked and fifteen school buildings razed. Many teachers relocated from rural to urban areas, leaving village schools understaffed and swelling the ranks of the unemployed in the cities and towns; about 2,000 teachers fled the country. The highly structured and controlled educational environment that the communist regime had painstakingly cultivated in the course of more than forty-six years was abruptly shattered.

Health and Welfare

Medical Care and Nutrition

The government credited itself with a revolutionary transformation of Albanian health standards. According to official statistics, the incidence of malaria and other debilitating diseases that affected large segments of the population before 1950 had been greatly reduced or eliminated, and average life expectancy had increased about twenty years by 1988 (see Population, this chapter). These successes were attributable primarily to large-scale inoculation programs, the extermination or reduction in number of disease-spreading pests, and a general expansion of health services. In 1987 Albania had about one physician or dentist per 577 inhabitants (compared to one per 8,154 inhabitants in 1950), and one hospital bed per 168 inhabitants (compared to one per 229 inhabitants in 1950). All medical services were free. However, further improvements in health care were obstructed by malnutrition, unsanitary conditions, and a rapidly deteriorating economy.

Although considerably decreased, the infant mortality rate—fifty deaths per 1,000 live births, according to data published by the United States government—was still much higher than that

Albanians drawing water from a spigot on a state farm in central Albania
Courtesy Charles Sudetic

Breadline in Elbasan
Courtesy Fred Conrad

of other Balkan states in 1991. Many of these deaths were caused by low birth weight. Because of food shortages and inadequate prenatal care, the proportion of premature births increased from 7 to 11 percent between 1987 and early 1992. Hospitals lacked essential medicines and equipment; the University of Tiranë Hospital, considered the best in the country, had only one incubator.

The United Nations Children's Fund (UNICEF) reported that fifty-seven out of every 1,000 Albanian mothers died during pregnancy or childbirth—roughly ten times the average rate in Western Europe. Contraceptives could not be obtained. Abortions, which were legalized in the summer of 1991, were performed with poorly sterilized instruments, as were Caesarean sections. Patients at Tiranë's maternity clinic sometimes had to share beds or bring their own food.

The food supply—a perennial problem because of poor soil, occasional drought, primitive methods of cultivation, and a lack of readily accessible resources—did not keep pace with population growth under communist rule. The typical diet lacked protein and other vital elements. Families, regardless of size, received meager rations of meat, usually three to four kilograms per month. Eggs, cheese, sugar, and coffee also were rationed. Nonrationed goods, such as milk, green vegetables, and fruit, were often difficult to come by, and émigrés reported having to stand in line many hours to purchase them. Farmers relied on small private plots of land to supplement their provisions.

The economic disintegration of the late 1980s and early 1990s, hastened by a severe drought in the summer of 1990, a general strike the following year, and widespread food riots, compelled the country to become totally dependent on foreign food aid. Jolted by a flood of Albanian refugees, Italy delivered 83,000 tons of food to its eastern neighbor between September 1991 and January 1992. Additional emergency aid was received from Germany, Switzerland, the United States, and other countries, as well as from international relief agencies.

Housing

Official sources indicated that, between 1945 and 1985, nearly 165,000 apartments were built by the state and more than 232,000 houses were constructed by individuals with state assistance. Nevertheless, living quarters became increasingly overcrowded because of rapid population growth. Families of four or more persons often lived in a single room. Newlyweds seeking a private home faced waiting periods of up to ten years. War and natural catastrophes added to the burden. During World War II, some 35,000

Housing blocks near the town of Lushnjë in central Albania
Courtesy Charles Sudetic

Albanian women on a state farm washing clothes at an open drain
Courtesy Charles Sudetic

dwellings had been destroyed. About 10,000 homes were damaged or destroyed by earthquakes in 1967 and 1969, and a powerful earthquake in 1979 demolished about 18,000 buildings and left 100,000 people homeless.

Rural houses were small, sparsely furnished, and simply constructed of natural rock or stone. Most had one or two rooms, and a hearth or sometimes a stove for heating and cooking. Urban houses and apartments usually were small; many lacked central heating. Kitchens and toilet facilities in apartments had to be shared by three or four families.

Social Insurance

The noncontributory social insurance program, administered by state organizations, included retirement pensions and compensation for disability and maternity leave. Funds for social insurance payments came from the state budget. Total expenditures increased from 13 million leks (for value of the lek—see Glossary) in 1950 to almost 1.8 billion leks in 1987, according to official statistics.

The government had granted retirement benefits to workers, including employees of state farms, since the late 1940s. Depending on job type, full retirement pensions (70 percent of an individual's average monthly earnings during any three consecutive years within the last ten years worked) were awarded to male workers between the ages of fifty and sixty after twenty to twenty-five years of work, and to female workers between the ages of forty-five and fifty-five after fifteen to twenty years of work. Pensions ranged from L350 to L700 (US$52 to US$104) monthly. Workers who reached retirement age but had worked less than the number of years required to receive full pension payments were eligible for partial pensions, computed on the basis of time in service. After the full collectivization of agriculture in 1972, social insurance benefits were extended to the peasants. Retirement pensions were granted to male peasants at the age of sixty-five, after twenty-five years of work, and to female peasants at the age of fifty-five, after twenty years of work.

Disability payments were made at the rate of 85 percent of average earnings for the last month worked; persons with less than ten years' service received 70 percent; temporary or seasonal workers received less. When a disability was directly work-related, compensation was granted at the rate of 95 percent for most trades and 100 percent for miners.

Pregnant women were entitled to a total of six months' leave. During that period, they received 75 to 95 percent of their regular earnings, depending on length of service, and were permitted to work reduced hours after returning to their jobs. Subsidized day-care facilities were provided for children six months of age or older. A woman could remain at home for limited periods to care for a sick child and collect 60 percent of her average pay. If it was considered medically necessary for a mother to stay in the hospital with her sick child, she received 60 percent of her average pay during the entire hospital stay.

In the early 1990s, the education and health care systems, indeed the structure of Albanian society, continued to deteriorate. Albanians began looking toward democratic opposition groups to replace their communist rulers and to lead the country toward a modern, civil society.

* * *

Albania: A Socialist Maverick, by Elez Biberaj, contains a good overview of contemporary Albanian society. A broad range of statistical data on past and present social structure may be found in the *Statistical Yearbook of the People's Socialist Republic of Albania,* and occasionally also in articles published by the English-language monthlies *New Albania* and *Albania Today.* Albania's diverse cultural history is explored in Stavro Skendi's *Balkan Cultural Studies. Conscience and Captivity: Religion in Eastern Europe,* by Janice A. Broun, provides valuable insights into the country's religious heritage and describes the communist regime's campaign against religion. Human rights violations are meticulously documented by the Minnesota Lawyers International Human Rights Committee in its 1990 report, *Human Rights in the People's Socialist Republic of Albania.* For a comprehensive analysis of Albania's postwar rural transformation, Örjan Sjöberg's *Rural Change and Development in Albania* is recommended. The *RFE/RL Research Report* (formerly Radio Free Europe/Radio Liberty's *Report on Eastern Europe*) regularly reviews recent sociopolitical and socioeconomic developments in Albania and neighboring Kosovo. (For further information and complete citations, see Bibliography.)

Chapter 3. The Economy

Albanian women working at computer terminals

EUROPE'S POOREST NATION by every economic measure, Albania has been isolated and underdeveloped for centuries. Economists estimated the gross domestic product per capita at about US$450 in 1990, a figure that placed Albania below Lesotho and above Sri Lanka as the world's thirty-second least developed country. Ironically, Albania possesses significant fossil fuel and mineral deposits, including oil and chromite, as well as a topography and annual rainfall suitable for generating hydroelectric power. Large-scale drainage projects begun after World War II turned marshes into fertile fields in Albania's lowlands, and the country's Mediterranean climate offers ideal conditions for cultivating fruits and vegetables. But Europe's highest birth rate and a mismanaged postwar industrial expansion, which failed to create enough productive jobs to absorb the flood of people entering the work force, left Albania with an abundance of literate but unemployed and unskilled workers. At the start of the 1990s, thousands of desperate Albanians fled abroad seeking jobs because of the wretched standard of living and limited economic opportunity at home.

Albania's communist economic system, with its strict central controls, egalitarian incentive system, and bias toward heavy industry, collapsed in the early 1990s, idling almost all of the country's production lines. In early 1992, the government was piecing together a new, market-based economic mechanism. The People's Assembly passed many new laws on privatization of state property and protection of free enterprise, private property, and foreign investments, and lawyers drafted new civil and commercial codes, banking and tax laws, and labor, antitrust, and social security regulations. The structure of Albania's productive capacity was clearly going to change radically as the government broke up collective farms and privatized state lands and enterprises and as managers adjusted to free-market conditions. Nevertheless, agriculture was certain to remain the economy's cornerstone for the foreseeable future. The farm sector produced over 30 percent of Albania's net material product (see Glossary) and employed over 50 percent of the work force before the centrally planned economy buckled. However, farm output failed to keep pace with the demands of Albania's burgeoning population, and the entire sociopolitical system began to crumble when the farm sector could no longer supply adequate food to urban areas or raw materials to factories.

The orthodox Stalinists of the ruling Albanian Party of Labor (APL) worshiped heavy industry and for decades offered it investment monies, which usually flowed from foreign coffers. That investment brought expansion and diversification to the country's entire industrial sector, but production was constrained by the mismanagement and inefficiency that characterize communist systems. Before the communist economy imploded in 1990, industry accounted for over 40 percent of Albania's net material product and employed about 25 percent of the nation's work force. The industrial sector's most important branches were petroleum production, electric-power generation, mining, engineering, and light industry. The transportation and trade sectors had registered improvements in absolute terms over prewar levels of development, but both lagged behind European standards.

Starting in the 1920s, Italy, Yugoslavia, the Soviet Union, and China in turn supported the Albanian economy before war or political spats prompted Tiranë to break off each relationship. Enver Hoxha, first secretary of the APL, launched a policy of strict autarky when the country's last foreign patron, China, stopped aid infusions in 1978. Rapid population growth and lagging farm and industrial output, however, soon brought hunger and economic chaos. Tiranë delayed significant economic reform until popular discontent threatened to explode into revolution. By 1991, a chain reaction of supply shortfalls had paralyzed the entire economy, and Albania cried out for humanitarian aid, this time from the West. Albania's opening to the world had a major impact on the freedom of enterprises and people to participate in foreign trade, but the country's escalating foreign debt and currency problems rendered it incapable of importing badly needed materials and equipment.

The totality of the collapse of Albania's communist economic system made introducing free-market reforms more difficult, in the view of some Western authorities, than in any other East European country. So critical was the need for heating fuel in the winter of 1991–92 that people stripped wood from park benches, and the nurses at an orphanage in Shkodër locked up branches and twigs to keep them from thieves. Mobs stormed warehouses, factories, bakeries, flour mills, shops, and hotels, taking everything they could carry and destroying much of what they could not. Italian soldiers escorting food convoys found that they had to guard their own garbage trucks after armed gangs descended on the vehicles to pick through their contents. Thieves stole medicine, medical equipment, and even ambulances from hospitals. Fires in storehouses and factories burned out of control because fire fighters had no equipment in good repair. Opposition political leaders blamed the communist APL for instigating unrest in hopes of demonstrating to the impressionable that the isolation and apparent order of the old regime were better than the present chaos and the ways of the wider world.

Despite Albania's economic dysfunction and backwardness, Western economists predicted that the country stood a good chance of prospering if its government could restore order and take advantage of the country's fertile lands, relatively rich mineral resources, favorable location, potential for tourism, and generally literate work force.

Albania's communist regime published few economic statistics, and Western scholars found that the sparse data made available were often neither accurate nor consistent. No statistical yearbook was issued for fourteen years after 1974, and data on performance of the oil industry were treated as a state secret after production began falling in the 1970s. Observers specializing in the Albanian economy have posited that the communist government released data only when performance results were positive and that data on aggregate economic growth were not published when they were close to or below the population growth rate.

Economic Policy and Performance

Despite significant progress in the twentieth century, Albania still lagged far behind the other European nations economically. A unified economy did not exist before the early 1920s, and the succession of foreign patrons had punctuated the country's erratic economic development since then. Heavy-handed domination by fascist Italy between 1925 and 1943 brought Albania scant economic progress. During its postwar rule of forty-six years, the Albanian government turned first to Yugoslavia, then to the Soviet Union, and then to China for assistance in imposing a Stalinist economic system. Enver Hoxha and his protégés used economic policy primarily to maintain political power and only secondarily to stimulate growth. They insisted on rigid centralization and forced industrialization despite Albania's small size and lack of skilled workers, able administrators, and farmers capable of producing key raw materials and enough grain to feed the population. Albania's leaders prescribed autarky when China shut off aid in 1978, but galloping population growth and lagging farm output rendered the policy and the regime bankrupt. Tiranë delayed radical economic reform until public discontent spilled onto the streets. By 1991, supply shortfalls had paralyzed the entire system.

The Precommunist Albanian Economy

The Albanians faced daunting developmental challenges when they declared independence in 1912 after some 500 years as part of the Ottoman Empire. Their medieval, patriarchal social structure necessarily stunted the growth of anything beyond the most rudimentary economic relationships. Subsistence and feudal agriculture so dominated Albania's economy in the state's early years that even trained carpenters, joiners, and blacksmiths were in short supply. Each family generally produced its own bread and meat as well as flax, wool, and leather. Many peasants used wooden plows and knew little about manures, artificial fertilizers, or crop rotation; most had no incentive to produce cash crops because they had no way to transport their output to a reliable market. A complete absence of good roads made interregional commerce almost impossible. The trip from Tiranë to Vlorë, for example, involved a sea journey; and although Shkodër's tradesmen exported skins by boat to Italy, their compatriots in Gjirokastër had to cross the Strait of Otranto to buy them from the Italians (see fig. 1). There were also no roads across the Greek or Yugoslav borders capable of handling commercial traffic.

Albania's leaders lacked accurate data on the country's agricultural output, as well as on the extent and characteristics of its farmland, livestock herds, and oil and mineral deposits.

President Ahmed Zogu (later king Zog) sought Italian protection for Albania in 1925, entering into economic agreements that Italy used to exploit Albania's oil, chromite, copper, and iron-ore reserves. Albania remained backward, however. In the late 1920s, agriculture contributed over 90 percent of the national income although only 8 percent of the country's land area was under cultivation and the entire farm sector could boast only thirty-two tractors (see table 3, Appendix). Even in 1938, Albania's industrial output amounted to less than 4 percent of national income, and annual per capita industrial production totaled about US$8. However, Italy did carry out extensive geological exploration, gauging for the first time the extent of Albania's mineral wealth. The Italians also improved Albania's infrastructure, modernizing Tiranë and constructing 1,500 kilometers of roads and several hundred bridges as well as Durrës harbor. World War II dealt Albania's economy severe setbacks except in the mining sector, where the mineral-hungry Italian and German occupying forces actually added to productive capacity. Durrës harbor and many of the country's roads and bridges, however, sustained damage during the war.

Imposition of the Stalinist System

As World War II drew to a close, Albania's provisional government, run by the Albanian Communist Party, predecessor of the APL and a communist-dominated front organization, wasted little time in taking full control of the economy. In December 1944, shortly after coming to power, the regime adopted new laws providing for strict state regulation of all industrial and commercial companies as well as foreign and domestic commercial relations. A "war-profits tax" and laws allowing the seizure of property belonging to anyone labeled an "enemy of the people" weakened the country's minuscule middle class. In early 1945, the Albanian authorities confiscated Italian- and German-owned assets, revoked all foreign economic concessions, nationalized all public utilities and means of transportation, and created a network of government-sponsored consumer cooperatives. Heedless of Albania's needs and comparative advantages, the party leaders followed Stalinism's dictates and pushed the development of heavy industry over agriculture and light industry.

The regime wooed the peasantry by curbing the power of the large landowners and granting concessions to peasants and sharecroppers. In January 1945, the new leaders canceled outstanding agricultural debts, slashed land-use charges by 75 percent, nationalized water resources, and offered peasants an opportunity to purchase irrigation water from the state at nominal fees. The Agrarian Reform Law of August 1945 destroyed what remained of the economic might of central and southern Albania's large landowners, replacing their sprawling estates with about 70,000 small farms. In effect, the government nationalized all forests and pasture lands and expropriated without compensation land belonging to individuals who had nonfarm sources of income. The land law allowed farmers to keep up to forty hectares if they earned their income exclusively from farming and worked the land with machinery. The landholdings of religious institutions and farmers without machinery were limited to twenty hectares. Landless peasants and people who owned less than five hectares of property received up to five hectares per family and additional hectarage for married sons who were household members. In some cases, the law required the new landowners to make nominal compensation to the former owners.

Another agricultural reform law enacted in 1946 limited rural property holdings to five hectares of arable land. In April of that year, military tribunals began giving prison sentences to peasants caught hoarding grain. The state also nationalized farm tools and draft animals, banned land sales and transfers, and required peasants to obtain government permission to slaughter animals. In June the authorities ordered peasants to deliver relatively high quotas of grain crops to state procurement centers at low, officially set prices. Using carrot-and-stick techniques, the government attempted to persuade peasants to join collective farms. Despite the fact that collective-farm members paid lower taxes and had smaller production quotas, the campaign succeeded in convincing only 2,428 peasant families to join collective farms by 1948. The government admitted that the campaign had failed. Poor yields, purges, and coercion characterized the agricultural sector for the next three years, and grain shortages became a chronic problem.

By early 1947, the government had in place much of the institutional framework required for a Stalinist economic system, nationalizing industries and seizing control of foreign trade and most domestic commerce. A currency reform delivered another blow to the embattled middle class. In April 1947, the Economic Planning Commission drew up the country's first economic plan, a nine-month set of selected production targets for the mining, manufacturing, and agricultural sectors denominated in terms of physical output rather than money. Albanian enterprises also began introducing the Soviet accounting system, and party zealots and teachers set about indoctrinating the population with the economic catechism of Marxism-Leninism.

Dependence on Yugoslavia, 1945–48

After World War II, just as before, Albania's economy relied heavily on foreign assistance. The United Nations Relief and Rehabilitation Administration granted Albania US$26.3 million in aid during 1945 and 1946, including large amounts of seed and enough grain to feed a third of the population in 1945; the United States supplied US$20.4 million of the United Nations relief. In July 1946, Albania and Yugoslavia signed a treaty of friendship and cooperation, which provided for establishment of an agency that would coordinate the two countries' economic plans. The agreement also called for the creation of a customs union and the standardization of the Albanian and Yugoslav monetary and pricing systems. A series of technical and economic agreements soon followed. In November, Tiranë and Belgrade signed an economic cooperation accord and an agreement on the creation of jointly owned companies. At least on paper, these documents transformed Albania into a Yugoslav satellite; but their implementation quickly ran into snags.

In early 1947, Tiranë began voicing serious objections to the economic arrangements with Belgrade, taking exception to the way the Yugoslavs weighed Albanian investment in the jointly owned companies and calculated the value of Albanian exports of raw material to Yugoslavia. The Albanians also charged that Yugoslavia's shipping enterprise was working to usurp control of their country's foreign trade. Tiranë sought investment funds to develop light industries and an oil refinery; Belgrade wanted the Albanians to concentrate on agriculture and the extraction of raw materials. Despite its objections to the economic relationship with Yugoslavia, in early 1948 Tiranë launched a one-year economic plan designed to bring Albania's economy into step with Yugoslavia's. But Albania abruptly cut economic links with its neighbor after the Soviet Union expelled Yugoslavia from the Cominform (see Glossary) in June.

Dependence on the Soviet Union, 1948–60

After breaking with Yugoslavia, Albania turned toward the Soviet Union, forming a twelve-year relationship. In September 1948, Moscow stepped in to compensate for Albania's loss of Yugoslav aid, and Albania's factories quickly became dependent on Soviet technology. Anxious to pay tribute to Joseph Stalin personally, the authorities in Tiranë implemented new elements of the Stalinist economic system. The regime introduced a Soviet-style three-step process for drawing up the national economic plan and adopted basic elements of the Soviet fiscal system, under which enterprises contributed to the state treasury from their residual income and retained only a share of earnings for authorized self-financed investments and other purposes. The Ministry of Finance thus won the authority to set each enterprise's investment policy and regulate its current activity through the state bank.

The First Five-Year Plan (1951–55) emphasized mining and electric-power production as well as transportation improvements. The plan called for an increase in industrial production at an average annual rate of 27.7 percent, including an increase of 26.5 percent in consumer-goods output and a 31-percent rise in production of goods consumed by producers. Shortfalls in agricultural production during the first year doomed the entire plan. The farm sector failed to meet output targets for raw materials, leaving the industrial sector unable to meet targets for consumer goods. Industrial productivity also lagged because recently urbanized peasants had not had enough time to learn to operate factory equipment. The regime then realigned planning priorities in favor of agriculture and consumer-goods production. Over the plan period, annual industrial output reportedly increased at an average of 22.8 percent; consumer-goods output rose 24.3 percent; and producer-goods output rose 20.7 percent. The Albanian economy's backwardness dashed the leadership's hopes of rapidly developing heavy industries, specifically the mineral-processing and capital-goods manufacturing branches, at the expense of the agricultural sector. Although their efforts brought partial success—the ratio between the values of agricultural and industrial production shifted from 82:18 in 1938 to 40:60 in 1953—70 percent of Albania's work force continued to till the soil.

Having relatively easy access to capital because of generous Soviet aid, the regime redoubled its industrialization drive and tightened control of the agriculture sector. Albania conducted all its foreign commerce with the other communist nations between 1949 and 1951 and over half its trade with the Soviet Union itself. The Soviet Union and its satellites wrote long-term "loans" to cover shortfalls in Albania's balance of payments. Soviet and other East European aid at first dovetailed with the Albanian leadership's ambition to industrialize the country. Tiranë's Second Five-Year Plan (1956–60) called for an annual increase of 14 percent in industrial production. Good results in 1956 and 1957 prompted the authorities to revise plan targets upward. Although the new goals went unattained, industrial production rose an average of about 17 percent annually over the five-year period. In 1955 private farms still produced about 87 percent of Albania's agricultural output, and the government reemphasized its farm collectivization drive. By 1960, however, the proportion of output from collective and state farms was unchanged. The farm sector continued to suffer from low productivity and poor worker motivation. Soviet aid was required, and wheat imports were depended on to meet as much as 48 percent of Albanian need.

Considering Enver Hoxha's obsession with heavy industry misguided, the new Soviet leadership balked at the idea of investing in large-scale industrial projects in Albania after Stalin's death in 1953. The Soviet Union and other communist countries had provided considerable investment and equipment to Tiranë from 1948. Especially after 1955, however, this aid was designed primarily to integrate Albania's economy into a "division of labor" established by the Soviet-led Council for Mutual Economic Assistance (Comecon—see Glossary). Albania's allotted role demanded that it foster agricultural growth and increase the extraction of raw materials and the production of consumer goods. The leadership in Tiranë considered Moscow's advice to concentrate on production of cash crops and raw materials a disparaging attempt to relegate Albania to the status of a Soviet colony in perpetuity. When Tiranë began to tilt toward China, Moscow and its satellites offered incentives to persuade Hoxha to remain in the Comecon fold. The disagreement over Albania's development policy soon became entangled in the animosities between the Soviet Union and China. In 1959 the two communist giants competing for Albania's hand poured capital into the tiny Balkan country so rapidly that it could not be absorbed. China extended Albania a US$13.8 million loan, Moscow followed with new credits totaling US$83.8 million, and other East European countries contributed another US$35 million.

Dependence on China, 1961–78

The Albanian leadership's fixation on heavy industry contributed significantly to its decision to break with the Soviet Union. Enver Hoxha gambled that China not only would be less likely than the Soviet Union to threaten his ascendancy but also would be more likely to provide investment money and equipment for his pet industrial projects. Albania's Third Five-Year Plan (1961–65) amounted to outright defiance of Soviet advice to concentrate mainly on agriculture. The plan allocated industry 54 percent of all investment and called for a 52-percent rise in overall industrial production, including increases of 54 percent and 50 percent in the output of producer and consumer goods, respectively. Moscow responded by canceling credits. The Albanian leaders foresaw that a cut in Soviet investment and aid would disrupt their economy but calculated that maintaining power and continuing industrialization would outweigh the failure of one five-year plan. The Soviet aid stoppage brought Albania's foreign trade to a near halt and delayed completion of major construction projects. Spare-parts shortages led to a 12.5-percent decline in labor productivity between 1960 and 1963. China compensated Albania for the loss of Soviet credits and supplied about 90 percent of the spare parts, foodstuffs, and other goods Moscow had promised. The Chinese, however, proved unable to deliver promised machinery and equipment on time.

In 1962 the Albanian government introduced an austerity program to keep the country's sputtering economy from stalling entirely. Official public appeals to cut costs and conserve resources and equipment netted a claimed 6 percent savings. The government also initiated a campaign of "popular consultation," asking individuals to submit suggestions for improving self-sufficiency. Years of state terror and still-rigid central control, however, had undermined the Albanians' willingness to assume personal responsibility. Party hard-liners, fearing they would lose their positions to a younger generation of more technically sophisticated managers, sabotaged cost-cutting measures.

The government launched a program to increase the amount and quality of arable land by terracing hillsides and draining swamps. A new phase of collectivization was initiated. However, agricultural output grew only 22 percent over the entire five years instead of the planned 72 percent. Overall industrial production grew a mere 14 percent in 1964 and 1965.

Fearful of a potential domestic power struggle and disappointed that heavy industry's output had failed to increase significantly overall between 1950 and 1965, the Albanian regime adjusted its Stalinist economic system in the mid-1960s. The government altered the planning mechanism in February 1966 by allowing for a small degree of worker participation in decision making and reducing by 80 percent the number of indicators in the national economic plan. The leadership also decentralized decision-making power from the Council of Ministers to the ministries and local people's councils and included a slight devolution of control over enterprise investment funds. The system was specifically designed, however, to ensure that resources were allocated in accordance with a central plan. At no time, at least in public, did Albania's rulers entertain the notion—heretical to all orthodox Stalinists—that economic decision making should be devolved to the enterprises.

In March 1966, an "open letter" from the Albanian Party of Labor to the Albanian people heralded radical changes in the egalitarian job allocation and wage regime. The authorities cut 15,000 jobs from the state bureaucracy, replaced executives, and shunted managers and party officials into the countryside. The government then eliminated income taxes and reduced the salaries of highly paid workers. Wages varied by industry, but the ratio between the lowest and highest salaries was only about 1:2.5. Reviving a scheme originally launched in 1958, the government began assigning all employees to perform "productive" physical labor. People engaged in "mental work"—for example, intellectuals, teachers, and party and state bureaucrats—were required to toil in the fields for one month each year. Even high-school students took part in "voluntary" construction and agricultural work. Only the party elite remained unaffected by the egalitarian reforms.

In emulation of China's Cultural Revolution, which was designed to rekindle the revolutionary fervor of the masses, Hoxha prescribed a regular rotation of managers to prevent "bureaucratic stagnation," "bureaucratism," "intellectualism," "technocratism," and a whole neologistic lexicon of other "negative tendencies." The campaign, called the Cultural and Ideological Revolution, also prescribed the replacement of men with women in the party and state administrations.

The government's economic adjustments militated against efficiency. Workers, who were given a voice in planning, lobbied for the easiest possible production targets and worked to overfulfill them in order to earn bonuses. But because one year's output figures became the basis for the next year's targets, they tried to limit overfulfillment to prevent the imposition of difficult targets in the next planning period. The government's campaign to send office workers out to the fields, mines, and factories encountered resistance. The policies of guaranteed full employment and extensive growth—expanding productive capacity rather than squeezing more from existing capacity—made huge numbers of workers redundant. The low quality and quantity of consumer goods and virtually flat income-distribution curve dampened incentive. Workers dealt in pilfered state property and rested at their official jobs in order to moonlight illegally. Although the government had herded all artisans into cooperatives by 1959, many craftsmen, including tailors, carpenters, and clothing dealers, earned undeclared income through private work. Black-market construction gangs even performed work at factory sites and collective farms for directors desperate to meet plan targets.

In the late 1960s, thanks mainly to massive capital inflows from China, the Albanian economy expanded. The Fourth Five-Year Plan (1966–70) called for an increase of about 50 percent in overall industrial production, with producer-goods production increasing by 10.8 percent annually and consumer-goods output rising 6.2 percent. Most sectors exceeded plan targets. Heavy industry's share of overall industrial production rose from 26 percent in 1965 to 38.5 percent in 1970, the largest increase registered in any five-year period in Albania's history (see table 4, Appendix). In 1967 the government launched a "scientific and technical revolution" aimed at improving self-sufficiency. For the first time, the Albanian Party of Labor made a serious attempt to take into account Albania's natural resources and other competitive advantages while planning industrial development. Government officials examined blueprints for coal-fired and hydroelectric power plants as well as plans for expanding the chemical and engineering industries. Despite chronic worker absenteeism, the engineering sector performed remarkably well, tripling output between 1965 and 1973. The late 1960s also saw changes in the agricultural sector. The authorities announced a farm collectivization drive in 1967 and, in an attempt to take advantage of economies of scale, amalgamated smaller collectives into larger state farms in 1967 and 1968. By 1970, Albania's power grid linked all the country's rural areas.

In the early 1970s, Albania's economy entered a tailspin when China reduced aid (see Shifting Alliances, ch. 4). During the period of close ties, the Chinese had given Albania about US$900 million in aid and had provided extensive credits for industrial development. In the mid-1970s, China accounted for about half of Albania's yearly US$200 million in trade turnover. The economic downturn after the aid reduction clearly showed that Albania's Stalinist developmental strategy failed to provide growth when levels of foreign aid were reduced. In the Fifth Five-Year Plan (1971-75), the government called for an increase of about 60 percent in the value of overall industrial production; producer-goods production was to increase by about 80 percent and consumer-goods output by about 40 percent. General results from the first two years of the plan were relatively satisfactory. But after China reduced aid to Albania substantially in 1972, many key sectors fell disastrously short of plan targets. Tiranë responded by launching an export drive to the capitalist West a year later. In 1974 the government criticized consumer-goods producers for failing to meet assortment and quality objectives. During the five-year period, overall industrial production rose just over 50 percent; producer-goods output, 57 percent; and consumer-goods output, 45 percent. Despite the obvious link with the curtailment of Chinese aid, the Albanian government offered no official explanation for the economic downturn. Widespread purges were reported in 1974, 1975, and 1976.

Isolation and Autarky

Besides triggering short-term disruptions in the Fifth Five-Year Plan, China's reduction of aid to Albania had a dramatic impact on the Balkan nation's broader economic policy after 1972. In official parlance, Albania's rulers implemented a strategy of "socialist construction based on the principle of self-reliance," that is, a policy of strict autarky. In 1976 the People's Assembly constitutionally barred the government from accepting any loan or credit from a capitalist source and from granting concessions to or setting up joint ventures with companies from the capitalist world. The Albanians publicly criticized Beijing beginning in the fall of 1976, and China ended economic aid to Albania altogether in July 1978. The break eliminated the source of half of Albania's imports. The country had no choice but to stimulate exports to make up the shortfall in the hard currency needed to purchase essential supplies. Just before the announced break, government planners prescribed a rapid increase in the production and export of Albania's four main sources of hard-currency income: oil, chromite, copper, and electric power. Between 1976 and 1980, exports jumped 33 percent over the preceding five-year period. In an act indicative of its xenophobia and economic priorities, the regime invested an estimated 2 percent of net material product in the construction and installation of thousands of prefabricated cement bunkers throughout the country from 1977 to 1981.

Tiranë took energetic, if extreme, steps to end Albanian dependence on food imports, even going to the point of requiring each of the country's districts to become self-sufficient in food production. In order to keep people on the farms, the authorities also made rural wages relatively more attractive and tightened travel restrictions on the rural population. The government reduced the size of the personal plots of collective-farm members. Police also increased harassment of peasants who attempted to sell produce in the cities. In late 1981, the government collectivized private livestock in the lowlands as well as all goats and sheep in the highlands. Disaster ensued when peasants undertook a wholesale slaughter of their herds; shortages of meat and dairy products soon plagued the cities. Overpopulation in farm communities further complicated efforts to achieve self-sufficiency.

Autarky proved an unsuccessful policy. The productivity growth rate fell slowly but steadily during the Seventh Five-Year Plan (1981–85), and the annual increase in net material product for the period 1981–88 averaged only 1.7 percent, a figure that did not even keep pace with the country's annual population increase of more than 2 percent. Albania's economy suffered two of its worst years in 1984 and 1985. In 1984, 1985, 1987, and 1988 the net material product decreased, and from 1986 to 1990 it declined 1.4 percent (see table 5, Appendix). Five years of drought between 1983 and 1988 dealt sharp setbacks to agricultural and hydroelectric power output. Power shortages and other acute problems afflicted two of Albania's main generators of hard-currency income, oil and chrome. As output fell, investment contracted and caused further drops in productivity. Insolvent enterprises turned to the state for bailouts. The shortage of goods circulating in the economy and the government's maintenance of fixed wage levels created repressed inflation and forced saving.

Despite clear portents of an economic catastrophe, the regime took no radical initiatives to pull Albania out of its economic nosedive until it was too late to avoid a major collapse. Ramiz Alia, who became chairman of the Presidium of the People's Assembly in November 1982, gradually assumed more decision-making power from Hoxha, who went into semiretirement in 1983 and died in April 1985. In 1986 the Albanian Party of Labor still fully supported a centrally planned economy. The party's official daily, *Zëri i*

Populllit, included the following proclamation in January 1986: "The execution of plan tasks . . . by every individual, sector, enterprise, agricultural cooperative, district, and ministry is a great patriotic duty, a party and state duty." A year later, Alia set to work to quash the right of the peasant collective-farm members who still had personal plots to sell their produce, denouncing the practice as a waste of time and a misguided stimulation of a private market. The ambitious Eighth Five-Year Plan (1986–90) called for an increase of about 35 percent in national income, a 30-percent increase in industrial output, a 35-percent improvement in agricultural output, and a 44-percent increase in exports. Targeted for investment were a hydroelectric power plant at Banjë in the south, a rail line connecting Durrës with the main chromite-mining area in central Albania, new superphosphate and ferrochrome plants, and the completion of nickel-cobalt and lubrication-oil plants.

By late 1989, the dismantling of the communist governments of Eastern Europe and the reintroduction of capitalism to the region were under way, and signs of change began to appear in isolated Albania. It was recognized that the attempt to introduce a completely socialized agricultural sector had failed and that livestock collectivization had been a huge blunder. Nevertheless, in September 1989 Alia told the Eighth Plenum of the Central Committee of the APL that the leadership would "never permit the weakening of common socialist property." The party will never, he said, "permit that the way be opened to the return to private property and capitalist exploitation." At the end of his address, however, Alia said that guaranteed employment, a cornerstone of the communist system, should be allowed to go by the wayside. Thus, he signaled that the leadership had indeed realized that radical changes to the country's Stalinist economic system were necessary.

In 1990 Alia attempted to strengthen the communists' weakening hold on power by initiating an economic reform from the top down. For the first time, the leadership proposed broadening private economic activity outside of agriculture and a role for market forces in determining resource allocations for state-owned industrial enterprises. The government relaxed central planning in agriculture, increased the maximum allowable size of personal plots to about 0.2 hectares, and ordered collective farms to return livestock to peasants. The reforms provided for an expansion of enterprise self-financing and allowed local governments to plan part of the industrial activity that took place in their districts.

In January 1990, at the Ninth Plenum of the Central Committee, party leaders disclosed a reform program that constituted an even more radical departure from their purely Stalinist rhetoric of only a few months earlier. Enterprises were divided into small units and made financially independent, with long-term bank credits replacing state subsidies. The package included decentralization of economic decision making. Workers won the right to choose and dismiss enterprise directors. Wages were to be based on plan fulfillment and enterprise profits. Supply and demand were to determine the prices of luxury goods. Citizens were permitted to undertake private construction for their own use. Agricultural cooperatives were allowed to sell food in towns and set their own prices. At the Tenth Plenum of the Central Committee in April 1990, Alia said that as a consequence of the reforms a significant turnover had occurred among the directors of Albania's enterprises. Resistance to the reforms came from administrative employees unwilling or unable to adapt to new job requirements. Some firms responded to the economic reforms by reducing their output targets in hope of increasing their bonuses; other firms, hoping to avoid penalties for sustaining unplanned losses, actually planned for losses in advance.

The government failed to implement the reforms quickly enough to stem the tide of popular unrest and prevent economic disaster. In the summer of 1990, the existence of unemployment became apparent in Albania. A new drought reduced supplies of electricity from Albania's hydroelectric dams and forced plant shutdowns. Thousands of Albanians demanding visas stormed Tiranë's few Western embassies. The first postwar opposition political movement emerged in December 1990; riots in Tiranë and Shkodër in April 1991 galvanized antigovernment forces; and thousands of Albanians fled to Greece and Italy, but most were later forcibly returned.

By mid-1991, only a quarter of Albania's production capacity was functioning. Industrial output in the third quarter was 60 percent less than in the third quarter of 1990. The foreign debt reached about US$354 million in mid-1991, up from US$254 million at the end of 1990 and US$96 million at the close of 1989. Despite the paralysis in production, the government fed inflation by issuing unbacked money to pay idle workers 80 percent of their normal wages. The opportunity to pilfer became one of the strongest factors motivating people to go to work, and the absence of clearly defined property rights and the breakdown of the rule of law fueled rampant theft of both private and state-owned property. The prolonged shutdown of production lines threatened serious damage to equipment and other capital goods, which suffered at least as much from plunder and cannibalization as from normal depreciation.

In the chaos, consideration of the transition costs inherent in the changeover from a socialist to a capitalist system became irrelevant. The coalition government that took office in June 1991 responded to the situation by announcing that it intended to carry out radical economic reforms including privatization of agricultural land, creation of a legal framework necessary for the functioning of a market economy, commercialization and privatization of economic enterprises, tight monetary and fiscal policies, price and foreign-trade liberalization, limited convertibility of Albania's currency, and the creation of a social safety net. However, the coalition government fell several months later. In April 1992, a victorious Albanian Democratic Party (ADP) took over the government and assumed the burden of implementing badly needed economic reforms.

Economic System

Change from a centrally planned economy to a free-market system necessarily entails hardship, job redistribution, income fluctuations, and a naturally unpopular abandonment of a false sense of security. Albania's Stalinist economic system, however, disintegrated so completely in the early 1990s that the people had little choice but to take cover as the government enacted sweeping free-market reforms. Article 1 of an August 1991 law on economic activity ripped the heart out of the Stalinist economic system, providing for the protection of private property and foreign investments and legalizing private employment of workers, privatization of state property, and the extension and acceptance of credit. Government officials set to work drafting a new civil code, a revised commercial code, new enterprise laws, and new banking, tax, labor, antitrust, and social security legislation. Widespread anarchy, an almost complete production shutdown, a paucity of capital, and a lack of managers trained to deal with the vagaries of a market economy slowed the reform process.

Governmental Bodies and Control

In its last months in power, Albania's communist regime engaged nine ministries in the battle to free up the country's paralyzed economy. The Council of Ministers and the Ministry of Finance formed the hub of economic decision making, and workers and managers at troubled enterprises regularly turned directly to them for direction. The Ministry of Finance took most responsibility for implementing the government's economic reform programs. It drew up accounting and tax regulations as well as rules on the documentation of business activity and contributions to

A man harvesting with a scythe in a field in the central coastal region
Albanians loading grass into a wagon near the town of Lushnjë in the central part of the country
Courtesy Charles Sudetic

social security funds. Inspectors from the Ministry of Finance, known as the "treasury police" or "financial police," enforced the country's economic laws, oversaw customs posts, and worked, albeit with little success, to curb black-market speculators and take action against violators of price ceilings. The other ministries concerned with the economy, such as agriculture, construction, industry, trade, and transportation, implemented plans affecting their respective sectors.

Ownership and Private Property

Albania's government sought to save itself during the collapse of the country's economy by abandoning its Stalinist ideology, reviving family farms, and allowing for the creation of small trade and service businesses. It launched reforms in early 1991 that legalized private ownership and gave statutory protection to joint ventures involving Albanian and foreign companies. In its June 1991 economic program, the coalition government called for the rapid privatization of state-owned property, including the relinquishment of agricultural land to private farmers and the transfer of ownership of industrial enterprises through a free distribution of shares in mutual funds or stock in holding companies. Later the government began auctioning off small enterprises, including shops and restaurants, as well as distributing apartments and homes to their current residents without requiring payment. The government also planned to liquidate unsalvageable enterprises.

The new government supported calls for a crash privatization program and the free granting of ownership rights to the "most natural recipients" by arguing that the economy sorely lacked independent decision makers and that no recovery could be expected until private property had been established. The economy's paralysis and widespread popular unrest underscored the urgency of going forward with some kind of privatization scheme. The law on economic activities provided for the privatization of industrial enterprises and firms dealing with handicrafts, construction, transportation, bank services, foreign and domestic trade, housing, culture and the arts, and legal services. The law, however, called for special legislation to regulate the privatization of Albania's energy and mineral extraction industries, telecommunications, forest and water resources, roadways and railroads, ports and airports, and air and rail transportation enterprises. The government created a National Privatization Agency to auction off enterprises; Albanians were to receive first option to buy.

Privatization proceeded in fits and starts, but within several months about 30,000 people found themselves employed in the nonagricultural private sector. The government privatized about 25,000 retail stores and service enterprises and about 50 percent of all small state enterprises in each sector, mostly through direct sales to workers. Also privatized were state firms engaged in handicrafts, a brick factory, bakeries, a fishery and fishing boats, a construction company, and six seagoing cargo vessels. The government also planned a large-scale privatization of workshops, production lines, and factories. The original plan called for the establishment of about five mutual funds and transformation of the surviving larger state enterprises into joint-stock companies. The shares in these companies would be distributed to the mutual funds, whose shares would in turn be distributed free to all adult citizens resident in Albania. Limited domestic capital, however, made privatization of large enterprises difficult.

Enterprises and Firms

Prior to the 1990s, the state owned and ran all enterprises. Reams of instructions sent from central planners constituted upper management. Enterprise directors did not have power over investment, employment, production, or any other decision-making areas but were responsible for maintaining initial capital stock. Competition among enterprises did not exist. In October 1990, however, as the economic system's breakdown became fully apparent, the government enacted a new enterprise law giving workers management, but not ownership, of the enterprises that employed them. In August 1991, the law on economic activity enabled persons seeking to open businesses to register at the court of the district in which they wished to operate. The court would, within a ten-day period, decide whether or not to grant an operating license. If denied a license, a registrant could appeal to a higher court, which had to decide on the matter within another ten days. The law on business activity also required private enterprises to abide by government standards for quality; weights and measures; safety, sanitary, and working conditions; and environmental protection.

With the help of consultants from the European Community (EC—see Glossary), the International Monetary Fund (IMF—see Glossary), and the World Bank (see Glossary), the Council of Ministers also began working on a new law on the activities of state enterprises. In draft, the law provided for the state to supervise the operation of surviving state-owned enterprises but allowed their managers a broad measure of independence. The draft also provided for the creation of a steering council for each enterprise, which would be nominated by the appropriate ministry or a local government. The council would make major management decisions; work up the enterprise's business plan; manage relations with the government, other enterprises, and employees; and set wages and bonuses. A delegate elected by fellow employees would represent the enterprise's workers on the steering council but would not have a vote. The draft bill also defined how net revenues would be divided among capital reserves, development funds, social assistance, and employee bonuses.

By freeing prices, eliminating barriers to trade, applying banking criteria to credits, and instituting new policies on interest rates, Albania's government gradually bolted together a new framework for assessing the potential viability of the country's enterprises. Western economists proposed a recovery program calling for infusions of aid, management supervision, and closure of loss-generating enterprises. The program included commitments by donor nations of US$140 million in spare parts and raw materials to jump-start paralyzed industries. Under the program, enterprises whose output was valued at less than the cost of inputs would not be restarted because halting production and paying full wages to idled workers would be less damaging to the overall economy than maintaining operations. The viability of restarted firms would be evaluated six to nine months after the introduction of free-market conditions. These enterprises would face either a rollover of capital credits, a rollover of working capital credits accompanied by an investment credit, or liquidation by the auctioning of assets.

Finance and Banking

Under the communist system, the government made all investment decisions, allocating monies to enterprises directly from state coffers. Enterprises were permitted only to manage their initial capital stock and were not allowed to dispose of or acquire new capital. Each enterprise redeposited a predetermined sum into the state budget to compensate for the cost of its fixed assets. The financing mechanism failed in the early 1990s because production rates plummeted and state enterprises generated far more losses than gains. As a consequence, government revenues and reserves rapidly shrank. By mid-1991 Albania's budget deficit was equal to almost half of the country's gross domestic product (GDP—see Glossary). Unbacked currency was issued to finance a large part of the banking system, and inflation soared. Decades of communist-enforced isolation had left few Albanians with an understanding of the pitfalls of complex financial transactions. In 1989 and 1990, according to the Council of Ministers, State Bank of Albania currency traders speculated recklessly on the world spot-money market. Taking on market commitments of up to US$2 billion in a single currency, these traders reportedly marked up losses of as much as US$170 million, a huge figure considering that the country's annual exports at the time amounted to about US$100 million.

The efficient replacement of government plan instructions by consumer preferences in determining resource allocation required the development of a true capital market in Albania. The August 1991 law on economic activity allowed private persons, for the first time since World War II, to finance businesses with lek (L; for value of the lek—see Glossary) investments and foreign currency through the State Bank of Albania, other state-owned banks, and domestic or foreign private banks. Albania joined the IMF in 1991 and thereafter worked to secure a standby credit agreement. In the absence of an effective domestic banking system, illegal money changers and black marketeers met the demand for credit and money-changing services on a bustling Tiranë street corner known locally as "the Bank," where an estimated US$60,000 to US$80,000 changed hands each day.

Albania's government, assisted by specialists from the IMF and World Bank, prepared a two-tier banking system to be governed by laws on the central bank and the commercial banking system. Under the draft banking laws, the National Bank of Albania, a reorganized version of the old State Bank of Albania, would issue and manage the national currency and oversee credit policies. The central bank would also manage foreign-exchange reserves, act as a fiscal agent for the government, maintain a securities exchange market, and license other banks to operate in Albania. The bank would be responsible to the People's Assembly and therefore maintain some distance from the government administration. The country's banking system would include the Albanian Commercial Bank, which took over commercial foreign-exchange transactions from the State Bank of Albania; the Savings Bank; and the Bank for Agricultural Development.

With a branch in every district, 130 rural offices, and 500 staff members, the main source of formal agricultural credit in Albania was the Bank for Agricultural Development. The government separated the farm bank from the State Bank of Albania in 1991. New banking laws excluded the Bank for Agricultural Development pending a parliamentary agreement with parliament. At issue was whether the bank would loan money and set interest rates according to bankers' criteria, the primary one being the potential for timely repayment at a profit, or give special treatment to small farmers and act as a government agent channeling funds to state farms and state-owned enterprises. The farm bank's portfolio included close to L4.0 billion (US$592 million) in bad loans to state farms, dissolved collectives, and state-owned enterprises. A debt-resolution agency was likely to assume responsibility for collection of these bad loans, 90 percent of whose face value had been underwritten by the state. The bank's only real assets were L320 million in loans to individuals and L254 million in deposits.

Currency and Monetary Policy

For decades Albania's government artificially maintained the exchange rate of the country's currency, the lek, at between L5 and L7 to US$1 without regard to production, prices, the external market, or other factors. Among the casualties of the economic collapse of the early 1990s was the government's control over public finances and monetary aggregates; another victim was the lek's facade of stability. An enormous budget deficit, brought on in part by huge government subsidies to money-losing enterprises during a period of almost complete breakdown in production, led to triple-digit inflation. The regime took steps to impose monetary discipline by suspending payment of wage increases. To slow inflation, the government promised to cut its budget and eliminate price supports and subsidies to loss-generating state enterprises.

The government's first tentative step toward currency convertibility came when the August 1991 law on economic activity legalized the exchange of foreign currency for leks at rates set by the State Bank of Albania or by the private foreign currency market. A month later, the government devalued the lek by 150 percent and pegged it to the European Currency Unit (see Glossary). The inflationary spiral quickly drove the lek's value downward. Foreign businesses had no choice but to reinvest lek profits, despite the government's announced intention of introducing a fully convertible lek, because the acute shortage of foreign-currency reserves made convertibility impossible.

Government Revenues and Expenditures

Tax collection had been a serious problem in the Albanian-populated lands at least since the Ottoman Empire extended its rule over the region and probably since Roman times. The government eliminated personal income taxes in 1967 and all personal taxes in 1970. For the next twenty years, central and local governments collected revenues primarily through turnover taxes and revenue deductions from state and collective enterprises. In 1984 these collections accounted for a record 96 percent of government revenue. Chaos overtook Albania's fiscal and taxation systems in 1990, revenues dried up, and the government had to issue unbacked currency to continue operations. In 1991 the government announced that the country's fiscal system had to be strengthened because "no market economy exists without taxes." The People's Assembly set to work on a battery of revenue measures, including a tax on profits, a sales tax, a business registration tax, a motor vehicle tax, and excise taxes on cigarettes, alcoholic beverages, and oil products. Predictably, talk of taxes fueled resentment among neophyte entrepreneurs.

The law on taxation of profits, which the government hoped to implement in early 1992, appeared to offer significant incentives to private enterprise and foreign investment. It required payment of a 30 percent tax on yearly profits but exempted private persons from payment for three years from the time they began business activities. Joint ventures and foreign-owned firms were required to pay a 30 percent profit tax. Upon completing ten years of business activity in Albania, a joint venture or foreign firm would receive tax reductions. Foreign enterprises and persons who reinvested profits in Albania received a 40 percent tax reduction on the amount reinvested. The proposed measure, however, would require all joint ventures and foreign-owned enterprises engaged in mining and energy production to pay a 50 percent profits tax. Foreign persons were required to pay a 10 percent tax on all repatriated profits.

With only limited capacity to generate tax revenues, the government emphasized reducing the overall budget deficit and public debt. Proceeds from the legitimate sale of international aid items were used to maintain essential government functions and the social safety net. Local government reform depended on the development of a new system of financing based on users' fees, local taxes, and central-government grants. Albania's local governments were in dire need of technical assistance to establish a local finance system and train government staff in planning and financial management.

Savings

Albania's communists claimed they had engineered the world's thriftiest society. One in three Albanians maintained a savings account. The volume of deposits in Albania's savings bank rose by 200 times between 1950 and the late 1980s, albeit from a minuscule base. Between 1980 and 1983, the savings rate grew 28 percent. The continual increases in personal savings indicated that the economy was not producing adequate quantities of consumer goods. The government-run banks offered a 2 percent interest rate on short-term deposits and 3 percent on long-term deposits. After the economic crash of the early 1990s, saving, at least in cash, was not an option for most of the population. The wage of an average

Albanian worker dropped to about US$10 per month; a day's pay bought a half kilogram of cheese.

Work Force and Standard of Living

Until the 1990s, Albania's working people played practically no meaningful decision-making role in the country's economic life. Most workers simply followed orders and scrambled to find necessities in the country's poorly stocked stores. Personal initiative too often either went unrewarded or was considered ideologically unsound and therefore hazardous to personal safety. The regime denied the existence of unemployment in Albania but kept thousands of redundant workers and managers on factory and government payrolls and dispatched young people entering the work force to labor manually on collective farms or elsewhere in the economy.

The collapsing economic system left most Albanians effectively jobless. Despair, fear of political repression, and television-fed expectations of an easy life in the West triggered waves of emigration to Europe's established free-market democracies, in particular Greece and Italy. The craving to leave Albania in search of work was so strong that in August 1991, long after the arrival of international food aid, tens of thousands of people converged on Durrës after rumors spread through the nearby countryside that a ship would take passengers from that port to Italy.

Prices and Wages

For many years, all prices and wages were fixed by the government, using annual economic plans. The leadership followed the Stalinist model of conveying general productivity gains to households by reducing retail prices rather than by raising wages, which would have allowed consumers a modicum of leverage in the marketplace and, if goods were unavailable or failed to attract purchasers, would have produced inflationary pressure, forced savings, and a black market. Between 1950 and 1969, the Albanian authorities lowered prices thirteen times. The 1970s witnessed no price cuts, but the government reduced some prices again in 1982 and 1983. Enterprises that sustained losses because of the governments' system of setting wages and prices were compensated with subsidies from the state budget.

The economic anarchy that followed the collapse of the centrally planned system ended the years of artificial price stability. The August 1991 law on economic activity removed price controls on the prices of all goods except bread, meat, dairy products, other essential food items, other goods in short supply, and products produced by monopoly enterprises. Also, the law required an annual review of price ceilings. Price controls became less effective as private food markets developed. The price freeze even failed to halt price increases for rationed food items because they disappeared from the shelves of state stores, where price restrictions were enforced, and found their way onto the black market, where speculators kept prices high. The Council of Ministers endorsed a draft law on prices, drawn up by the Ministry of Finance, which would free retail, wholesale, and producer prices for all but a few agricultural commodities and monopoly controlled products. The authorities introduced trade liberalization to stimulate supply increases and competition, which they hoped would maintain downward pressure on prices. The government also planned gradual elimination of subsidies for money-losing firms in an attempt to stop hyperinflation.

Under the communist system, Albania's government had maintained one of the world's most egalitarian wage structures. The central authorities fixed the number of workers at an enterprise, assigned them to particular jobs, and set the wage fund, which for the nation as a whole translated in 1983 to a monthly pay of about L400 for a worker and about L900 for a manager. By 1988 average worker earnings grew to between L600 and L700 (US$89–US$104); and pay for top officials reached L1,500 (US$223). In the early 1990s, the regime modified the wage system, creating incentives for overfulfillment of plan targets, and allowing for a 10 percent pay cut for management if enterprises failed to attain plan targets.

Economic liberalization spawned a private sector without wage controls. Market-driven price hikes forced the government to raise wages for state workers twice in mid-1991. During the economic chaos, negotiators for Albania's newly independent trade unions demanded that the government automatically increase wages to keep pace with price hikes. At state factories and farms idled by disruptions in deliveries of raw materials, workers' salaries were reduced only 20 percent, a move strongly criticized by the country's main opposition party as inherently inflationary. The opposition called for fixed wages for workers at state enterprises and an absolute limit on subsidies to money-losing enterprises, as two means of slowing the bidding-up of wages and inflation. In the chaos, the average monthly income for Albanian workers plummeted to the equivalent of about US$10.

Enver Hoxha and his followers enforced frugality on Albanians for decades. The regime made few significant attempts to turn the product mix of the country's industrial sector away from heavy industrial goods and toward consumer goods, especially durable consumer goods. Instead of absorbing personal savings by producing and selling more consumer items, the government lowered the incomes of the few highly paid and skilled workers. People who complained often lost their jobs and were sent to state farms. The policy eased inflationary pressures but had dire consequences for worker motivation and willingness to accept responsibility. The Albanian economy's reliance on domestic monopolies made it especially susceptible to shortages. The country's only glass factory, for example, shut down in mid-1990. Lacking hard currency to purchase imported glass, Albanians had to live without bottles and replacement windows. When Italy delivered plate glass as part of relief supplies, it was discovered that the Albanians had no glazing putty.

Domestic consumption at first slowed with the collapse of the Stalinist economic system. In 1991 state shops were practically empty of goods, if they were open at all. Milk, butter, eggs, and medicines were in short supply. People had to squeeze through metal-barred windows at bakeries just to buy loaves of bread. Private stores and black marketeers had a relatively wide variety of goods, including pasta, peeled tomatoes, soap, fruit juices, and toilet paper, but with one kilogram of spaghetti costing a tenth of the average monthly salary, these goods were far beyond the purchasing power of the vast majority of the population. The government introduced general rationing, but by mid-1991 widespread fear that supplies of basic food items would run out caused crowds to begin plundering warehouses and retail outlets. Hopes for increased supplies and broader choices in the marketplace grew with the emergence of the private sector, which almost immediately began bringing in products that previously were unavailable, and often banned.

Domestic Consumption

Even the communist government's sparse official statistics could not hide the fact that the Albanians suffered a low living standard. From the mid-1970s, the economy struggled to produce enough food and consumer goods to supply the quickly growing population. In the early 1990s, serious difficulty in simply feeding the country forced the government to scrap its Stalinist economic policies and to appeal for foreign humanitarian relief to avert widespread hunger. Saving became an impossibility for almost the entire population.

Standard of Living

In the late 1980s, the average pay for an Albanian worker was about US$89 to US$104 monthly at the official exchange rate of

US$1 to L6.75. The government supplemented low incomes by annually allocating about 25 percent of the annual budget, about L4,000 (US$595) for each family, to the population's cultural and social needs, including everything from price subsidies for necessities like children's clothing to library construction. The state provided free education and health care and absorbed 65 percent of tuition for day care and kindergarten and 18 to 35 percent of the cost of meals in workers' cafeterias.

Under the communist regime, the cost of living for the average Albanian was generally low. Food was generally inexpensive but in chronically short supply. The Albanians' staple diet consisted of bread, sugar, pasta, and rice, which were sold at or near cost. Production shortfalls limited supplies of meat, dairy products, and other protein-rich foods. Albanians enjoyed increasing supplies of clothing in the late 1980s, but price, quality, and style left much to be desired. The state subsidized the prices of children's clothing and shoes, but a man's shirt could cost about L200 (US$30), a suit L675 (US$100), and a woman's sweater L150 (US$22). A farmer had to work about two weeks to buy a pair of the most inexpensive shoes. Durable goods carried exorbitant price tags. A bicycle sold for about L900 (US$134); a motorbike, L2,700 (US$402); a radio, L1,000 (US$149); a television, L4,000 (US$595). The ever-vigilant state required that purchasers of televisions and refrigerators obtain permits. Housing rents were low, usually amounting to between 1 percent and 3 percent of an average family's income. In 1980, for example, the monthly rent for an apartment in Lezhë came to L40 (US$7.50). Public transportation also cost little.

Officials estimated that the standard of living for town dwellers with average monthly incomes dropped by about half in 1991. Government statistics showed that a typical family with an average monthly income of L1,300 in December 1990 would need more than L4,500 to keep up with inflation over the same period. In 1991 a kilogram of spinach sold for L60 at Tiranë's produce market; oranges cost L200 per half kilogram; and a bottle of orange drink, L600. Per capita annual meat consumption in cities totaled about 11.7 kilograms in 1990, down from about 14.6 kilograms in 1975; rural meat consumption in 1990 was about 9.0 kilograms per capita, actually an improvement from 7.3 kilograms per capita in 1975. Furniture prices give some indication of how personal incomes failed to maintain pace with prices in 1991. In one Tiranë store, a table cost L60,000; a bed, L130,000; a door, L150,000.

Population and Work Force

Growing at least 2 percent annually during the 1980s, Albania's population reached 3.2 million by 1990. Males accounted for about 51.5 percent of the Albanian populace. About 60 percent of the country's men and 55 percent of its women were of working age. Natural growth added about 45,000 persons to the working-age population annually in the 1980s, about a 3.5 percent average yearly increase. The work force officially numbered about 1 million people in 1980 and about 1.5 million when the economy collapsed in 1990. Albania's principal industries were labor-intensive, but there were ample labor reserves in the agricultural population. Workers officially put in a six-day, forty-eight-hour week with at least two weeks of annual vacation. People who fled Albania during the communist era, however, reported that ten-hour workdays were the minimum at many farms and factories (see Social Structure under Communist Rule; Social Insurance, ch. 2).

The government also assigned almost everyone to special "work actions," which entailed gathering harvests and building irrigation systems and railroad embankments; "volunteer" work details scavenged scrap metal and beautified public parks on "Enver Days" to honor the "father of the nation." Labor productivity declined about 1.7 percent per year from 1980 to 1988, an indication that the economy was failing to create enough jobs to absorb the increasing numbers of working-age people. Apart from diplomatic staff and émigrés, no Albanian nationals were working abroad before the communist system's decline.

Albania's employment profile was clearly that of a developing country. In 1987, Albania's agriculture sector employed 52 percent of the country's workers; industry, 22.9 percent; construction, 7.1 percent; trade, 4.6 percent; education and culture, 4.4 percent; and transportation and communications, 2.9 percent (see table 6, Appendix). The failure of the communist economy, however, rocked the structure of Albania's work force. Except for workers in the government bureaucracy, schools and hospitals, the military and police, basic services, and private firms, the turmoil left only a handful of Albanians with productive jobs. The doors slammed shut, for example, at almost all the enterprises in the mountainous Kukës District, including a profitable chromite mine, a copper-smelting plant that closed for lack of coal, and a textile factory that ran out of wool and thread. Albania's government reported unemployment at about 30 percent, but unofficial 1991 estimates indicated that about 50 percent of the work force was

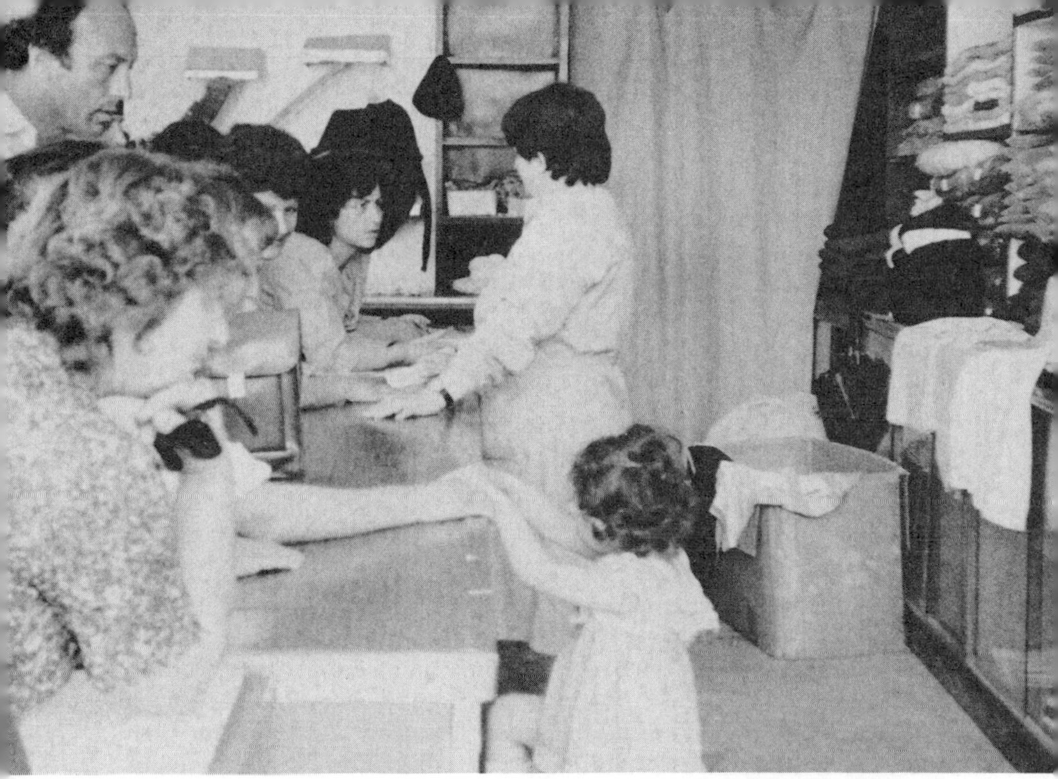

Woman at work in a clothing store in the port city of Durrës
Courtesy Charles Sudetic

Women at a loom in the port city of Durrës
Courtesy Charles Sudetic

jobless. Idled factory workers tilled private plots, sought jobs in new private retail outlets and handicraft workshops, or attempted to leave the country to search for work abroad. Officials appealed to the international community to provide material inputs necessary to jump-start Albanian factories and hoped that a US$10 average monthly wage, one of the world's lowest for a literate labor force, would entice foreign investors.

Women in the Work Force

The female proportion of the country's wage-earning work force increased markedly after World War II, although women continued to bear most of the responsibility for maintaining Albanian's households. Women had played a subservient role in traditional Albanian society and were for hundreds of years considered little more than beasts of burden. During Albania's Cultural and Ideological Revolution, which began in 1966, the regime encouraged women to take jobs outside the home in an effort to overcome their conservatism and compensate for labor shortages. An enormous increase in the number of preschools facilitated the entry of women into paying jobs. By late in the decade, the regime was struggling to overcome male resistance to the appointment of women to government and party posts once held exclusively by men. Women accounted for about 41 percent of the overall rural labor force in 1961 and 51.3 percent in 1983. Despite Albania's high annual birth rate in the late 1980s, women made up about 47 percent of the country's overall work force, including 53 percent of the labor force in agriculture; 43.5 percent in industry; 55 percent in trade; 80 percent in health care; and 54 percent in education and culture. In mountain areas, women made up a significantly higher proportion of farm labor. In 1981 women accounted for 70.7 percent of the collective-farm work force in Pukë District and constituted a similarly disproportionate segment in Kukës, Tropojë, Mat, and Librazhd.

Trade Unions

Albanian workers and enterprise managers had little significant influence until the old order began breaking down in 1990. Workers for decades had no recourse but to rely on government-controlled trade unions to protect their interests, but the ruling party used these unions only as mouthpieces to implore workers to produce more and accept more sacrifices. Independent trade unions arose from the ashes of the official labor organizations in each of the economy's major sectors. In 1991 union representatives pressed government officials for concessions on issues of wages and working conditions, a general labor contract, and wage indexing to mitigate the effects of inflation. They also demanded social security guarantees, reestablishment of electrical service in many towns, and deliveries of raw materials to idle factories. Management often backed the workers' demands to the government. There were strikes as well as mass protests in central Tiranë and elsewhere. In mid-1991, the Council of Ministers drafted a law on labor relations that eliminated the job security Albanian workers had enjoyed under the communist system, allowing firms to dismiss workers who violated disciplinary standards.

Agriculture

The Albanian economy's traditional mainstay, agriculture, generated a third of the country's net material product and employed more than half the work force in 1990. Domestic farm products accounted for 63 percent of household expenditures and 25 percent of exports in that year. While striving for self-sufficiency in the 1970s and 1980s, the Hoxha regime created the world's most strictly controlled and isolated farm sector. But as the government force-fed investment funds to industry at the farm sector's expense, food output fell short of the needs of the rapidly increasing population. The government triggered acute disruptions in food supplies by reducing the size of personal plots, collectivizing livestock, and forbidding peasants to market their produce privately. By the early 1990s, the country's farms were no longer supplying adequate amounts of food to urban areas; they were also failing to meet the needs of Albanian factories for raw materials. The regime responded by stimulating agricultural production through a program of land privatization and free-market measures, cognizant that the success of its broader economic reform program depended heavily on the agricultural sector's ability to feed the population and provide the input-starved production lines with raw materials.

The Land

In 1991 cultivable land in Albania amounted to about 714,000 hectares, about 25 percent of the country's total area. Arable land and permanent croplands totaled about 590,000 hectares and 124,000 hectares, respectively; permanent pasturelands accounted for another 409,528 hectares. More than 100,000 hectares of the cultivable land had a slope greater than 30 percent and was allocated almost entirely to permanent tree crops such as olives. Forests and woodlands covered more than 1 million hectares, or 38 percent of the total land area. The soils of the coastal plain and eastern plateau were fertile, but acidic soils were predominant in the 200,000 hectares of cropland in hilly and mountainous areas.

Irrigation and desalination projects, terracing of highlands, and drainage of marshes, often carried out by forced labor, added considerably to the country's cultivable land after 1945. Large population increases, however, reduced the amount of cultivable land per capita by 35 percent between 1950 and 1987 and by 20 percent between 1980 and 1988. About 423,000 hectares were irrigated in 1991, up from about 39,300 hectares in 1950. The economic disruptions of the early 1990s, however, left only about 40 percent of the country's irrigation system functional and 20 percent in complete disrepair. Albania also invested substantially in imported Dutch greenhouses during its drive for food self-sufficiency.

Land Distribution and Agricultural Organization

Following Enver Hoxha's 1967 proclamation that the regime had collectivized all of Albania's private farmland, the country's only legal forms of agricultural production were state farms, collective farms, and personal plots granted to members of collective farms. The first Albanian state farm grew out of a large experimental farm set up by Italian colonists in the 1930s. After World War II, the government amalgamated small collective farms and transformed them into state farms in each district. The 216 state farms, which still controlled 24 percent of the arable land in 1991, functioned like industrial organizations; thus, state farm workers, like factory workers, toiled for set wages. The state farms received the best land and equipment and a disproportionate amount of investment monies. Collective farms were the result of government campaigns to coerce peasants into signing over their private holdings to cooperatives and working the land in common, according to the instructions of the central government's economic planners. The authorities later took gradual steps to transform collective farms into "higher-type" farms more closely resembling state farms in their organization. Faced with dire food shortages, the regime in 1990 attempted to reform the agricultural system by lifting a 200-square-meter limitation on the size of the personal plots of collective farm-members.

In July 1991, the government enacted a law that nullified old property claims and regulated redistribution of the expropriated farmlands given to collective farms after 1946. The law granted landownership rights to members of the former collective farms and their households without requiring compensation; it also granted land-use rights to up to 0.4 hectares to other qualifying residents of villages attached to collective farms. The law provided for the inheritance of property but banned land sales and leases, thereby blocking voluntary consolidation of tiny landholdings and limiting farmers' access to credit by precluding the use of land as collateral.

The government established the National Land Commission to oversee the land reform. The minister of agriculture chaired the commission and reported on its activities to the Council of Ministers. District and village land commissions demarcated the land, issued ownership titles, and compiled a land registry.

Albania's land redistribution program proceeded rapidly but unevenly. It met especially stiff resistance in the country's mountainous northeastern regions where clans anxious to stake out the boundaries of their traditional family lands tried to stop large numbers of postwar immigrants from gaining title to them. Land disputes threatened to trigger blood feuds. Local officials also impeded the reform process. The central government countered by threatening to prosecute anyone who seized land illegally. Under the land-distribution program, Albania's agricultural sector would gain about 380,000 small family farms averaging about 1.4 hectares in size and often made up of two or three plots. In mountain areas, the parcels were significantly smaller. In Pukë, for example, the average size was just over 0.5 hectares, and in Kukës, almost 0.9 hectares. Western economists estimated that 35 percent of the new farms would not be economically viable and expressed concern that, unless restrictions on land sales were lifted, inheritance would lead to land fragmentation and hamper development. Fearing that smallholdings would not provide sustenance, the government amended the land law to provide for income support of farmers in mountainous areas. As privatization progressed, some families and owners of contiguous fields began to form private cooperatives to take advantage of economies of scale.

Left in limbo by the land reform were the 216 state farms and their 155,000 employees, who accounted for about 20 percent of the agricultural labor force. State farms contributed about 30 percent of the value of the country's agricultural output and supplied city dwellers with most of their dairy products, fruits, and vegetables. The state farms' yields normally outstripped those of the cooperative farms by a third or more because the state farms benefited from richer soils, more mechanization, and easier access to farm services, government finance, and transportation. The breakdown of the communist structure dealt the state farms serious setbacks. By mid-1991 lines of authority had snapped, equipment and buildings had been plundered, and the amount of cultivated land had decreased by half. Although it planned to dissolve sixty money-losing state farms in the mountainous northeast, the government generally spared the state farms from redistribution because their breakup would lead to serious land fragmentation problems and reduce urban food supplies. Pasturelands and forests were also exempted. Western economic analysts concluded that some of the state farms could turn a profit and that foreign companies might follow the lead of one Italian firm that had entered into a joint venture with a state farm.

Structure and Marketing of Agricultural Output

Before the 1990s, Albania's main food crops were wheat, corn, fruits, and vegetables (see table 7, Appendix). However, planners were devoting increasing attention to tobacco, olives, and oranges. Between 1989 and 1991, the country's crop structure underwent a radical transformation. The new private farmers took responsibility for transporting and selling their output and began basing their production and marketing decisions on free-market conditions. Low state procurement prices, a shortage of livestock feed, the breakdown of the transportation system, and a lack of demand from idled processing plants led to steep declines in the hectarage sown with wheat and such industrial crops as tobacco, sugar beets, sunflowers, and cotton. Disputes arising out of the government's land-privatization program, shortages of funds for seeds and agricultural machinery, and the hasty privatization of the enterprises that provided farmers with machinery and fertilizers also had an effect. In the first third of 1991, milk production was down 50 percent compared to the corresponding period in 1990; bread-grain production was down 67 percent; and areas sown with cotton and tobacco had decreased by 80 percent and 50 percent, respectively.

The farmers' choice of which crops to plant was motivated primarily by the need to feed their families and only secondarily by the cash market. In mid-1991, 10 to 15 percent of Albania's cultivable land lay fallow mainly because the state enterprises were not giving small farmers seed, fertilizers, and other necessary inputs. Transportation breakdowns and other problems continued to force farmers away from crops requiring processing, leaving wheat, sugar, and vegetable oils in short supply. Production on newly privatized plots grew, however, despite input shortages. Corn production increased, and meat, egg, and vegetable output seemed to be on the rise. Western economists expected agricultural production to begin recovering in 1992 as the private sector began solving transportation problems and reorganizing production in response to demand. Despite these grounds for optimism, domestic production in 1992 was projected to meet only about 88 percent

Tractor plowing a field just outside Tiranë
Courtesy Charles Sudetic

of the country's need for meat, 48 percent for wheat, 30 percent for sugar, and 5 percent for vegetable oils. The production shortfalls would force donor countries to commit additional food aid to avert serious hunger.

Livestock and Pasturelands

A botched campaign to collectivize livestock in the late 1970s and early 1980s led to a wholesale slaughter and chronic production shortfalls. When meat and dairy product shortages in the larger towns grew critical, Albania's communists retraced their steps. The regime gave animal husbandry a high priority in the Eighth Five-Year Plan (1986-90). In July 1990, the government decided to allow collective-farm members to raise cattle on their private plots and instructed the administrators of collective farms to transfer a portion of their stock animals to members. The government also recommended that collective farms in mountainous areas grant members 0.2 hectares of land each, in addition to their private plots, in order to increase livestock production. In mid-1991, shortages of feed severely hampered livestock production and forced farmers to allocate much of their land to cultivation of forage and feed corn. The animals raised on this diet were deficient in protein and generally of poor quality. Despite the ban on food exports, herdsmen were reportedly smuggling about 1,000 head of calves, cows, sheep, and other livestock across the Greek and Yugoslav borders each day because they lacked fodder and sought to take advantage of high prices on foreign markets. An additional challenge to Albanian stockmen was a serious shortage of artificial-insemination and other veterinary services.

Albania's 409,528 hectares of pastureland remained state-owned despite the land reform, and in the chaos of 1991 the government set to work on a new law to reassert state control of pasturelands and give managers new guidelines. The Ministry of Agriculture's eighteen pasture enterprises managed grazing lands at the district level and charged customers, including private herdsmen and farmers, a seasonal fee. Price liberalization did not boost grazing fees even though the enterprises were operating at a loss in 1991. Ministry officials estimated that grazing fees could have to increase fourfold before the pasture enterprises could break even. Western economists projected that pressure on Albania's pasturelands would increase as livestock herds grew and as expanding communities sought land for residential and recreational purposes.

Mechanization

Faithful to Stalin's teachings on agricultural organization, Albania's communist regime allowed state farms to possess tractors but gave collective farms access to machinery only through machine tractor stations (see Glossary). These stations remained a cornerstone of Albania's collective agricultural sector for decades. In 1991 the thirty-three machine tractor stations controlled about 63 percent of Albania's 10,630 tractors and 25 percent of its 1,433 combine harvesters; state farms controlled the rest. Official inventories also listed 1,857 threshers. As the old order collapsed, the tractor stations metamorphosed into state-owned "agricultural machinery enterprises" that offered their services to peasant customers on a contractual basis. These enterprises often ignored state limitations on service charges, demanding exorbitant fees as well as compensation for fuel at prices higher than those charged at the pump. Some tractor drivers bought older Chinese tractors and offered their services at prices up to 40 percent more than those charged by the state enterprises. More than 75 percent of Albania's tractors were over fifteen years old in 1991; most tractors were in disrepair because plant closures had cut off supplies of spare parts.

Fertilizers, Pesticides, and Seeds

During peak years, Albania had used fertilizers less than almost any other nation in Eastern Europe. Nevertheless, in the early 1990s the agricultural sector experienced a fertilizer shortage; supplies of pesticides and hybrid seed also ran low. In 1989 Albanian farmers had applied about 158 kilograms of active ingredients per hectare, but the country's economic breakdown pushed the total down to 135 kilograms in 1990 and 38 kilograms in 1991. A lack of hard currency caused fertilizer supplies to drop 80 percent and pesticide reserves to fall 63 percent. Ironically, intensive application of lindane and other pesticides as well as disinfectants for treating soil at seeding time, in combination with monocropping of wheat and corn, had destroyed many pests' natural enemies and increased dependency on pesticides. Although Albania's agricultural research institutes produced sufficient foundation seed, obsolete sorting and cleaning equipment lowered seed quality. Varietal improvement was dependent on the crossing of local strains. The breakup of collective farms, which produced most of the wheat and corn seed, forced farmers to seek new seed suppliers.

Forests

Albania has soils and a climate favorable to an extensive lumber industry. Although the postwar government invested heavily in afforestation, it developed an inefficient wood products industry. In the early 1990s, the thickest woodlands were in the central and northern mountain ranges. The country's southern half was mostly deforested, a consequence of the clear-cutting of oak trees to build the merchant ships of old Venice and Dubrovnik, the destruction of woodlands to create pastures, the burning of wood for fuel, and the expansion of villages onto hillsides. Albania's nine state forestry industry complexes produced an estimated 2.3 million cubic meters of roundwood annually between 1976 and 1988; its twenty-eight sawmills cut about 200,000 cubic meters of wood annually between 1977 and 1988. Outdated sawmills, however, wasted raw materials and were situated too far from sources of raw materials. The pulp, paper, and fiberboard industries enjoyed little competitive advantage and did considerable environmental damage. The country's high dependency on wood for heating—amounting to 100 percent of household energy needs in mountainous areas and over 90 percent in the cities in 1991—contributed to the overexploitation of forests. Unchecked cutting by people so desperate for fuel that they hacked tree stumps to below ground level caused serious damage to woodlands.

Fisheries

Albania's fishing industry, which was underdeveloped and poorly managed, consisted of four state-owned fishing enterprises, sixteen aquaculture enterprises, and two shellfish enterprises. The government foresaw little trouble in privatizing all of the country's fishing vessels but anticipated difficulty in selling off the three fish canneries and the only shipyard servicing the fishing and coastal transportation fleet. World Bank and European Community economists reported that Albania's fishing industry had good potential to generate export earnings because prices in the nearby Greek and Italian markets were many times higher than those in the Albanian market. Albania's coastal waters were overfished, and foreign economists advised the Albanian government to protect its piscine resources from illegal exploitation by vessels from other European countries.

Industry

Albania's rigid Stalinists considered heavy industry the force driving all developed economies. For years, the government fed the lion's share of investment money and technology imports to industrial behemoths, which had domestic monopolies and too often lacked distinct objectives. Especially from the 1960s onward, the government spent most investment funds on the production of minerals for export and the manufacture of import-substitution products. The effort succeeded in expanding and diversifying Albania's industrial sector, but without the discipline imposed by a free market; the resulting creation was inefficient and structurally distorted (see table 8; table 9, Appendix). In the early 1990s, industry accounted for about 40 percent of Albania's GDP and employed about 25 percent of the nation's work force. The industrial sector's most important branches were food products, energy and petroleum production, mining, light industry, and engineering. All of Albania's industrial branches suffered from obsolete equipment, inadequate infrastructure, and low levels of worker skill and motivation. Shortages of energy, spare parts, and raw materials stopped industrial production almost entirely in the early 1990s.

Energy and Natural Resources

Since classical times, people have exploited the fossil-fuel and mineral deposits present in the lands that now constitute Albania. Petroleum, natural gas, coal, and asphalt lie in the sedimentary rock formations of the country's southwestern regions. The predominantly igneous formations of the northern mountains yield chromite, ferronickel, copper, and cobalt. Albania also has deposits of phosphorite, bauxite, gold, silver, kaolin, clay, asbestos, magnesite, dolomite, and gypsum. Salt is abundant. About 70 percent of Albania's territory is about 300 meters above sea level, twice

A power plant for a textile mill complex on the outskirts of Tiranë
Courtesy Charles Sudetic
Elbasan Steel Combine
Courtesy Fred Conrad

the average elevation of Europe. Jagged limestone peaks rise to over 2,700 meters. These great heights, combined with normally abundant highland rainfall, facilitate the production of hydroelectric power along rivers.

With its significant petroleum and natural-gas reserves, coal deposits, and hydroelectric-power capacity, Albania has the potential to produce enough energy for domestic consumption and export fuels and electric power. Mismanagement led to production shortfalls in the early 1990s, however, and forced the government to import both petroleum and electric power. For years after production dropped in the late 1970s, Albania's government considered statistics on the performance of its petroleum industry a state secret; as a consequence, data on the oil industry vary radically (see table 10). Known petroleum reserves at existing Albanian drill sites totaled about 200 million tons, but in 1991 recoverable stocks amounted to only 25 million tons. Albania's petroleum reserves generally were located in the tertiary layers in southwestern Albania, mainly in the triangle-shaped region delimited by Vlorë, Berat, and Durrës. The principal petroleum reserves were in the valley of the lower Devoll; in the valley of the Gjanicë near Patos in the southwest, where they lay in sandy Middle or Upper Miocene layers; and in Marinëz, between Kuçovë and Fier. Petroleum was refined in Ballsh, near Berat; Cërrik near Elbasan; and Kuçovë.

In the 1980s, the petroleum and bitumen enterprises employed 10 percent of Albania's industrial work force, controlled 25 percent of the country's industrial capital, and received almost 33 percent of its industrial investment funds. Nevertheless, the industry's share of the country's gross industrial production fell from 8.1 percent in 1980 to 6.6 percent in 1982 and perhaps as little as 5 percent in 1985. Albania produced only between 1.5 million tons and 2.1 million tons of petroleum annually in the 1970s, according to reliable estimates. Output sagged further during the 1980s when extraction became increasingly difficult. Albania's wells pumped only 1.2 million tons of petroleum in 1990. At some sites, obsolete drilling equipment was extracting only 12 percent of the available petroleum in situations where modern drilling and pumping equipment would permit the extraction of as much as 40 percent.

Petroleum was the first industry to attract direct foreign investment after the communist economic system broke down. In 1990 and 1991, the Albanian Petroleum and Gas Directorate entered into negotiations with foreign drilling and exploration firms for onshore and offshore prospecting. In March 1991, the Albanian government and a German company, Denimex, signed a US$500 million contract for seismological studies, well drilling, and production preparation. Albania also negotiated exploration contracts with Agip of Italy and Occidental Petroleum, Chevron, and Hamilton Oil of the United States.

Albania's known natural-gas reserves have been estimated at 22,400 million cubic meters and lie mainly in the Kuçovë and Patos areas. The country's wells pumped about 600,000 cubic meters of natural gas annually during the late 1980s. Fertilizer plants consumed about 40 percent of Albania's annual natural-gas production; power stations consumed about another 15 percent. Planners projected an increase in natural-gas production to about 1.1 million cubic meters per year by 1995, but output tumbled during the first quarter of 1991.

Albania's unprofitable coal mines produced about 2.1 million tons in 1987. The coal, mainly lignite with a low calorific value, was being mined mainly in central Albania near Valias, Manëz, and Krrabë; near Korçë at Mborje and Drenovë; in northern Tepelenë at Memaliaj; and in Alarup to the south of Lake Ohrid. Coal washeries were located at Valias and Memaliaj. Albania imported about 200,000 tons of coke per year from Poland for its metalworks. Conditions inside Albania's coal mines were deplorable, with much of the work done by manual labor. Albania used most of its coal to generate electric power.

About 80 percent of Albania's electric power came from a system of hydroelectric dams built after 1947 and driven by several rivers that normally carried abundant rainfall. Electric power output was estimated by Albanian officials at 3,984,000 megawatt hours in 1988. Outfitted with French-built turbines, Albania's largest power station, the Koman hydroelectric plant on the Drin River, had a capacity of about 600 megawatts. The hydroelectric stations at Fierzë and Dejas, also on the Drin River, had capacities of 500 megawatts and 250 megawatts, respectively, and used Chinese-built turbines. Albania had no capacity to generate nuclear power, but in the early 1990s a research nuclear reactor was reportedly under construction with United Nations funds. In 1972 high-tension transmission lines linked Albania's power grid with Yugoslavia's distribution system. Albania's first 400-kilovolt high-tension line carried power from Elbasan over the mountains to Korçë, where a 220-kilovolt line carried it to Greece.

Droughts in the late 1980s and in 1990 brought an energy crisis and a sharp drop in earnings from electric-power exports. In 1991 heavy rainfall allowed Albania to resume electric-power exports to Yugoslavia and Greece. In the early 1990s, labor strikes and transformer burnouts—caused by the overloading of circuits when many Albanians turned to electricity to heat apartments after other fuel supplies ran out—regularly resulted in blackouts in towns across the country, and even sections of Tiranë, producing disruption for months at a time. Although the electrical grid reached rural areas by 1970, the amount of power per household in farm areas was limited to 200 watts, only enough to power light bulbs. The chaos caused by economic collapse led to the destruction of about 25 percent of Albania's 30,000 kilometer power-distribution network.

Albania's mineral resources are located primarily in the mountainous northern half of the country. Albanian miners extract mainly chromium ore, ferronickel, copper, bitumen, and salt. Obsolete equipment and mining techniques have hampered Albania's attempts to capitalize on its mineral wealth. High extraction and smelting costs, as well as Albania's overall economic collapse, have forced mine and plant closures. The government repeatedly has promised to take steps to reopen mines.

Some production estimates placed Albania just behind South Africa and the former Soviet Union in the output of chromite, or chromium ore, which is vital to the production of stainless steel. Foreign studies estimated that Albania had more than 20 million tons of chromite reserves, located mainly near the towns of Korçë, Mat, Elbasan, and Kukës. Export of chrome and chromium products provided one of Albania's most important sources of hard-currency income. Albania's chromite industry, however, consistently failed to meet plan targets and came under severe criticism in the waning years of the communist regime. Estimates for chromite output during 1989 ranged from 500,000 to 900,000 tons. The drought-related power cuts in 1990 and economic chaos in 1991 forced the closing of ferrochrome enterprises at Burrel and Elbasan, and the government desperately sought sources of foreign capital to invest in technological improvements.

Albania's high-grade chromite reserves had been largely exhausted by 1990. The poor quality of the remaining ore accounted for the country's worsening position in world markets. Impurities present in Albania's highest-grade chrome were largely the byproduct of poor mining and smelting techniques and the use of antiquated Chinese equipment. The country's chromium industry also suffered because of inadequate transportation facilities. In the late 1980s, construction was under way on a rail link connecting the main chromium-ore production center at Bulqizë, in central Albania with the port of Durrës and the main line to Yugoslavia. In the late 1980s, Albania exported its chrome products mainly to Sweden, the United States, the Federal Republic of Germany (West Germany), Yugoslavia, and other East European countries.

A dilapidated industrial plant on the main road between the Yugoslav border and Tiranë
Courtesy Charles Sudetic

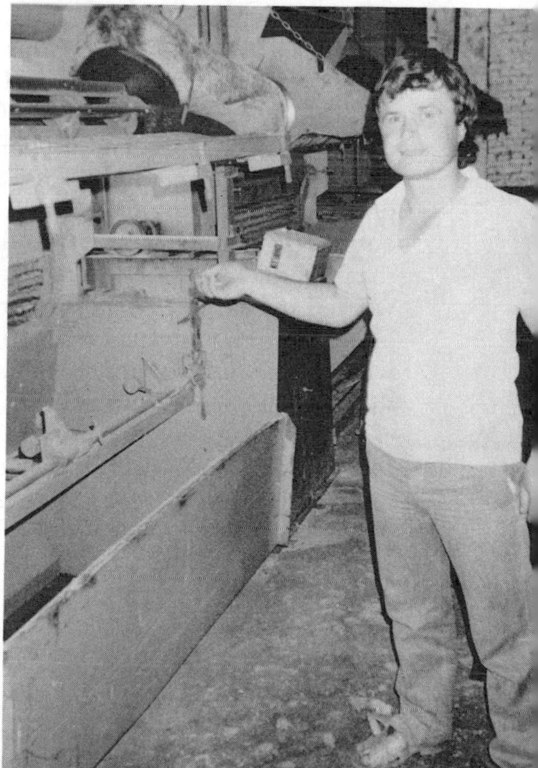

Repairman in front of the cotton gin at a textile plant in the central coastal region
Courtesy Charles Sudetic

In 1980 Albanian chrome sales to the United States accounted for about 75 percent of the approximately US$20 million in trade between the two countries. Despite its reported profitability, the chromium industry suffered from a lack of worker incentive because miners frequently went unpaid. In 1991 one of Albania's top economists revealed that the country had never earned more than US$60 million a year from chrome exports.

Albania also produced copper, iron, and nickel. The main copper deposits, estimated at about 5 million tons, were located near the northern towns of Pukë, Kukës, and Shkodër. During the 1980s, although the quality of copper ores was generally low, copper was the most successful industry in Albania's mineral-extraction sector. Copper production rose from about 11,500 tons in 1980 to 17,000 tons in 1988. The government aimed to export copper in a processed form and built smelters at Rubik, Kukës, and Laç. The industry's product mix included blister copper, copper wire, copper sulfate, and alloys. Albania's principal iron ore deposits, estimated at 20 million tons in the 1930s, were located near Pogradec, Kukës, Shkodër, and Peshkopi. The Elbasan Steel Combine was Albania's largest industrial complex. In operation since 1966, the steelworks had obsolete Chinese equipment. Annual nickel output ranged from 7,200 to 9,000 tons in the 1980s.

Albanian bitumen and asphalt deposits were located near the town of Selenicë and in the Vjosë River valley. Bitumen and asphalt production rose significantly after World War II, and most of the output was used for paving and waterproofing materials and in the manufacturing of insulators and roofing shingles. Miners had worked the Selenicë deposits continuously for centuries before a lack of soap, boots, and basic equipment forced operations to cease when the centrally planned economy stalled. Geologists estimated that the Selenicë deposits would not be exhausted until several decades into the twenty-first century at normal production rates. Albania also possessed abundant deposits of salt, found near Kavajë and Vlorë. Limestone, a principal raw material for Albania's construction industry, was quarried throughout the country.

Manufacturing

Chemicals

Albania's chemical industry was geared mainly toward producing agrochemicals and chemicals for minerals processing. During the effort to achieve economic self-reliance in the 1970s and 1980s, Albania's government frantically tried to increase fertilizer output at plants in Krujë and Fier, which produced nitrogen and phosphate from imported rock phosphate. Nitrogen and phosphate fertilizer production totaled about 350 billion tons between 1985 and 1990. A lack of spare parts and raw materials, especially natural gas, halted production in mid-1991. Western economists estimated that the US$3 million needed for the main phosphate plants' rehabilitation might be too high a price to pay because domestic deposits of key raw materials were projected to last only three to five years at normal production rates. One of Albania's two ammonia-urea plants planned to restart operations in 1992, but it desperately needed spare parts and environmental protection equipment. The country's lone pesticide plant, which did not stop producing DDT until 1982, made lindane as well as products based on sulfur, zinc, copper, and mercury. In 1991 the facility was working at less than 10 percent of capacity, and production was not likely to be stepped up because the plant was in poor condition and environmentally unsafe. Other chemical enterprises included a plastics-fabrication facility at Lushnjë, a rubber and plastics works at Durrës, and a paint and pigment factory in Tiranë.

Engineering

During Albania's long effort to achieve autarky, economic planners focused the country's engineering industry on producing tools, equipment, and spare parts for machinery that would substitute for imports. However, product standards suffered because of the poor quality of domestically produced materials, especially steel, and because of Albania's complete isolation from world technological advances. The continuing operation of machinery long obsolete in the outside world, including a textile mill in Tiranë reminiscent of sweatshops in the turn-of-the-century United States, was a testament to the ingenuity of the workers in the engineering branch who fabricated spare parts. In addition to spare parts, several plants produced finished products, including the Enver Hoxha Auto and Tractor Plant in Tiranë, which produced 75-horsepower tractors, refrigerator compressors, and other products; the Drini Engineering Works in Shkodër, which turned out heavy machinery; the Durrës shipyards and agricultural machinery works; a precision-tool factory in Korçë; and a textile equipment works in Tiranë.

Light Industry

Statistics released in 1989 showed that the light industry sector met about 85 percent of domestic demand for consumer goods and provided about 22 percent of the state's revenue. The sector's output increased markedly from 1960 to 1990. Albanian light industry included textile plants, shoe factories, bicycle assembly plants, and a host of other factories. The communist government scattered textile plants throughout the country. The largest textile factory, the Tiranë Textile Combine—formerly called the Stalin Textile Combine because it was built with Soviet aid—was shut down frequently by workers striking for higher wages, better local transportation, and a regular supply of steam to run their antiquated equipment. In the early 1990s, Greek businessmen began setting up clothing and yarn factories in Gjirokastër and Sarandë. Also, many Albanian businessmen established workshops producing handicrafts, carpets, weavings, and souvenirs for tourist shops and export. Albania's light industry branch also included nineteen furniture factories, whose production was slashed to 15 percent of capacity or less in 1991 because of a lack of material inputs.

Food Processing

In the early 1990s, Albania's food-processing industry had at least one processing facility for the cereal, meat, and dairy branches in each of the country's twenty-six administrative districts without regard to efficiency or economies of scale. These facilities, which employed about 25,000 people, relied on the Ministry of Light Industry to allocate raw materials, arrange transportation, and market products. Years of depreciation and inadequate investment had left the 200 largest food-processing enterprises and about 750 smaller plants with obsolete, broken-down equipment. As a result, managers had little experience in obtaining materials or marketing, and the plants functioned inefficiently and produced low-quality goods. Minimal hygiene and sanitation standards went unmet. Shortages of raw materials and spare parts, along with transportation problems, forced many food-processing enterprises to curtail operations; in 1991 alone, output fell 35 percent from the previous year. When the government loosened controls on food and vegetable prices in 1991, the official marketing network collapsed, cutting off the supply of raw materials to the country's thirty-one canneries. As unofficial prices rose, supply flows to the twenty-seven state-owned slaughterhouses dried up. The thirty-two district-level and 550 village dairies survived only by paying unofficial prices for milk and cooperating with private traders.

In the early 1990s, Albania's thirty-eight flour mills normally employed between thirteen and 257 people and could grind between eight tons and 160 tons of flour per day. The seventy state-owned bakeries in urban areas produced about 370,000 tons of bread annually. The government privatized many of the country's village bakeries, which had a 200,000-ton total annual production capacity. Albania's lone modern yeast factory could produce about

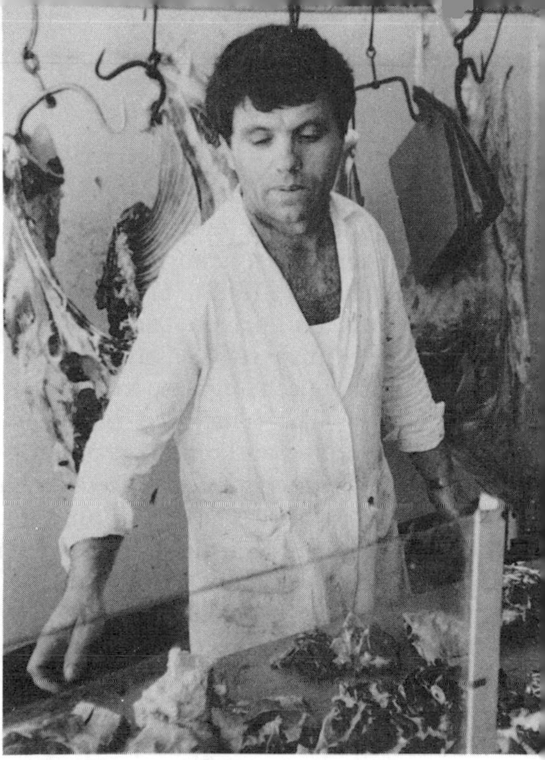

Butcher at work in a private shop in central Tiranë, 1991
Courtesy Charles Sudetic

600 tons annually, which was inadequate to meet the country's needs. Albania had ten pasta factories and two starch factories. Free-market prices four times higher than official levels left state-owned mills and bakeries unable to compete with private millers and bakers for available grain supplies.

State-farm managers and private farmers radically reduced the amount of hectarage producing oilseed, cotton, and tobacco because state prices were low and there were no private markets offering higher prices. Tobacco and sugar-beet production decreased less drastically because state enterprises, including the Durrës tobacco factory and the country's only sugar-beet refinery, offered farmers advance purchase contracts at relatively attractive prices. Albania's vegetable-oil industry consisted of twenty-seven olive-oil plants capable of pressing 755 tons of olives daily; eleven sunflower-oil plants with a daily capacity of 262 tons of seeds; seventeen oil-extraction plants with a daily capacity of 270 tons of olive, cotton-seed, corn, and sunflower pulp; and ten obsolete oil-refinery units with a daily capacity of 110 tons of sunflower oil and soya oil. Town and district plants bottled edible oils. The country also had four soap factories and one margarine plant.

Construction

In the late 1980s, Albania's construction enterprises, which concentrated mostly on adding to the country's housing stock and industrial capacity, built about 14,000 dwellings annually. Uncertainties about landownership and problems with supplies of building materials, financing, and wages halted the construction industry in the early 1990s. The government legalized private construction firms, and private companies and individuals began applying to the Ministry of Construction for building permits soon after questions concerning property ownership were resolved. Reports in the national press included complaints that many people were constructing homes and buildings on property they did not own or on land better suited to mechanized agriculture. The government proposed a draft law to govern zoning and construction standards.

Cement factories were located in Elbasan and Vlorë, and there was a production facility for prefabricated concrete structures in Tiranë. Brick kilns were located in Tiranë, Elbasan, Korçë, Lushnjë, Dibrë, and Fier.

Environmental Problems

The communist regime's policy of developing heavy industry at all costs caused significant environmental problems. Air and water pollution went unchecked. Despite the scarcity of traffic, a pall of diesel fumes lingered over the country's main roads, a by-product of the poorly refined fuel that powered Albania's trucks and buses. The Elbasan Steel Combine, Albania's largest industrial complex, represented a typical industrial polluter. Proclaimed a symbol of Albania's "second liberation" when it became operational in 1966, the steelworks was equipped with 1950s-vintage Chinese furnaces that filled the Shkumbin River valley with smoke, poisonous gases, and orange-colored particulate. The cyanic acid, ammonia, phenol, and other pollutants that the mill dumped into the river itself rendered it practically lifeless. A United Nations team recommended closing the facility because of the pollution problem.

Transportation and Communications

In the early 1990s, the rock-strewn roadways, unstable rail lines, and obsolete telephone network crisscrossing Albania represented the remnants of the marked improvements that were made after World War II. Enver Hoxha's xenophobia and lust for control had kept Albania isolated, however, as the communications revolution transformed the wider world into a global village. Even internal travel amounted to something of a luxury for many Albanians during communism's ascendancy. For years, peasants needed special passes to visit nearby districts, and until 1990 the government banned private ownership of automobiles. Urban mass transit consisted primarily of bus lines for ferrying workers between home and work. Breakdowns in Tiranë's bus lines sometimes forced employees to walk to work or pay for rides in the beds of passing trucks. The communications system sustained severe damage in the chaos of the economic collapse as people ripped down telephone lines to use as fencing. Despite generally deteriorating conditions, the importation of fleets of used cars and buses and popular hunger for contact with the outside world raised hopes that matters would improve.

Road Transportation

In 1987 Albania had about 6,700 kilometers of paved roads and between 9,000 and about 15,000 kilometers of other roads suitable for motor vehicles (see fig. 7). The total length of Albania's roads had more than doubled in about three decades, and by the 1980s almost all of the country's remote mountain areas were connected, at least by dirt roads, with the capital city and ports. The country's roads, however, were generally narrow, poorly marked, pocked with holes, and in the early 1990s often crowded with pedestrians and people riding mules, bicycles, and horse-drawn carts. Even in tiny villages, hundreds of people of all ages gathered daily along main roads waving their arms seeking rides, and gangs of children often blocked rural highways hoping to coax foreign travelers into tossing them candy. Heavy snowfalls cut off some mountain areas for weeks at a time. Central government funding of local road maintenance effectively ended in 1991, and the breakdown of repair vehicles because of a lack of spare parts threatened to close access to some remote areas. A group of Greek construction companies signed a protocol with the Albanian government in July 1990 to build a 200-kilometer road across the southern part of the country, extending from the Albanian-Greek border to Durrës. The project was scheduled to last four years and cost US$500 million.

Despite the appalling quality of Albania's roads, most of the country's freight was conveyed over them in a fleet of about 15,000 smoke-belching trucks. According to official figures, in 1987 Albania's roadways carried about 66 percent of the country's total freight tonnage. In 1991 the Albanian government lifted the decades-old ban on private-vehicle ownership. The country's roads, once almost devoid of motor traffic, began filling up with recklessly driven cars that had been snapped up in used-car lots across Europe. Car imports numbered about 1,500 per month, and a black-market car lot began operating just off Tiranë's main square. Traffic in the capital remained light, but traffic lights and other control devices were urgently needed to deal with the multiplying number of privately owned cars. Albanian entrepreneurs also imported used Greek buses and started carrying passengers on intercity routes that did not exist or had been poorly serviced during the communist era. Gangs of hijackers and thieves, who preyed on truck and automobile traffic, made road travel hazardous in some regions.

Railroads

In 1991 Albania's 509 kilometers of standard-gauge rail lines linked Shkodër with Durrës, Tiranë, Elbasan, Pogradec, Ballsh, and Vlorë. The country's only international rail link, opened in 1986, connected Shkodër with Yugoslavia's rail system. Albania's communist government focused on developing new rail lines to serve mining regions and the coastal plain. According to official figures, in 1987 and 1988 Albania's railroad carried about 33 percent of the country's total freight tonnage for that period. The opening of the rail link with Yugoslavia facilitated the movement of goods to Europe, and Yugoslav railroads reportedly shipped 174,300 tons of Albanian goods in the first half of 1990, a 19.4 percent increase over the first half of 1989. None of Albania's railroads was electrified. In 1991 vandals and thieves caused so much damage to the tracks and rolling stock that the rail system's transport capacity was cut in half; operations later ceased altogether.

Air Transportation

In 1977 Albania's government signed an agreement with Greece, opening the country's first air links with noncommunist Europe. By 1991 Tiranë had air links with many major European cities, including Paris, Rome, Zurich, Vienna, and Budapest. Tiranë was served by a small airport located twenty-eight kilometers from the capital at the village of Rinas. Albania had no regular domestic air service. A Franco-Albanian joint venture launched Albania's first private airline, Ada Air, in 1991. The company offered flights in a thirty-six-passenger airplane four days each week between Tiranë and Bari, Italy, and a charter service for domestic and international destinations.

Water Transportation

Albania's main seaports are Durrës, Vlorë, Sarandë, and Shëngjin. By 1983 there was regular ferry, freight, and passenger service from Durrës to Trieste, Italy. In 1988 ferry service was established between Sarandë and the Greek island of Corfu. A regular lake ferry linked the Macedonian town of Ohrid with Pogradec. The estimated total displacement of Albania's merchant fleet was 56,000 tons in 1986. The limited capacity of the wharves at Durrës

caused severe bottlenecks in the distribution of foreign food aid in 1991.

Telecommunications

Until 1990 Albania was one of the world's most isolated and controlled countries, and installation and maintenance of a modern system of international and domestic telecommunications was precluded. Callers previously needed operator assistance even to make domestic long-distance calls. Albania's telephone density was the lowest in Europe, at 1.4 units for every 100 inhabitants. Tiranë accounted for about 13,000 of the country's 42,000 direct lines; Durrës, the main port city, ranked second with 2,000 lines; the rest were concentrated in Shkodër, Elbasan, Vlorë, Gjirokastër, and other towns. At one time, each village had a telephone but during the land redistribution of the early 1990s peasants knocked out service to about 1,000 villages by removing telephone wire for fencing. Most of Albania's telephones were obsolete, low-quality East European models, some dating from the 1940s; workers at a Tiranë factory assembled a small number of telephones from Italian parts. In the early 1990s, Albania had only 240 microwave circuits to Italy and 180 to Greece carrying international calls. The Albanian telephone company had also installed two U–20 Italtel digital exchanges. The exchange in Tiranë handled international, national, and local calls; the Durrës exchange handled only local calls. Two United States firms handled direct-dial calls from the United States to Tiranë.

The communist regime used radio and television for propaganda purposes. In 1992 the Albanian government owned and operated seventeen AM radio stations and one FM station that broadcast two national programs and various regional and local programs. An estimated 514,000 Albanians had radio receivers in 1987, according to the United States government. Nine television stations, also controlled by the communist regime, broadcast to the approximately 255,000 television sets owned by Albanians in 1987. Although the regime gave minimal support to domestic communications, it provided for an extensive external shortwave and medium-wave system. Programs were broadcast in eight foreign languages, in addition to Albanian, and reached Africa, the Middle East, North America, South America, and Europe. Albania's external broadcast service was one of the largest such services in the world. The programming was heavily propagandist, according to Western observers.

Retail Trade, Services, and Tourism

Retail shops and service businesses opened all over Albania after the communists surrendered control of domestic trade and released their stranglehold on private economic initiative. Thousands of fruit and vegetable mongers converged on the streets of towns and cities. Private entrepreneurs bought out formerly state-run stores and restaurants and threw open the doors to new shops and workrooms. Import restrictions and price controls on food stimulated a lively black market. The Albanian Stalinists' aversion to the outside world had stunted the development of a tourism industry. From 1991, however, the government worked desperately to attract foreign visitors to replenish its hard-currency coffers.

Retail Trade and Services

Albania's militaristic supply distribution system had little in common with the retail trade sector in the capitalist world before 1990. The state fixed prices, determined which goods would appear on store shelves, and paid shop managers and clerks set salaries. The distribution system grew considerably after World War II, with the ratio of shops to inhabitants increasing from 1:896 in 1950 to 1:278 in 1988. There were two supply networks: one operated directly by the state, the other administered by local collectives under state supervision. The state-run supply network carried a narrow range of consumer goods that were, except in rare cases, domestically produced. The Ministry of Domestic Trade controlled about 85 percent of the state network. The balance fell under the jurisdiction of the Ministry of the Communal Economy, which managed repair and other workshops; the Ministry of Health, which operated pharmacies; and the Ministry of Education, which ran bookshops and art and handicraft stores. The collective-run shops dealt mostly in farm-related products but greatly improved the supply of consumer goods in rural areas.

The limited assortment and supply of consumer products available through retail outlets forced Albanians to become expert at improvising and dealing with shortages. The government imposed a rationing system on all consumer items in September 1946 and did not lift restrictions on nonfood items until 1956 and on food items until 1957. Cutoffs of Soviet and Chinese aid and failures in the agricultural sector led to severe food shortages in the early 1960s and again in the early 1980s, when the authorities reimposed meat rationing. The rural population clearly depended to a large extent on the personal plots of collective-farm members for basic

Typical city bus waiting at a turnaround near the port city of Durrës
Courtesy Charles Sudetic

Old Albanian man riding a donkey
Courtesy Charles Sudetic

food items for extended periods. The state distribution system failed to compensate for the loss from urban markets of produce grown on personal plots after the government restricted plot sizes in the 1980s. Sales of food products made up about 61.5 percent of the retail trade at about 10,600 shops in 1983. The total did not take into account the commerce in goods within agricultural cooperatives. Albania's economic planners neglected the country's service sector to an extent unknown even in other centrally planned economies.

The economic reforms of the early 1990s broke down the barriers that for decades had kept would-be private entrepreneurs from the retail marketplace. At first, peasants began setting up roadside fruit and vegetables stands or carrying their produce to markets in the towns and cities. Later, small shops, restaurants, and workrooms opened their doors and began hiring workers. Soon after the communist economic system broke down, the government privatized about 25,000 retail stores and service enterprises—about half of the small state enterprises in the retail and service sectors—mostly through direct sales to workers. One businessman, using French capital, opened up import shops and duty-free stores in the country's largest hotels. But supply problems hampered retail operations. The new entrepreneurs also encountered problems with local officials who arbitrarily imposed fees and license requirements based on obsolete communist-era laws or on no laws at all. The owner of Tiranë's first private restaurant, for example, complained that officials demanded an annual license fee equivalent to about US$10,000. In 1991 government officials were at work on a commercial code.

Black Market

The food shortage, price controls on staple items, and the ease with which foreign food aid could be diverted from normal distribution channels produced ideal conditions for a brisk black market. Basic food items, which officially still had government-fixed prices, became difficult, and often impossible, to purchase at stores but appeared at significantly higher prices on the black market alongside items pilfered from aid consignments. Nonfood items looted from warehouses were available from black-market dealers at many times normal prices. Fines for trafficking in smuggled and stolen goods were trivial compared to the potential profits.

Tourism

No serious consideration was given to developing a tourism industry until several years after Enver Hoxha's death. After 1989 the government viewed tourism as offering one of the country's best chances to earn hard currency relatively quickly. In 1989 and 1990, record numbers of tourists visited Albania, although the totals themselves were unimpressive. About 14,400 foreigners were permitted to enter the country in 1989 and about 30,000 in 1990. Most of these tourists, however, were single-day visitors on excursions from the Greek island of Corfu. Albanian officials expected the country's seacoast and mountains to draw significantly greater numbers of visitors. But potential tourist areas, with the possible exception of Tiranë, lacked even the most basic amenities. Tiranë itself lacked hotel capacity, and there were few foreign investors willing to risk funds on an Albanian venture. Furthermore, the country's seacoast and mountains were not sufficiently pristine to support predictions of a coming boom in tourism.

Foreign Economic Relations

Enver Hoxha's regime had maintained a legal stranglehold on the country's foreign commerce since World War II through state-run trading enterprises. For decades Albania had maintained no representative commercial offices in Western countries, and so deep was the Albanian dictator's animus toward the Soviet Union that the two countries carried on no trade at all for decades after their split in the early 1960s. Hoxha and his protégés created a formidable barrier to economic relations with the West in 1976 by incorporating into the country's constitution an amendment banning borrowing from capitalist countries. Trade with the West increased after Hoxha's death in 1985, but it was not until the end of the decade that Albania's government surrendered its monopoly on foreign trade. Lawlessness and graft soon made a mockery of almost all legal controls on foreign transactions. In mid-1991 the government was working to set up a free-market-based foreign trade system. After more than a decade of "self-reliance," during which balanced trade had been an essential element of Hoxha's economic doctrine, the country's economic collapse forced its foreign-trade balance and balance of payments deeply into the red. Albanians had to rely on outside aid just to feed themselves.

Foreign Trade Organization

Until 1990 Albania's government exercised a monopoly on foreign trade and controlled it through a highly centralized management mechanism. Following Stalin's model, all external transactions were conducted through foreign-trade enterprises under the guidance of the Ministry of Foreign Trade. In the 1980s, six government foreign-trade enterprises dealt in commodities; five covered services; and two more were concerned with foreign copyrights and licensing agreements. Domestic firms paid for imported goods at fixed wholesale prices that bore little relationship to world prices; they also received fixed wholesale prices for exports. The state bank retained all foreign-currency earnings and covered any losses the foreign-trade enterprises sustained. As a matter of policy, the regime stressed exports and maintained strictly balanced trade on an ongoing, country-by-country basis until 1990. Foreign companies could win or lose contracts depending on Albania's current trade balance with their home country. Albanian traders generally purchased only vital goods and usually paid in cash. Western trade restrictions on East European countries applied to Albania for years because the country never formally withdrew its membership from Comecon, even though it did not participate in Comecon activities.

The downfall of the centrally planned economic system brought sweeping changes to Albania's method of conducting foreign trade. The government abandoned its strict monopoly on foreign commerce in August 1990, when it began allowing state-owned enterprises to conduct foreign trade, retain foreign-exchange earnings, and maintain foreign-currency accounts. Private Albanian companies won the right to carry on foreign trade a year later when the government announced that domestic firms would be permitted to export everything except certain food items. Strapped by a balance of payments deficit and mounting external debt, the authorities continued, however, to limit imports. Tiranë also imposed customs duties ranging from 10 percent for food to 30 percent for new machinery and equipment. The Ministry of Foreign Economic Relations, which replaced the Ministry of Foreign Trade, attempted to stimulate exports by establishing a department for trade consultation that provided data on world prices, product availability, types of trade, and other information to state and private enterprises as well as to foreign firms interested in doing business with Albania. The authorities planned to streamline the tariff system and abolish state trading enterprises.

In the lawlessness that beset Albania after the communist order began to break down, trade laws were generally ignored by the country's private businessmen and black marketeers, especially ethnic Albanians from Serbia's province of Kosovo (see Glossary) and émigrés in Europe and the United States. Graft pervaded the customs service. Italian soldiers said customs officers who inspected containers of aid from Italy left the Durrës dockyards with food jammed into their clothing. High-ranking government officials resigned after disclosures that they had smuggled to Greece 1,000 tons of Italian cooking oil sent as food aid. Peasants also smuggled

The docks in the port city of Durrës
Courtesy Charles Sudetic

livestock to markets across the Greek order, and border officials in Yugoslavia and Greece complained of Albanians coming across and burglarizing homes.

Foreign Trade Balance and Balance of Payments

After more than a decade of autarky and trade surpluses, the force of Albania's economic collapse pulled the country's foreign-trade balance and balance of payments into the red. Albania's exports slipped more than 50 percent to about US$120 million in the early 1990s, and the influx of emergency food and commodity aid contributed almost half of a 20 percent increase in imports. In 1991 Albania's external current-accounts deficit, excluding official transfers, widened to more than US$250 million, which equaled about 30 percent of the country's GDP before the economy seized up. In an effort to narrow the gap, the authorities practically depleted Albania's meager foreign-currency reserves. In the late 1980s, the government began ignoring the constitutional ban on foreign credits, and by mid-1991 the country's total convertible-currency debt was soaring toward US$400 million. Shortfalls in the output of electric power, minerals, and other goods set off another significant slide in export earnings. Officials hoped remittances from the thousands of Albanians who had fled to Greece and Italy would help return Albania's balance of payments to an even keel, but in the early 1990s these émigrés were mostly sending home hard goods, such as used cars, unavailable in the homeland.

Trade Partners

In the mid-1980s, Albania claimed to be carrying on trade with more than fifty countries although the value of the goods exchanged with most of them was small. Trade with IMF member countries, however, was in some cases substantial (see table 11, Appendix). Neighboring Yugoslavia accounted for about 18 percent of Albania's trade volume; the remainder was divided almost evenly between the communist and capitalist countries. Tiranë's main trading partners in Eastern Europe were Romania, Poland, Bulgaria, and Czechoslovakia. In the late 1970s, Albania's break with China forced its commercial representatives to redouble their efforts to find new trading partners in the free-market world. The value of Albania's trade with the West stood at about US$200 million by the late 1980s. In 1988 its main Western trading partners were Italy (US$65 million in trade turnover), West Germany (US$52 million), Greece (US$16.4 million), and France (US$14 million).

Albanian-Yugoslav trade, torpid throughout a decades-long chill in the two countries' relations, revived after Albania's break with

China. The chamber of commerce of each nation opened offices in the other's capital city, and in 1986 a new rail line to Yugoslavia linked Albania with the European rail network for the first time. Albanian imports from Yugoslavia included reinforcing steel, railroad track, steel piping, cables, bricks, pharmaceuticals, electronics, textiles, food, and capital goods. Yugoslavia imported electric power, tobacco, chrome, bitumen, gasoline, natural gas, cognac, and food from Albania. The fallout from the political crisis in Yugoslavia's Kosovo province, populated mainly by ethnic Albanians, had surprisingly little effect on Albanian-Yugoslav trade until the early 1990s, when war erupted between Croatia and Serbia. In 1991 the Albanian government and leaders of the ethnic Albanian community in Kosovo worked toward establishing a joint, Tiranë-based commission to promote stronger economic ties.

After its break with the Soviet Union in 1960, Albania played no part in the activities of Comecon. Trade with the Eastern bloc—with the glaring exception of the Soviet Union, with which Albania maintained no trade relations—increased after Albania broke with China. Generally, Albania supplied its communist-world trading partners with metal ores and agricultural products; it imported machinery, transportation equipment, and some consumer goods. The Albanians obtained rolled steel and coking coal from Poland, pumps from Hungary, trucks and tires from Czechoslovakia, sheet steel from Bulgaria, and textile machinery and fertilizers from East Germany. The Albanians also signed a contract with Hungary to build a pharmaceuticals plant in Tiranë. After a five-year hiatus, China and Albania resumed trade activities in 1983; the new relationship, however, lacked the intimacy of the twelve-year period of close cooperation in the 1960s and early 1970s. Albania carried on a modicum of trade with the Democratic People's Republic of Korea (North Korea) and Cuba.

In the mid-1980s, the growing interest of small import firms in the Albanian market accounted for a sharp increase in trade with Italy and West Germany. Italy was Albania's largest Western trading partner in the late 1980s. Italian exports to Albania accounted for about 20 percent of the West's exports to Albania in 1985, and Italy purchased 16.5 percent of Albania's exports to Western countries. Italy sold Albania metalworking and food-processing machinery, chemicals, iron and steel, metal products, vehicles, and plastics. The Italians imported petroleum products, chrome, copper, nickel and iron ore, and farm products from Albania. In the mid-1980s, West Germany accounted for about 15.5 percent of Western exports to Albania and 15 percent of Western purchases from Albania. Chromium ore and concentrates represented about

50 percent of Albania's exports to West Germany in 1985. The Albanians bought machinery, transportation equipment, and manufactured goods from West Germany. The collapse of Albania's Stalinist economic system opened the door for greater trade with Western Europe. In 1991 Tiranë was negotiating its first economic agreement with the European Community, under which each party would grant the other most-favored-nation status (see Glossary).

For decades Albania was subject to all United States controls on exports to East European nations. The country did not have most-favored-nation treatment and was not eligible for credits or loan guarantees from the Export-Import Bank of the United States (Eximbank). Nevertheless, the volume of United States trade with Albania grew from about US$1 million in 1973 to over US$20 million in 1982; it fell, however, to US$7.7 million in 1986. In 1991 the United States exported coal, wheat, butterfat, powdered milk, and other products to Albania with a total value of about US$18 million; to the United States, Albania exported primarily spices and fruit preserves worth about US$3.2 million. In 1991 Albania was attempting to conclude an economic agreement with the United States by which each nation would extend to the other most-favored-nation status.

Albania's trade with developing countries, which was driven mostly by a need to find and nurture political alliances, amounted to only about US$10 million out of a total trade turnover of US$513 million reported in 1982. Trade with developing countries was hindered because Albania sold its raw materials to and bought vital manufactured goods from wealthier, industrialized nations. Algeria, Costa Rica, Egypt, Iran, Libya, Mexico, and Turkey had had trade agreements with communist Albania.

Commodity Pattern of Trade

Raw materials, fuels, and capital goods accounted for the bulk of Albania's foreign trade before the communist system fell apart (see table 12; table 13, Appendix). The communist regime strove to increase the value of the country's exports by producing and selling industrial and semifinished products instead of raw materials and foodstuffs. In the late 1980s, raw materials and industrial goods made up about 75 percent of exports, which mainly consisted of petroleum, chromite and chrome products, copper wire, nickel, and electric power. Albania's light industries contributed export earnings from sales of bicycles, textiles, handicrafts, souvenirs, wood products, briar pipes, and rugs. Cognac, cigarettes, fruit, olives, tomatoes, canned sardines, anchovies, and other agricultural products also accounted for a share of exports. In 1989 Albania imported about US$245 million in goods from the West, up from US$165 million in 1988. It imported mainly capital goods, semifinished products, and replacement parts necessary to keep industries, especially export-producing industries, functioning. Imports included locomotives, trailers, machinery, textiles, synthetic fibers, lubricants, dyes, plastics, and certain raw materials. Consumer goods such as components for television sets and equipment to outfit enterprises serving foreign tourists accounted for a smaller percentage of imports.

Activities of Foreign Companies in Albania

Albania's 1976 constitution specifically prohibited joint ventures between Albanian enterprises and foreign firms. However, the severe economic crisis of the early 1990s persuaded the government to create a rudimentary framework for regulating the business activities of foreign firms on Albanian soil. Decrees were issued providing for investment protection and the creation of joint ventures between Albanian and foreign companies. At least in theory, the August 1991 law on economic activity allowed foreign companies to repatriate, in foreign currency, accumulated capital and profits from economic activities. More than two dozen foreign companies had already signed joint-venture contracts by August 1991. Almost half of the joint ventures involved small investments in shoe and textile manufacturing, fishing, retail trade, tourism, and construction. Foreign petroleum companies also signed agreements to explore for petroleum reserves beneath the Adriatic Sea. Other potential investors came from Italy and Greece, the Albanian émigré community in the West, and Kosovo's community of ethnic Albanians.

In October 1991, Albania joined the IMF and afterward worked to secure the IMF standby credit agreement prerequisite to receipt of credits from the World Bank and other international institutions. Albania also became a member of the Multilateral Investment Guarantee Agency, a part of the World Bank Group; signed bilateral trade accords and foreign-investment protection agreements with Italy, Germany, Greece, and Turkey; and signed an agreement with the Overseas Private Insurance Corporation, which insures foreign investments by United States companies. Greek businessmen also began operating clothing and yarn factories, and Greek firms signed agreements to transport natural gas as well as contracts for road construction, machinery sales, and shipping. Albania also signed import-credit arrangements with Turkey, which agreed to give Albania technical assistance in banking and other areas.

Foreign Assistance

Throughout its modern history, with the exception of the disastrous "self-reliance" period in the 1970s and 1980s, Albania has relied on foreign aid to achieve economic growth. Each interruption of aid has had immediate and dramatic effects. Between 1955 and 1960, foreign assistance augmented Albania's state budget 233 percent, and industrial output rose by an average of 16.5 percent annually; between 1960 and 1965, aid augmented the budget 130 percent, and yearly industrial output rose only by an average 6.8 percent annually.

The Stalinist economic system's breakdown left Albania with acute shortages of many of the basic necessities of life, especially food. Having no choice but to turn to the West for aid, Albania's leaders got responses from the United States, the member states of the European Community, and Turkey; Greece and Italy were particularly forthcoming. Italy, which was interested in providing assistance mainly in order to stem inflows of Albanian job seekers, pledged more than US$300 million in food, raw materials, and replacement parts alone. Western economists estimated that in 1992 Albania would need some US$500 million worth of food, basic consumer goods, and materials for its factories. Law-enforcement problems and poor, often predatory, local administrations complicated aid deliveries, and on occasion mobs stormed and looted food warehouses and trucks. In many areas, the local communist bosses controlled the only aid-distribution network. They often stole relief supplies and denied deliveries to ordinary people. In mid-1991 the Italian army launched "Operation Pelican," sending 750 troops to protect convoys delivering aid from the ports of Vlorë and Durrës to Albania's twenty-six district centers. Western aid to Albania was also directed at longer-term goals. In July 1991, the European Community enrolled Albania in its program for technical assistance to the former communist countries. Germany granted assistance to improve health services, the drinking-water supply, and student housing.

Prospects for Reform

In 1992, after close to fifty years of communist-imposed isolation following five centuries of Ottoman domination, the Albanian people had little awareness of the outside world and possessed Europe's least developed trade network. The Albanians faced the daunting task of reviving their moribund factories and workshops and learning the realities of modern capitalism while building a market economy from scratch. Burgeoning unemployment, falling output, acute food shortages, and widespread lawlessness eroded most grounds for optimism in the prospects for rapid success. Individual Albanian factories could not switch on assembly lines because idled plants, farms, mines, and generators elsewhere in the production chain were not supplying essential inputs. For most enterprises, importing these inputs was impossible because Albania's nascent foreign-exchange market was not yet fully operative. Despite Albania's dire circumstances, World Bank and European Community economists projected that the country's resource base and labor force could provide the basis for an escape from poverty if the government, with the international community's financial help, took urgent steps to establish the institutions and infrastructure needed to support a market economy and stimulate small-scale private entrepreneurship in the farm sector.

The government's immediate objective was to restore a secure food supply for the general population and provide income and employment for rural inhabitants. Albanian leaders turned to the international community for direct food aid and technical and material assistance for the farm sector. Boosting agricultural output was also a prerequisite for resuming industrial production because many factories needed inputs of raw materials produced in the farm sector. Overall resumption of production had to be coordinated between state enterprises so as to create economic demand and establish a smooth flow of supplies. In 1992, despite the country's inability to pay its international creditors, Albania looked to the IMF, World Bank, and individual Western countries to lend the money needed to jump start and stabilize the economy. Over the longer term, the Albanian economy's fate depends on the country's political leadership restoring law and order, attracting private investors from abroad, and obtaining credits and aid from Western governments for the modernization of industry and agriculture. The last task is especially important because the lack of expertise in international trade and poor quality of Albania's exports preclude the country's earning the foreign exchange necessary to improve infrastructure and increase production. Chronic unemployment is almost certain to be a reality in Albania until urbanization significantly slackens population growth.

* * *

Despite Albania's small size and its communist regime's almost pathological yearning for secrecy, a surprising amount of literature is available on the Balkan state's economy. The best descriptions of Albania's Stalinist system are Adi Schnytzer's *Stalinist Economic Strategy in Practice* and Örjan Sjöberg's *Rural Change and Development in Albania.* Stavro Skendi's *Albania,* Peter R. Prifti's *Socialist Albania since 1944,* and Robert Owen Freedman's *Economic Warfare in the Communist Bloc* offer valuable historical insights into Albania's economic development. Gramoz Pashko, the Albanian economist best known in the West, has also contributed several clearly written, compelling papers on Albania's communist economic system, including "The Albanian Economy at the Beginning of the 1990s." Both the Economist Intelligence Unit and Business International publish regular studies of the Albanian economic situation; the studies are particularly useful to persons exploring the possibility of trading with the country or setting up business operations there. (For further information and complete citations, see Bibliography.)

Chapter 4. Government and Politics

Albanian citizens celebrating victory after announcement that regime would permit multiparty elections, December 1990

ALBANIA WAS THE LAST COUNTRY in Eastern Europe during the early 1990s to undergo a transition from a totalitarian communist regime to an incipient system of democracy. Because Albania was isolated from the outside world and ruled by a highly repressive, Stalinist-type dictatorship for more than four decades, this transition was especially tumultuous and painful, making a gradual approach to reform difficult.

Following the establishment of the People's Republic of Albania in January 1946, Albania became a rigid police state, dominated completely by the communist party and by Marxism-Leninism. Although Albania operated under the facade of constitutional rule, the communist party, led by Enver Hoxha, who was also president of Albania, actually controlled all aspects of the political, social, and economic systems. Hoxha pursued a repressive internal policy, while at the same time implementing a highly isolationist foreign policy. His reliance first on the financial aid and political protection of a sequence of patron states, then insistence on Albania's economic self-reliance and a highly centralized economic system caused Albania to lag far behind its neighbors in terms of economic development.

After Hoxha died in 1985, his hand-picked successor, Ramiz Alia, who became party leader while retaining his post as titular head of state (chairman of the Presidium of the People's Assembly), at first appeared to be carrying on Hoxha's tradition of hard-line policies. But it soon became clear that he was more flexible than his predecessor and was willing to institute badly needed political and economic reforms that attempted to prevent the country from collapsing into anarchy. These reforms, however, were largely cosmetic and insufficient to meet the demands of the growing radical elements in the population. By 1991, popular dissatisfaction with Alia's regime had mounted, causing considerable political instability and social unrest. The civil war in neighboring Yugoslavia (see Glossary) served only to exacerbate the growing political and social tension within Albania. Alia resigned following his party's resounding defeat in the spring 1992 multiparty election, and a new government undertook the task of building democracy in a country that for close to five decades had been isolated from the outside world, dominated by a highly repressive political system, and devoid of free-market, private enterprise.

Origins of the Political System

The communists gained a foothold in Albanian politics during World War II, when they became the founders and leaders of the National Liberation Movement (NLM), which came into existence during the Italian and German occupations. Hoxha, a former schoolteacher who became first secretary of the Albanian Communist Party (ACP) in 1941, was a prominent wartime resistance leader and was largely responsible for the success of the communists in achieving a position of political dominance towards the end of the war.

As leaders of the NLM, the Albanian communists were successful in arousing active opposition to the Italian army and, after September 1943, to the German army. Toward the end of the war, the communists worked unceasingly to ensure that they would exercise political power in liberated Albania. In October 1944, the renamed National Liberation Front transformed itself into the provisional democratic government of Albania, with Hoxha as prime minister. By the time German troops had withdrawn from Albania in November 1944, almost all organized resistance to communism had been crushed.

Albania after World War II

The People's Republic of Albania was proclaimed on January 11, 1946, by a newly elected People's Assembly. The assembly, which was elected in December 1945, initially included both communists and noncommunists. Within a year, however, all noncommunists had been purged from the assembly and were subsequently executed. The communists had a monopoly of power by the end of 1946.

The new regime acted swiftly to consolidate its position by breaking up the power of the middle class and other perceived opponents. The communist party tried before special tribunals those classified as "war criminals," a designation that came to include anyone who was unsympathetic to the new government. Members of the landed aristocracy and tribal chieftains were arrested and sent to labor camps. More than 600 leaders were executed during the new government's first two weeks in power. In an effort to strengthen its grip on the economy, the government promulgated a series of laws providing for strict state regulation of all industrial and commercial enterprises and foreign and domestic trade. The laws legalized the confiscation of property of political opponents in exile and anyone designated an "enemy of the people" and levied a crushing "war-profits tax" against the economically prosperous members of the population. As part of its program to nationalize industry, the government confiscated all German and Italian assets in Albania and revoked all foreign economic concessions. All means of transportation were also nationalized. As far as the peasantry was concerned, the new government was cautious. The Agrarian Reform Law of 1945 nationalized all forests and pasturelands, but landowners who possessed farm machinery were allowed to keep up to forty hectares for farming (see Communist Albania, ch. 1).

The Hoxha Regime

Hoxha was the most powerful leader in modern Albania, occupying at times the posts of prime minister, minister of defense, and commander in chief of the armed forces, while continuing to serve as first secretary of the ACP. He was head of state from 1944 until 1985. His main rival in the initial period of his rule was the minister of internal affairs and head of the dreaded secret police, Koçi Xoxe. Xoxe was close to the Yugoslavs and was arrested in 1948 as a Titoist (see Glossary) following Albania's break with Yugoslavia. The next most influential political figure was Mehmet Shehu, who became prime minister when Hoxha relinquished this post in July 1954.

Hoxha's efforts to impose a rigid, repressive political and government structure on Albania met with little active resistance until the country's declining standard of living and poor economic performance led to such dissatisfaction that unrest began to spread in 1965–66. In response, the Hoxha government initiated the Cultural and Ideological Revolution in February 1966, which was an attempt to reassert communist party influence on all aspects of life and rekindle revolutionary fervor. By 1973 demands for a relaxation of party controls and for internal reforms were creating considerable pressure on Hoxha. The pressure led him to launch a series of purges of top cultural, military, and economic officials. In 1977, for example, an alleged "Chinese conspiracy" was uncovered, which resulted in the dismissal and arrest of several top military officials.

In keeping with its Stalinist practices, Albania's government pursued a rigorously dogmatic line in domestic policy, instituting highly centralized economic planning and rigid restrictions on educational and cultural development. In 1976 a new constitution was promulgated, the third such constitution since the communists came to power. The 1976 constitution, which changed the official name of the country to the People's Socialist Republic of Albania, was little different from the 1950 version. It paid lip service to such institutions as the Supreme Court and the People's Assembly, but it affirmed the primary role of the communist party, known as the Albanian Party of Labor (APL) from 1948 until 1991.

Whatever gains the Hoxha leadership achieved in socioeconomic terms were diminished by the sharp repression in all areas of life, and Hoxha's decision to keep Albania isolated retarded the country's technological growth to such an extent that it became economically inferior to all of its neighbors (see Economic Policy and Performance, ch. 3).

The early 1980s were marked by further purges in the government and party in preparation for the impending succession to Hoxha, who was in ill health. Although Prime Minister Shehu had been regarded as the second most powerful leader, especially because he had significant support in the police and military, Hoxha decided against naming him as his successor. Instead, Hoxha began a campaign against him, which culminated in Shehu's alleged suicide in December 1981. Hoxha then proceeded to arrest all of Shehu's family and supporters.

Alia Takes Over

Before Hoxha died in April 1985, after more than forty years as the unchallenged leader, he had designated Ramiz Alia as his successor. Alia was born in 1925 and had joined the Albanian communist movement before he was twenty years old. He had risen rapidly under Hoxha's patronage and by 1961 was a full member of the ruling Political Bureau (Politburo) of the APL. Hoxha chose Alia for several reasons. First, Alia had long been a militant follower of Marxism-Leninism (see Glossary) and supported Hoxha's policy of national self-reliance. Alia also was favored by Hoxha's wife Nexhmije, who had once been his instructor at the Institute of Marxism-Leninism. Alia's political experience was similar to that of Hoxha; and inasmuch as he appeared to share Hoxha's views on most foreign and domestic issues, he easily accommodated himself to the totalitarian mode of ruling. That he had managed to survive several waves of extensive purges bespoke his political prowess and capacity for survival.

The second-ranking member of the leadership after Hoxha's death was Prime Minister Adil Çarçani, a full member of the Politburo since 1961. Among the fifteen candidate and full members of the party's Politburo in 1985, nine were members of the postwar generation and most had made their political careers after Albanian-Soviet ties were severed in 1961. By late 1986, both the Politburo and the party's other administrative organ, the Secretariat, were dominated by Alia's supporters.

When Alia took over as first secretary of the APL, the country was in grave difficulty. Political apathy and cynicism were pervasive, with large segments of the population having rejected the regime's values. The economy, which suffered from low productivity and permanent shortages of the most basic foodstuffs, showed no sign of improvement. Social controls and self-discipline had eroded. The intelligentsia was beginning to resist strict party controls and to criticize the regime's failure to observe international standards of human rights. Apparently recognizing the depth and extent of the societal malaise, Alia cautiously and slowly began to make changes in the system. His first target was the economic system. In an effort to improve economic efficiency, Alia introduced some economic decentralization and price reform in specific sectors. Although these changes marked a departure from the Hoxha regime, they did not signify a fundamental reform of the economic system.

Alia did not relax censorship, but he did allow public discussions of Albania's societal problems and encouraged debates among writers and artists on cultural issues. In response to international criticism of Albania's record on human rights, the new leadership loosened some political controls and ceased to apply repression on a mass scale. In 1986 and 1989, general amnesties brought about the release of many long-term prisoners. Alia also took steps to establish better ties with the outside world, strengthening relations with Greece, Italy, Turkey, and Yugoslavia. A loosening of restrictions on travel and tourism resulted in a more promising outlook for Albania's tourist trade.

By the late 1980s, Alia was supporting a campaign for more openness in the press and encouraging people to talk freely about Albania's problems. As a result, controversial articles on a range of topics began to appear in the press. Not everyone, however, was happy with Alia's cautious program of reform. The entrenched party bureaucrats were worried that they would lose their powers and privileges and hence resisted many of the changes. Thus Alia's regime was not able, or willing, to attempt changes that would put an end to the repressive elements of the system.

Albania's Communist Party

Albania's communist party, in early 1992, was in a state of transition, and its future remained uncertain. Known from 1941 to 1948 as the Albanian Communist Party, from November 1948 as the Albanian Party of Labor (APL), and from June 1991 as the Socialist Party of Albania (SPA), the communist party was organized along lines similar to the Communist Party of the Soviet Union.

The 1976 constitution recognized the special status of the APL, which controlled the political, cultural, and economic life in the country. According to Article 3 of the constitution, the party is the "leading political force of the state and of the society." The party was organized on the principle of democratic centralism (see Glossary), under which the minority had to submit to the majority and could not express disagreement after a vote. The highest organ of the party, according to the party statutes, was the party congress, which met for a few days every five years. Delegates to the party congress were elected at party conferences held at the regional, district, and city levels. The party congress examined and approved reports submitted by the Central Committee, discussed general party policies, and elected a Central Committee. The latter was the next highest echelon in the party hierarchy and generally included all key officials in the government, as well as prominent members of the intelligentsia. The Central Committee directed party activities between party congresses and met approximately three times a year.

As in the Soviet Union, the Central Committee elected a Politburo and a Secretariat. The Politburo, which usually included key government ministers and Central Committee secretaries, was the main administrative and policy-making body and convened on a weekly basis. Generally the Central Committee approved Politburo reports and policy decisions with little debate. The Secretariat was responsible for guiding the day-to-day affairs of the party, in particular for organizing the execution of Politburo decisions and for selecting party and government cadres.

The Ninth Party Congress of the APL was convened in November 1986, with 1,628 delegates in attendance. Since 1971, the composition of the party had changed in several respects. The percentage of women had risen from 22 percent in 1971 to 32.2 percent in 1986, while 70 percent of APL members were under the age of forty. The average age of members in the newly elected Central Committee was forty-nine, as compared with an average age of fifty-three in the previous Central Committee. The new Central Committee elected a Politburo of thirteen full and five candidate members. In his speech at the Ninth Party Congress, Alia did not indicate any significant departure from the policies of Hoxha, but he launched a campaign to streamline the party bureaucracy and improve its efficiency. Alia urged that standards of cadre training and performance be raised in an effort to rid the system of bureaucrats who were so concerned with protecting their privileges that they blocked the implementation of new economic policies. The Politburo also instituted a policy whereby cadres in positions

Speaker at the Tenth Party Congress of the Albanian Party of Labor, June 1991
Courtesy Charles Sudetic

that were vulnerable to graft and corruption would be rotated on a regular basis.

At the Ninth Plenum of the Central Committee in January 1990, Alia announced further modest reforms. Meetings of all lower-level party organizations would be open to the masses, secretaries of party organizations could serve no longer than five years, one-third of the membership in state organs had to be renewed each legislative term, and at each congress of the APL a third of the delegates would be replaced.

These reforms, however, appeared to be ineffectual after Albania underwent radical changes in its political culture in 1990–91. As was the case in the Soviet Union and in other countries of Eastern Europe, attempts at cautious reform in response to unrest gave rise to widespread manifestations of discontent. On December 11, 1990, student protests triggered the announcement at the Thirteenth Plenum of the Central Committee of the APL that a multiparty system would be introduced in time for the general elections set for February 1991. Following the multiparty election in the spring of 1991, the APL, later the SPA, emerged as the dominant partner in a coalition government (see Reform Politics, this ch.). The SPA was defeated in the spring 1992 general election, receiving only 26 percent of the vote.

The Government Apparatus

The government apparatus, like that of the party, was in a transitional, reformist phase in early 1992. Following the upheavals of 1990 and 1991, which left the economy shattered, much of the country's infrastructure damaged, and parts of the education and welfare systems inoperative, the regime was becoming more democratic and more responsive to the demands of the Albanian people. This shift was reflected, above all, in the introduction of a new electoral system, which for the first time allowed people to choose among several candidates in electing representatives to the legislature. The organs of government described here were provided for in the 1976 constitution. However, changes were introduced in April 1991, when the People's Assembly passed the Law on Major Constitutional Provisions (see Multiparty System, this ch.).

People's Assembly

The supreme organ of the state was, according to the 1976 constitution, the People's Assembly, a unicameral legislative body whose 250 members were elected for four years from a single list of approved candidates. All legislative power was vested in the assembly, which met twice a year for a few days. The People's Assembly had the authority to appoint commissions, to carry out special functions, and to conduct investigations. Between sessions the fifteen-member Presidium of the People's Assembly took charge. Proposals for legislation could be made by the Presidium of the People's Assembly, the Council of Ministers, or members of the assembly itself. In order for a bill to become law, a majority of the People's Assembly had to affirm support for it. Rarely did the assembly express anything other than unanimous approval for a bill. The chairman of the Presidium of the People's Assembly was Alia, who thus merged the functions of party and government leader in one person.

Council of Ministers and People's Councils

The Council of Ministers, formally approved by the People's Assembly, served as the executive branch of the government, taking charge of activities in the social, economic, and cultural spheres. The APL's Politburo actually chose the Council of Ministers, which in early 1991 consisted of twenty-one members. At the same time, some ministers were members of the Politburo, and all belonged to the APL. This fact enabled the party to exercise strong supervision and direction over the Council of Ministers, and, indeed, the council's main function was to ensure that Politburo decisions were carried out. The Council of Ministers was headed by a chairman, the de facto prime minister, who was chosen by the party leadership. In January 1982, Adil Çarçani succeeded Mehmet Shehu as prime minister and was, in turn, replaced by Fatos Nano in February 1991.

People's councils, elected for three-year terms, were responsible for government at twenty-six district levels as well as regional and city levels. They maintained order, enforced laws, and were charged with protecting citizens' rights. The councils met twice a year for a few days, and between sessions their work was conducted by executive committees.

Courts

The highest judicial organ was the Supreme Court, whose members were elected to a four-year term by the People's Assembly in a secret ballot. The Supreme Court consisted of a chairman, deputy chairmen, and assistant judges and made its decisions collegially. Officers of courts at the lower levels—district and regional courts—were elected in a similar manner by people's councils. Trials were generally open to the public and were often held in places of employment or in villages in order to make them accessible.

After abolishing the Ministry of Justice in the 1960s, the Albanian leadership placed supervision of the country's legal and judicial system in the hands of the prosecutor general. Then in 1983, the Ministry of Justice's Office of Investigations, charged with investigating criminal cases, was placed under the direct supervision of the Presidium of the People's Assembly, ostensibly to make the legal system more responsive to the needs of the people. Whatever organizational changes occurred, the courts themselves had little independence in practice because of party interference in both the investigative process and court proceedings. In 1990 the Ministry of Justice was reestablished, with a mandate for supervising the courts and coming up with a program of judicial reform. As of early 1992, the creation of such a program was still underway.

Mass Organizations

According to Enver Hoxha, mass organizations were "levers of the party for its ties with the masses," and they carried out political, executive, and organizational work in such a way as to enable party directives to be correctly understood and implemented by the population at large. Because less than 4 percent of Albania's population belonged to the APL as of 1990, the leadership relied heavily on mass organizations to achieve political socialization. They were controlled by APL cadres and used public funds for their maintenance. However, by early 1992, the importance of these organizations had diminished because a multiparty system had been established and members of the public had the democratic means through which to channel their political expressions.

Democratic Front

Among the most important of Albania's mass organizations was the Democratic Front, which in August 1945 succeeded the National Liberation Front (previously the National Liberation Movement) as the party's most important auxiliary. As the broadest mass organization, the Democratic Front was supposed to give expression to the political views of the population and to carry out mass political education. The main tasks of this organization were to strengthen the political unity between the party and the people and to mobilize the masses in favor of the implementation of the APL's policies. Ideological indoctrination, the spreading of Marxist-Leninist ideas, was another goal of the front. The Democratic Front, as an umbrella organization for cultural, professional, and political groups, was open to all citizens who were at least eighteen years old. It was chaired until December 1990 by Hoxha's widow, Nexhmije, herself a member of the APL Central Committee.

Union of Albanian Working Youth

Described officially as the "greatest revolutionary force of inexhaustible strength" and a "strong fighting reserve of the party," the Union of Albanian Working Youth was another key organization for political socialization and indoctrination. The union operated directly under the APL, with its local organs supervised by the relevant district or city party committees. Founded in 1941, the union was considered one of the most important auxiliaries of the party. Organized in the same way as the party, the union had city and district committees, and higher organs, including the Politburo and Central Committee. It was patterned after the All-Union Lenin Communist Youth League, known as Komsomol, in the Soviet Union. The more than 200,000 members of the union ranged in age from fifteen to twenty-five. The union was responsible for controlling all Pioneer organizations, which embraced children from seven to fourteen years of age; for implementing party directives among youth; and for mobilizing so-called volunteer labor brigades to work on special economic projects. Membership in the union was a prerequisite for those aspiring to a career in the party or state apparatus.

Union of Albanian Women

The Union of Albanian Women was another important mass organization. The union was headed in 1990 by Lumturie Rexha, a member of the Central Committee of the APL. Its tasks included controlling and supervising the political and social activities of the country's women, handling their ideological training, and leading the campaign for the emancipation of women. This campaign, initiated in 1966 by Hoxha, had considerable success in securing equal social and political rights for women. As part of the campaign, women from the cities were dispatched to rural regions to explain to the party's line on the role of women. By the late 1980s, women accounted for 47 percent of the labor force and about 30 percent of deputies to the People's Assembly. Women held responsible jobs at all levels of government and received equal pay in most jobs. Nonetheless, Albanian society remained behind the West in its attitudes toward women and had a long way to go to achieve total equality for women (see Traditional Social Patterns and Values, ch. 2; Women in the Work Force, ch. 3).

United Trade Unions of Albania

Founded in 1945, the United Trade Unions of Albania had tasks that were similar to those of the Democratic Front, but on a more limited scale. The organization's main goal was to carry out political and ideological education of the work force and to mobilize support for the implementation of the party line. The United Trade Unions of Albania consisted of three general unions: the Union of Workers of Industry and Construction, the Union of Education and Trade Workers, and the Union of Agriculture and Procurements Workers. The unions operated according to the principle that the interests of the workers and the state were one and the same. But toward the end of the 1980s, it became increasingly clear that workers no longer identified with the state. Growing disillusionment with social values was reflected in the significant increase in theft of socialist property, corruption, and violation of labor discipline (see Trade Unions, ch. 3).

Mass Media

The mass media had long served as an important instrument for the government's efforts to revolutionize society along communist lines. One of the first acts of the communists when they came to power in 1944 was to seize control of the media, although formal nationalization of media operations did not occur until 1946.

Thereafter the press, radio, and later television were used to justify communist rule and instil Marxist values in the population.

The press, radio, and television were also used to mobilize the population to support and participate in the implementation of regime programs, such as economic plans, antireligious policies, or campaigns to promote literacy. In order to appeal to the sentiments of the masses, much of the media's message had a nationalist content, evoking feelings of loyalty and pride associated with Albanian independence. The media also served to keep party and government officials in check through exposure of corruption and inefficiency.

The media were closely controlled by the party through the exercise of vigorous censorship until 1990, when the leadership began to moderate policies and to gradually allow for the expression of views that ran counter to the official line. Before 1990 all individuals who worked in the mass media, whether editors, film directors, or television and radio producers, were subject to strict party discipline and rigid guidelines.

The most important daily newspaper was *Zëri i Popullit* (Voice of the People), published by the party's Central Committee. As a result of the democratic changes that began in 1990, *Zëri i Popullit* lost its substantial circulation to the new, liberal papers that started to emerge. By 1991 several opposition papers had emerged, including the popular and outspoken *Rilindja Demokratike*. In response to the changing public mood, *Zëri i Popullit* dropped the hammer and sickle insignia from its masthead, along with the Marxist slogan "Proletarians of the World Unite." It then joined with opposition newspapers in the campaign to expose and denounce the corruption and privileges of the ruling elite.

Reform Politics

Albania held out against political reform longer than any other country that had been considered to be in the Soviet Union's sphere of influence, but significant indicators of change in the country's politics began to occur in 1989. Pressure for reform originated from several sources: the intelligentsia and university students, workers, Politburo members antagonistic to Alia, other East European countries, and institutions such as the army and security police. Alia gradually responded to these pressures, but in general the reforms he initiated were too little too late.

Initial Stages

In 1990 Albania had the youngest population in Europe, with the average age at twenty-seven. Albanian youth had been discontented and restless for some time before the regime began to make changes. Although efforts were made to keep Albania isolated from the rest of the world, television broadcasts from other European countries reached Albanian citizens, and the young could see "bourgeois" lifestyles and the political ferment that was occurring elsewhere in Eastern Europe. In addition, the working class was suffering the dire consequences of Albania's declining economy, and conditions were worsened by a terrible drought in 1989. In October 1989, workers and students in the southern district of Sarandë staged protests against the regime's policy of work incentives, and several protesters were arrested. A more serious protest had occurred in May 1989 at the Enver Hoxha University at Tiranë. At first students were simply demanding better living conditions, but their grievances soon acquired a more political character and were treated as a distinct threat by the regime. Although the protest eventually ended without bloodshed, it caused the regime to reassess its policy toward young people and to consider such measures as improving living standards and educational facilities in order to ease the discontent that had been building up among students (see Education under Communist Rule, ch. 2).

Alia and his colleagues dismissed the Soviet Union's concepts of *glasnost'* (see Glossary) and *perestroika* (see Glossary) as irrelevant to the Albanian experience. Demonstrating his ideological purity, Alia claimed that communism collapsed in Eastern Europe because these states deviated from orthodox Marxism. At the Ninth Plenum of the party's Central Committee in January 1990, however, Alia announced some modest political reforms (see Albania's Communist Party, this ch.). In addition, he presented limited economic reforms that called for some management authority at state farm and enterprise levels and for improvements in wage and price regulations to increase the role of material incentives.

In general, Alia's reforms suggested that the party leadership was nervous and defensive, and Alia seemed anxious to convince the Central Committee that Albania should not follow the path of other East European countries. Albanian leaders seemed to fear that anything but very limited reform could lead to the social and political upheaval that had occurred elsewhere in Eastern Europe. But Alia's half-measures did little to improve the economic situation or to halt the growing discontent with his regime.

Some Albanian intellectuals, such as the sociologist Hamit Beqeja and the writer Ismail Kadare, recommended more radical changes, particularly with regard to democracy and freedom of the press. As their demands grew, these intellectuals increasingly clashed with the conservatives in the party and state bureaucracy. In October

1990, it was announced that Kadare, Albania's most prominent writer, had defected to France. The defection dealt a blow to Albania's image both at home and abroad, especially since the writer had sent a letter to Alia explaining that he had defected because he was disillusioned with the slow pace of democratic change in the country. The official reaction to Kadare's defection was to condemn it as a "grave offense against the patriotic and civil conscience" of Albania, but his work continued to be published within the country.

Human Rights

Albanian citizens had few of the guarantees of human rights and fundamental freedoms that have become standard in Western democracies. A large and very effective security service, whose name was changed in July 1991 from the directorate of State Security (Drejtorija e Sigurimit te Shtetit—Sigurimi) to the National Information Service (NIS), helped to support the rule of the communist party by means of consistently violating citizens' rights and freedoms. According to Amnesty International, political prisoners were tortured and beaten by the Sigurimi during investigations, and political detainees lacked adequate legal safeguards during pretrial investigations. Most investigations into political offenses lasted for several months. Such violations were described in Kadare's literary works.

Alia's regime took an important step toward democracy in early May 1990, when it announced its desire to join the Conference on Security and Cooperation in Europe (CSCE—see Glossary), while at the same time introducing positive changes in its legal system. A prerequisite for membership in the CSCE is the protection of human rights. The United Nations Human Rights Committee had severely criticized Albania for its human rights abuses in 1989, and in May 1990 the secretary general of the United Nations (UN) visited Albania and discussed the issue of human rights. The results of these efforts were mixed, but in general the leadership became more tolerant of political dissent.

Deputy Prime Minister Manush Myftiu announced in 1991 a long list of legislative changes that were designed to improve Albania's human rights record. Among the reforms were the right to a speedy trial, legal defense, and appeal; the reduction of the number of crimes punishable by death; the right of all nationals to obtain passports for travel abroad; and the removal of loopholes in the definition of crimes against the state. The government also eased its persecution of religious practice and even allowed some religious activity and "religious propaganda" (see Religion, ch.

2). Restrictions on travel were liberalized, and the number of passports issued was increased significantly. In addition, foreign broadcasts, including those from Voice of America, were no longer jammed.

Further Moves Toward Democracy

The communist regime faced perhaps its most severe test in early July 1990, when a demonstration by a group of young people in Tiranë, the nation's capital, led about 5,000 to seek refuge in foreign embassies. To defuse the crisis, in July 1990 the Central Committee held a plenum, which resulted in significant changes in the leadership of party and state. The conservatives in the leadership were pushed out, and Alia's position was strengthened. Alia had already called for privatizing retail trade, and many businesses had begun to operate privately. Then in late July, the Politburo passed a law stating that collective-farm members should be given larger plots of land to farm individually (see Land Distribution and Agricultural Organization, ch. 3).

In a September 1990 speech to representatives of Albania's major social and political organizations, Alia discussed the July crisis and called for electoral reform. He noted that a proposed electoral law would allow all voting to take place by secret ballot and that every precinct would have at least two candidates. The electors themselves would have the right to propose candidates and anyone could nominate candidates for the assembly. Alia also criticized the bureaucratic "routine and tranquility" of managers and state organizations that were standing in the way of reform.

Despite Alia's efforts to proceed with change on a limited, cautious basis, reform from above threatened to turn into reform from below, largely because of the increasingly vocal demands of Albania's youth. On December 9, 1990, student demonstrators marched from the Enver Hoxha University at Tiranë though the streets of the capital shouting slogans and demanding an end to dictatorship. By December 11, the number of participants had reached almost 3,000. In an effort to quell the student unrest, which had led to clashes with riot police, Alia met with the students and agreed to take further steps toward democratization. The students informed Alia that they wanted to create an independent political organization of students and youth. Alia's response was that such an organization had to be registered with the Ministry of Justice.

The student unrest was a direct consequence of the radical transformations that were taking place in Eastern Europe and of Alia's own democratic reforms, which spurred the students on to make more politicized demands. Their protests triggered the announcement on December 11, 1990, at the Thirteenth Plenum of the APL Central Committee, that a multiparty system would be introduced in time for the general elections that were set for February 1991. The day after the announcement, the country's first opposition party, the Albanian Democratic Party (ADP), was formed.

The Thirteenth Plenum of the APL Central Committee also announced an extensive shakeup in the party leadership. Five of the eleven full members of the Politburo and two alternate members were replaced. Among those dismissed was Foto Cami, the leading liberal ideologist in the APL leadership. Cami's ouster came as a surprise because he was on close terms with Alia, but apparently Alia was dissatisfied with his failure to deal with the intellectuals effectively.

The student unrest that began in Tiranë gave rise to widespread riots in four of the largest cities in northern Albania. Violent clashes between demonstrators and security forces took place, resulting in extensive property damage but, surprisingly, no fatalities. Apparently Alia had given the police strict orders to restrain themselves during confrontations with demonstrators. However, Alia issued stern public warnings to the protesters on television, claiming that they had been misled by foreign influences and opportunistic intellectuals.

The crisis was analyzed in the Albanian press in an usually candid manner. On December 17, the Democratic Front's daily newspaper, *Bashkimi,* described what had occurred and then warned that such violence could lead to a conservative backlash, suggesting that conservative forces posed a real threat to the process of democratization in the country. The outspoken nature of the article, the first instance of open criticism of the security agencies, indicated that the government was prepared to allow intellectuals and reformers to express their views in the media. Later that month, the Council of Ministers set up a state commission to draft a law on the media and formally define their rights, thus reducing the APL's direct control over the press. The council also authorized the first opposition newspaper, *Rilindja Demokratike.*

Another important sign of democratization was the publication on December 31 of a draft interim constitution intended to replace the constitution of 1976. The draft completely omitted mention of the APL. It introduced a system with features similar to those of a parliamentary democracy, while at the same time strengthening the role of the president, who would be elected by a new People's Assembly. The president was to assume the duties of commander in chief of the armed forces and chairman of the Defense Council, positions previously held by the party first secretary. Also on December 31, the government eased restrictions on private trade in the service and light industry sectors, indicating a general trend toward a less centralized economy.

In his traditional New Year's message to the Albanian people, Alia welcomed the changes that had been occurring in the country and claimed that 1991 would be a turning point in terms of the economy. But despite positive signs of change, many Albanians were still trying to leave their country. At the end of 1990, as many as 5,000 Albanians crossed over the mountainous border into Greece. Young people motivated by economic dissatisfaction made up the bulk of the refugees.

Multiparty System

Alia and his political colleagues did not respond to demands by reformers for a multiparty system until the pressure became too great to resist. After the government was finally forced to introduce political pluralism and a multiparty system, several opposition parties were created. The first was the Albanian Democratic Party (ADP), formed on December 12, 1990. One of the founders of the party was the thirty-five-year-old Gramoz Pashko, an economist and a former APL member and son of a former government official. The party's platform called for the protection of human rights, a free-market economy, and good relations with neighboring countries. At the end of 1990, the ADP started organizing rallies in various cities intended to help people overcome their fear of expressing political views after decades of authoritarian control. Thousands of people attended the rallies. The ADP supported the rights of the large Albanian population in Kosovo, a province in the Serbian Republic of Yugoslavia, and advocated a reduction of the length of military service.

By early February 1991, the ADP had an estimated membership of 50,000 and was recognized as an important political force both at home and abroad. The ADP was led by a commission of six men, the most prominent of whom were Sali Berisha, a cardiologist, and Pashko. Berisha, a strong nationalist, vigorously defended the rights of the Albanian residents of Kosovo, and Pashko was an outspoken advocate of economic reform. The party's newspaper, *Rilindja Demokratike,* was outspoken in its political commentary. Its first issue, which appeared on January 5, 1991, criticized the government very aggressively.

The second main opposition party, the Republican Party, headed by Sabri Godo, was founded in January 1991. The Republican Party, which soon had branches in all districts of the country, advocated a more gradual approach to reform than that espoused by the ADP. Several other opposition parties with reform platforms were formed; they included the Agrarian Party, the Ecology Party, the National Unity Party, and the Social Democratic Party.

Albania held its first multiparty elections since the 1920s in 1991. The elections were for the 250 seats in the unicameral People's Assembly. The first round was held in February, and runoff elections took place on March 31; a final round was held in April. Staff members of the CSCE observed the voting and counting of ballots. They found that the process was orderly, although some complaints of irregularities were reported. The turnout was an extremely high 98.9 percent. The APL emerged as the clear victor, winning some two-thirds of the seats. The margin enabled it to maintain control of the government and choose a president, Ramiz Alia, who had previously been chairman of the Presidium of the earlier People's Assembly.

The ADP captured 30 percent of the seats in the People's Assembly, as opposed to 67.6 percent acquired by the APL. Although the APL bore the burden of being the party responsible for past repression and the severe economic woes of Albania, it nonetheless represented stability amidst chaos to many people. This fact was particularly true in the countryside, where the conservative peasantry showed little inclination for substantial changes in their way of life. Another advantage for the APL was its control of most of the media, particularly the broadcast media, to which the opposition parties had little access. It was therefore able to manipulate radio and television to its advantage.

Although many conservative leaders won election to the People's Assembly, Alia lost his seat. Alia had surprised many people by adopting a new, apparently pragmatic, approach to politics in the months leading up to the election. He had faced a serious challenge in mid-February, when unrest erupted again among students at the Enver Hoxha University at Tiranë. Approximately 700 students went on a hunger strike in support of a demand that Hoxha's name should be removed from the university's official name. The demand was a serious attack on the country's political heritage and one that Alia refused to countenance. He resisted student demands and stressed the necessity of preserving law and order, thereby antagonizing those who had expected him to be more moderate.

In April 1991, Albania's new multiparty legislature passed transitional legislation to enable the country to move ahead with key political and economic reforms. The legislation, the Law on Major Constitutional Provisions, was in effect an interim constitution, and the 1976 constitution was invalidated. The words "socialist" and "people's" were dropped from the official title of Albania, so that the country's name became the Republic of Albania. There were also fundamental changes to the political order. The Republic of Albania was declared to be a parliamentary state providing full rights and freedoms to its citizens and observing separation of powers. The People's Assembly of at least 140 members elected for a four-year term is the legislature and is headed by a presidency consisting of a chairman and two deputies. The People's Assembly elects the president of Albania by secret ballot and also elects the members of the Supreme Court. The president is elected for five years and may not serve more than two consecutive terms or fill any other post concurrently. The president does, however, exercise the duties of the People's Assembly when that body is not in session. The Council of Ministers is the top executive body, and its membership is described in the interim constitution. The law on Major Constitutional Provisions is to operate as Albania's basic law until adoption of a new constitution, to be drafted by a commission appointed by the People's Assembly.

Although he lost his seat in the legislature, the People's Assembly elected Alia president. The constitutional changes of April 1991 made it obligatory that Alia resign from all of his high-level posts in the APL in order to accept this post, and the amendments depoliticized other branches of government, including the ministries of defense, foreign affairs, and public order. The People's Assembly also gained regulation of the radio, television, and other official news media.

The Coalition Government of 1991

Prime Minister Fatos Nano, a moderate communist, did well in the spring 1991 elections, and he was able to set up a new government to replace the provisional administration that he established in February 1991. His postelection cabinet consisted mostly of new faces and called for radical market reforms in the economy. In outlining his economic program to the People's Assembly, Nano presented an extremely bleak picture of the economy. He said that the economy was in dire straits because of the inefficiencies of the highly centralized economic system that had existed up to that point, and he advocated extensive privatization as a remedy. He also announced government plans to reform and streamline the armed forces.

Nano's twenty-five-member cabinet and his progressive economic and political program were approved in early May 1991. But the outlook for his administration was clouded by the fact that a general strike had almost completely paralyzed the country and its economy.

Indeed, the situation became so dire that Nano was ousted and a "government of national salvation" was created, in which the communists were forced to share power with other parties in the executive branch for the first time since the end of World War II. The new government, led by Prime Minister Ylli Bufi, was a coalition of the communists, the ADP, the Republican Party, the Social Democratic party, and the Agrarian Party. It took office in June 1991.

Just days later, also in June 1991, the Tenth Party Congress of the APL took place in Tiranë. Delegates voted to change the name of the party to the Socialist Party of Albania (SPA) and elected a reformist leadership under Nano. Former Politburo member Xhelil Gjoni gave the keynote address to the congress. He openly attacked the late dictator, Hoxha, and even went so far as to criticize Alia. His speech was a milestone for the Albanian communists and signified the end of the Stalinist line pursued by the party until that time. The new program adopted by the party stressed the goal of making a transition to a modern, democratic socialist party.

Alia also gave a speech at the party congress, in which he, too, sanctioned a significant reform of the party. But it appeared as though he were under a political shadow. By July 1991, he had come under severe attack from various political quarters. Serious and highly damaging allegations were made by several of Alia's former associates. One detractor charged that Alia had given orders for police to fire on unarmed demonstrators in February 1991, and others openly questioned his claims to have started the process of democratization in Albania. The campaign against Alia was apparently designed to discredit him and force him to step down.

In response, Alia made a great effort to portray himself as a real reformist. In early August 1991, he addressed the nation on television to talk about the attempted coup in the Soviet Union. He said that Mikhail S. Gorbachev's ouster only encouraged all kinds of dictators and he deplored the actions of the self-declared Soviet State Committee for the State of Emergency. The subsequent defeat of the Soviet coup was described by Alia and others as a victory for the forces of reform.

An earlier sign that the government was making an attempt to break with the nondemocratic traditions of the past was the announcement in early July that the notorious Sigurimi, the Albanian secret police, had been dissolved and replaced by a reformed security organization (see Security Forces, ch. 5). The new institution, the National Information Service (NIS), was to be far more attentive to individual rights than its predecessor had been. The move to disband the Sigurimi and form the NIS coincided with a steep rise in crime and a wave of Albanians fleeing to Italy, an

The forced return of Albanian refuge-seekers from Italy at the port of Durrës, June 1991
Courtesy Charles Sudetic

exodus that the NIS was unable to stem. The refugee problem reached epidemic proportions in August 1991, with 15,000 Albanians seeking asylum in Italy; most were later returned to Albania.

In many respects, Alia was a political survivor. He had managed to remain a key political figure throughout several political crises. Although he had some genuine concerns for stability and continuity, he was not inflexible. He changed in response to the circumstances and accommodated the demands of the reformers. Nonetheless, with Albania in the throes of a grave economic crisis, Alia had to face challenges that he could not surmount. After the collapse of the coalition government in December 1991 and the ADP's landslide victory in the spring 1992 general election, he resigned as president on April 3, 1992. On April 9, the People's Assembly elected ADP leader Sali Berisha as Albania's new head of state.

Foreign Policy

Historically, Albania's foreign policy objectives have not been far-reaching. Ideology has not been a driving force in determining Albania's relations with the outside world. Rather, its main concern has been to preserve its territorial integrity and independence. The strategy pursued by Enver Hoxha was to rely on alliances with communist states that could give Albania large amounts of foreign aid and at the same support his regime. His successor, Alia, modified this strategy by pursuing a more varied foreign policy, reaching out to a number of Albania's neighbors.

Shifting Alliances

Several factors contributed to Albania's foreign policy, but nationalism was probably the single most important factor. Albanian nationalism had developed over years of domination or threat of domination by its more powerful neighbors: Greece, Italy, and Yugoslavia. The partition of Albania in 1912, when Kosovo and other Albanian-inhabited territories were lost, left the country with a deep sense of resentment and hostility to outsiders. Traditional fears of being dismembered or subjugated by foreigners persisted after World War II and were aggravated by Hoxha's paranoia about external enemies.

To offset the influence of Yugoslavia, Hoxha made an effort to improve relations with the Western powers, but was largely unsuccessful. Following the 1946 purge of Sejfulla Maleshova, the leader of the party faction that advocated moderation in foreign and domestic policy, Albania's relations with the West deteriorated, and both the United States and Britain withdrew their foreign envoys from Tiranë. Albania's application to join the UN was also rejected (Albania did join the UN in December 1955). Hoxha made peace with Josip Broz Tito, Yugoslavia's president, and in July 1946 signed the Treaty of Friendship, Cooperation, and Mutual Aid with Yugoslavia. Yugoslav influence over Albania's party and government increased considerably between 1945 and 1948. Yugoslavia came to dominate political, economic, military, and cultural life in Albania, and plans were even made to merge the two countries.

Yugoslavia's expulsion from the Cominform (see Glossary) in 1948 gave Hoxha an opportunity to reverse this situation, making his country the first in Eastern Europe to condemn Yugoslavia. The treaty of friendship with Yugoslavia was abrogated; Yugoslav advisers were forced out of Albania; and Xoxe, the minister of internal affairs and head of the secret police, was tried and executed, along with hundreds of other "Titoists." As a result of these changes, Albania became a full-fledged member of the Soviet sphere of influence, playing a key role in Stalin's strategy of isolating Yugoslavia. In 1949 Albania joined the Council for Mutual Economic Assistance (Comecon—see Glossary) and proceeded with a program of rapid, Soviet-style, centralized economic development.

Tiranë's close relations with Moscow lasted until 1955, when the post-Stalin leadership began pursuing a policy of rapprochement with Yugoslavia. As part of the de-Stalinization process, Moscow began to pressure Tiranë to moderate its belligerent attitude toward Yugoslavia and relax its internal policies. Hoxha managed to withstand this challenge and to resist the pressure to de-Stalinize, despite the fact that the Soviet Union resorted to punitive economic measures that caused Albania considerable hardship. In 1960 the Soviets attempted to engineer a coup against Hoxha, but were unsuccessful because Hoxha had learned of their plans in advance and had purged all pro-Soviet elements in the party and government.

By 1960 Albania was already looking elsewhere for political support and improving its relations with China. In December 1961, the Soviet Union, while embroiled in a deep rift with China, broke diplomatic relations with Albania, and other East European countries sharply curtailed their contacts with Albania as well. Throughout the 1960s, Albania and China, countries that shared a common bond of alienation from the Soviet Union, responded by maintaining very close domestic and foreign ties. China gave Albania a great deal of economic aid and assistance, while the latter acted as China's representative at international forums from which the Chinese were excluded. Although Tiranë's break with Moscow had been very costly in economic terms, Albania made no effort to reestablish ties with the Soviet Union. In an address to the Fifth Congress of the APL in November 1966, Hoxha made it clear that Albania intended to stay close to China.

The 1968 Soviet invasion of Czechoslovakia, however, marked the beginning of a gradual estrangement between Albania and China, primarily because Hoxha realized that an increased Soviet military threat could not be offset by an alliance with a country that was far away and militarily weak relative to the superpowers. Hoxha sanctioned a cautious opening toward neighboring countries such as Yugoslavia and Greece, although he continued to be concerned about the domestic effects of moving too far from foreign policy that excluded all countries except China.

Another cause of the estrangement was the realization that Chinese aid was not enough to prevent Albania from having serious economic problems. Albania's experience with financial assistance from communist powers from 1945 to 1978 had begun to make it wary of becoming so dependent on any outside entity. A chill in relations with China began to occur following the death of Mao Zedong in September 1976, and in July 1978 China terminated all economic and military aid to Albania, an action that left Albania without a foreign protector.

In the late 1970s, Albania embarked on a policy of rigid self-reliance. Having broken ties with the two leading communist states, Albania aspired to total economic independence and declared itself the only genuine Marxist-Leninist country in the world. The government was actually forbidden to seek foreign aid and credits or to encourage foreign investment in the country. Hoxha rigidly adhered to Marxism-Leninism, seeing the world as divided into two opposing systems—socialism and capitalism. But he also led Albania in a two-front struggle against both United States "imperialism" and Soviet "social-imperialism." For example, Albania refused to participate in CSCE talks or sign the Helsinki Accords (see Glossary) in 1975 because the United States and the Soviet Union had initiated the negotiating process.

Changes in the 1980s

Hoxha had basically used the threat of external enemies to justify a repressive internal policy. His primary goal was to stay in power, and an isolationist foreign policy suited this goal. But some members of the APL leadership began to question the efficacy of such a policy, particularly in view of its adverse economic consequences. At the end of the 1970s, Hoxha was pressured into sanctioning a cautious effort to strengthen bilateral relations with Albania's neighbors, in particular Yugoslavia. Bilateral cultural contacts between the two countries increased, and by 1980 Yugoslavia had replaced China as Albania's main trading partner. In the early 1980s, however, Yugoslavia's military suppression of ethnic Albanians demonstrating in the province of Kosovo led to a chill in Albanian-Yugoslav relations. Approximately two million ethnic Albanians lived in Kosovo, and Albania supported Kosovo's demands that it be granted the status of a republic. Yugoslavia responded by accusing Albania of interfering in its internal affairs, and cultural and economic contacts were severely reduced. Trade between the two countries stagnated.

In the early 1980s, a diplomatic shift toward Italy, Greece, and Turkey occurred. In November 1984, Alia, as Hoxha's heir apparent, gave a speech in which he expressed an interest in expanding relations with West European countries. He noted that "Albania is a European country and as such it is vitally interested in what is occurring on that continent." Relations with Italy and Greece became noticeably stronger in the early and mid-1980s. In 1983 Albania signed an agreement with Italy on establishing a maritime link between the ports of Durrës and Trieste. The two countries also ratified a long-term trade agreement, whereby Albania would send Italy raw materials in exchange for industrial technology. Albania entered into a long-term economic accord with Greece in December 1984, and the two countries also signed a series of agreements on road transportation, cultural exchanges, scientific and technological cooperation, telecommunications, and postal services. Albania's closer relations with Italy and Greece caused Yugoslavia concern, primarily because it appeared preferable to Belgrade to have Albania isolated. But Albania worried that West European countries would allow Yugoslavia to dictate its policies if it failed to develop strong relations with other countries in the region.

Alia's Pragmatism

On succeeding to Hoxha's party leadership post in 1985, Alia reassessed Albania's foreign policy. He realized that it was imperative for Albania to expand its contacts with the outside world if it were to improve its economic situation. He was eager in particular to introduce Western technology, although limited foreign-currency reserves and constitutional bans on foreign loans and credits restricted Albania's ability to import technology.

Alia's public statements indicated that in pursuing his country's foreign policy objectives he would be less rigid than his predecessor and put political and economic concerns ahead of ideological ones. Thus, at the seventy-fifth anniversary of Albania's independence in 1987, Alia stated, "We do not hesitate to cooperate with others and we do not fear their power and wealth. On the contrary, we seek such cooperation because we consider it a factor that will contribute to our internal development."

In February 1988, Albania participated in the Balkan Foreign Ministers Conference, held in Belgrade. The participation was a clear sign of a new flexibility in Albania's foreign policy. During the 1960s and 1970s, Albania had refused all regional attempts to engage in multilateral cooperation, but Alia was determined to end Albania's isolation and return his country to the mainstream of world politics. This new approach entailed an improvement of relations with Yugoslavia. Indeed, Alia apparently realized that Albania had nothing to gain from confrontation with Yugoslavia over the Kosovo issue, and he ceased endorsing Kosovar demands for republic status in his public statements. The government's conciliatory approach to Yugoslavia was expressed fully in a declaration by Minister of Foreign Affairs Reis Malile at the conference. Malile said that the status of Kosovo was an internal Yugoslav problem.

Trade and economic cooperation between Albania and Yugoslavia increased greatly toward the end of the 1980s. But Kosovo again became a source of tension when the Yugoslav government imposed special security measures on the province and dispatched army and militia units in February and March 1989. These actions resulted in violent clashes between Yugoslav security forces and the Albanian inhabitants of Kosovo. Albania denounced Yugoslavia's "chauvinist policy" toward Kosovo and noted that if the oppression continued, it would adversely affect relations between Albania and Yugoslavia. For its part, Yugoslavia threatened to close down Albania's only rail link to the outside world, a move that would have caused great hardship to Albania. In December 1989, a Yugoslav newspaper reported alleged unrest in northern Albania; President Alia denounced this report and similar ones as a foreign "campaign of slander" against Albania. He denied reports of unrest and said that Yugoslavia was trying to stir up trouble to divert attention from ethnic troubles in Kosovo.

By the late 1980s, Albania began to strengthen further its relations with Greece. The substantial Greek minority in Albania motivated Greek concern for better communications with Albania (see Ethnicity, ch. 2). It was especially important for Greece that Albanian nationals who were ethnically Greek should be allowed to practice the Greek Orthodox religion. Greece offered Albania hopes of economic and political ties that would offset the deterioration in relations with Yugoslavia. Albania and Greece had already signed a military protocol on the maintenance and repair of border markers in July 1985. In August 1987, Greece officially lifted its state of war with Albania, which had existed since World War II, when Italy had launched its attack on Greece from Albanian territory. In November 1987, the Greek prime minister visited Tiranë to sign a series of agreements with Albania, including a long-term agreement on economic, industrial, technical, and scientific cooperation. In April 1988, the two countries set up a ferry link between the Greek island of Corfu and the Albanian city of Sarandë. In late 1989, however, their relations began to worsen when some Greek politicians began to express concern about the fate of the Greek minority in Albania, and a war of words began. This hostility marked a sharp departure from the trend over the previous decade.

Albania's relations with both Turkey and Italy improved after the death of Hoxha. In May 1985, Prime Minister Çarçani sent a message to the Italian prime minister, Bettino Craxi, stating that he hoped cooperation between the two countries could be increased. In late 1985, however, there was a slight setback in Italian-Albanian relations when six Albanian citizens sought refuge in the Italian

Embassy in Tiranë and the two countries found it difficult to settle the dilemma. The six were allowed to remain in the embassy until Albania finally gave assurances that they would not be persecuted.

An important step toward ending Albania's isolation and improving its relationships with its neighbors was Tiranë's offer to host the Balkan Foreign Ministers Conference in October 1990. The conference was a follow-up to the Belgrade conference of 1988 and was the first international political gathering to take place in Albania since the communists came to power. The conference came at a good time for the Albanian leadership, which was attempting to project a new image abroad in keeping with the democratic changes beginning to take place within the country. For Albania it was an opportunity to increase its prestige and boost its international image in the hopes of becoming a full-fledged member of the CSCE. In fact, the latter aim was not achieved by the conference, and it was not until June 1991, after a visit by CSCE staff members to observe Albania's first multiparty elections, that Albania was accepted as a full member of the CSCE.

Albania Seeks New Allies

By the mid-1980s, Alia recognized that in order to ameliorate Albania's serious economic problems, trade with the West had to be significantly expanded. The Federal Republic of Germany (West Germany) was on the top of the list of potential economic partners. In 1987 Albania established diplomatic relations with West Germany, after first dropping claims for war reparations. Albania hoped to obtain advanced technology from West Germany, along with assistance in improving its agricultural sector and modernizing its transportation system. In November 1987, Albania signed an agreement with West Germany, which enabled it to purchase West German goods at below market prices; and in March 1989, West Germany granted Albania 20 million deutsche marks in nonrepayable funds for development projects.

Albania initiated discussions with many private Western firms concerning the acquisition of advanced technology and purchase of modern industrial plants. It also asked for technical assistance in locating and exploiting oil deposits off its coast. But the problems for Albania in pursuing these economic aims were considerable. The main problem was Albania's critical shortage of foreign currency, a factor that caused Albania to resort to barter to pay for imported goods. Tied to this problem was the economy's centralized planning mechanism, which inhibited the production of export commodities because enterprises had no incentive to increase the country's foreign-exchange earnings. An even greater problem until the 1990s was the provision in the 1976 Albanian constitution prohibiting the government from accepting foreign aid.

In addition to paying more attention to Albania's close neighbors and Western Europe, Alia advocated a reassessment of relations with other East European countries. A more flexible attitude was adopted, and relations with the German Democratic Republic (East Germany), Czechoslovakia, and Bulgaria significantly improved in the late 1980s. In June 1989, the East German foreign minister Oskar Fischer visited Albania; he was the first senior official from the Soviet bloc to visit the country since the early 1960s. Alia personally received Fischer, and a number of key agreements were signed that led to expanded cooperation in industry and the training of specialists. By 1990 long-term trade agreements had been signed with most East European states. The Comecon countries were willing to accept Albania's shoddy manufactured goods and its low-quality produce for political reasons. After 1990, however, when these countries were converting to market economies, they no longer had the same willingness, which made it considerably more difficult for Albania to obtain much-needed foreign currency. The Albanian media, nonetheless, greeted the revolutions in Eastern Europe with favor, covering events with an unusual amount of objectivity. The government in Tiranë was among the first to attack Romanian dictator Nicolae Ceauşescu and to recognize the new government in Romania. As far as the Soviet Union was concerned, however, Albania continued to be highly critical of its former ally and denounced Gorbachev's policy of *perestroika.* Apparently Albania was also concerned about what it saw as Soviet support for Yugoslavia's handling of the Kosovo issue. Nevertheless, the Soviet Union continued to call for improved relations with Albania.

Albania's attitude toward the United States traditionally had been very hostile. Relations with Washington were broken in 1946, when Albania's communist regime refused to adhere to prewar treaties and obligations. Alia showed a different inclination, however, after a visit to Tiranë in 1989 by some prominent Albanian Americans, who impressed him with their desire to promote the Albanian cause. In mid-February 1990, the Albanian government reversed its long-standing policy of having no relations with the superpowers. A leading Albanian government official announced: "We will have relations with any state that responds to our friendship with friendship." No formal contacts between the United States and Albania existed until 1990, when diplomats began a series of meetings that led to a resumption of relations. On March 15, 1991, a memorandum of understanding was signed in Washington

Statue of Stalin in storage in Tiranë
Courtesy Fred Conrad

reestablishing diplomatic relations between the two countries. United States secretary of state James Baker visited Albania in June 1991, following the CSCE meeting in Berlin at which Albania was granted CSCE membership. During his visit, Baker informed the Albanian government that the United States was prepared to provide Albania with approximately US$6 million worth of assistance. He announced that the United States welcomed the democratic changes that were taking place in Albania and promised that if Albania took concrete steps toward political and free-market reforms, the United States would be prepared to offer further assistance.

Alia's pragmatism was also reflected in Albania's policy toward China and the Soviet Union. The Albanian Deputy Minister of Foreign Affairs made an official visit to China in March 1989, and the visit was reciprocated in August 1990. On July 30, 1990, Albania and the Soviet Union signed a protocol normalizing relations, which had been suspended for the previous twenty-nine years. The Soviet-Albanian Friendship Society was reactivated, and Alia met with the Soviet foreign minister, Eduard Shevardnadze, when they were both in New York to visit the United Nations in September 1990. No longer were the United States and the Soviet Union considered to be Albania's most dangerous enemies.

Alia's trip to the UN was the first time that an Albanian head of state had attended an official meeting in the West. The purpose of the trip was to demonstrate to the world that Albania had a pragmatic and new foreign policy. While at the UN, Alia delivered a major foreign policy address to the General Assembly in which he described the changes that had taken place in Albania's foreign policy and emphasized that his country wanted to play a more active role in world events. In his address, Alia discussed the ongoing efforts of the Albanian leadership to adjust the external and internal politics of Albania to the realities of the postcommunist world.

The internal politics of Albania, driven by a collapsed economy, social instability, and democratic ferment, portend continued changes in the institutions of government in the early to mid-1990s and in the relationship between the country's leaders and its citizens.

* * *

Materials on Albania are not as readily available as those on other countries in Eastern Europe. Nonetheless, a few useful monographs on Albanian politics and government have appeared. *The Albanians: Europe's Forgotten Survivors,* by Anton Logoreci, and *Socialist Albania since 1944,* by Peter R. Prifti, both of which were published during the 1970s, provide useful accounts of political developments in Albania since World War II. *Albania: A Socialist Maverick,* by Elez Biberaj, offers a more up-to-date picture of the political scene in Albania, pointing out the positive and negative aspects of the changes taking place there. Among the more useful articles on Albanian politics is Biberaj's "Albania at the Crossroads," which analyzes political events in 1991 and offers a perspective on what might be expected for Albania's future. Also of value are the regular articles on Albanian politics by Louis Zanga, appearing in the Munich weekly *Report on Eastern Europe,* published by Radio Free Europe/Radio Liberty. (For further information and complete citations, see Bibliography.)

Chapter 5. National Security

The black, double-headed eagle, a traditional symbol of Albania

ALBANIA BECAME INDEPENDENT in 1912 when the Great Powers of Europe decided that its formation would enhance the balance of power on the continent. Small, weak, and isolated, Albania faced persistent threats of domination, dismemberment, or partition by more powerful neighbors, but struggled to maintain its independence and territorial integrity through successive alliances with Italy, Yugoslavia (see Glossary), the Soviet Union, and China. The Albanian Communist Party (ACP—from 1948 the Albanian Party of Labor) used the perception of a country under siege to mobilize the population, establish political legitimacy, and justify domestic repression. Yet it claimed success in that, under its rule, Albania's allies guaranteed its defense against external threats and were increasingly less able to dominate it or interfere in its internal affairs. After a period of isolation between 1978 and 1985, however, Albania looked to improved relations with its neighbors to enhance its security.

The modern armed forces grew out of the partisan bands of World War II, which fought the Italians and Germans as well as rivals within the resistance. By the time the Germans withdrew their forces from Albania in November 1944, the communist-led National Liberation Front (NLF) held the dominant position among the partisan groups and was able to assume control of the country without fighting any major battles. The armed forces in 1992 were under the control of the Ministry of Defense, and all branches were included within the People's Army. Total active-duty personnel strength was about 48,000 in 1991. Most troops were conscripted, and approximately one-half of the eligible recruits were drafted, usually at age nineteen. The tanks, aircraft, and other weapons and equipment in the inventory of the armed forces were of Soviet or Chinese design and manufacture. The People's Army, consisting of professional officers, conscripted soldiers, mobilized reserves, and citizens with paramilitary training, was organized to mount a limited territorial defense and extended guerrilla warfare against a foreign aggressor and occupation army. However, it remained the weakest army in Europe in early 1992.

Albania lacked the industrial or economic base to maintain its army independently and required external assistance to support its modest armed forces. After World War II, it relied on Yugoslavia and the Soviet Union, in turn, for military assistance. When Albania split from the Soviet Union in 1961, China became its main ally and supplier of military equipment. Chinese assistance was sufficient to maintain equipment previously furnished by the Soviet Union and to replace some of the older weapons as they became obsolete. However, this aid was curtailed in 1978, and Albania lacked a major external patron after that time.

After becoming first secretary of the Albanian Party of Labor and president of Albania when longtime leader Enver Hoxha died in 1985, Ramiz Alia gradually relaxed the Stalinist system of political terror and coercion established and maintained by his predecessor. The impact of changes in the Soviet Union and the subsequent collapse of communism in Eastern Europe, particularly in Romania, combined to increase pressure for internal liberalization in Albania during the late 1980s and early 1990s.

The Ministry of Internal Affairs controlled the police and security forces until it was abolished and replaced by the Ministry of Public Order in April 1991. Although details of the organization of the Ministry of Public Order were not generally known, some observers believed it had the same basic components as its predecessor. They were the National Information Service (successor to the hated Sigurimi, more formally Drejtoria e Sigurimit te Shtetit or Directorate of State Security), the Frontier Guards, and the People's Police.

The security forces traditionally exerted even more rigid controls over the population than those exercised by similar forces in other East European states. However, under Alia they did not enforce the communist order as they had when Hoxha ruled Albania. Alia curtailed some of their more repressive practices, and they ultimately failed to protect the regime when the communist party's monopoly on power was threatened in 1990 and ended in 1991. In large part, that threat came from a crippled economy, shortages of food and medicine, manifestations of new political freedoms (including strikes and massive public demonstrations that occurred with impunity), and calls by the new democratic movement for eliminating repression by the security forces, releasing political prisoners, and establishing respect for human rights.

Development of the Armed Forces

Albania's military heritage antedating World War II is highlighted by the exploits of its fifteenth-century national hero known as Skanderbeg, who gained a brief period of independence for the country during his opposition to the Ottoman Empire (see Glossary). In the seventeenth century, many ethnic Albanians, most notably members of the Köprülü family, served with great distinction in the Ottoman army and administration (see Albanians under Ottoman Rule, ch. 1). National feelings, aroused late in the nineteenth century, became more intense during the early twentieth century, and fairly sizable armed groups of Albanians rebelled against their Ottoman rulers. However, Albania achieved national independence in 1912 as a result of agreement among the Great Powers of Europe rather than through a major military victory or armed struggle.

Hardy Albanian mountaineers have had a reputation as excellent fighters for nearly 2,000 years. Nevertheless, they rarely fought in an organized manner for an objective beyond the defense of tribal areas against incursions by marauding neighbors. Occasions were few when Albanians rose up against occupying foreign powers. Conquerors generally left the people alone in their isolated mountain homelands, and, because a feudal tribal society persisted, little, if any, sense of national unity or loyalty to an Albanian nation developed (see Traditional Social Patterns and Values, ch. 2).

The Romans recruited some of their best soldiers from the regions that later became Albania. The territory of modern Albania was part of the Byzantine Empire, and the Bulgars, Venetians, and Serbs took turns contesting their control of Albania between the tenth and the fourteenth centuries. As the power of the Byzantine Empire waned, the forerunners of modern Albania joined forces with the Serbs and other Balkan peoples to prevent the encroachment of the Ottoman Empire into southeastern Europe. The Ottoman victory over their combined forces at Kosovo Polje in 1389, however, ushered in an era of Ottoman control over the Balkans.

The Albanian hero Skanderbeg, born Gjergj Kastrioti and renamed Skanderbeg after Alexander the Great, was one of the janissaries (see Glossary) who became famous fighting for the Ottoman Turks in Serbia and Hungary. He was almost exclusively responsible for the one period of Albanian independence before 1912. Although it endured for twenty-four years, this brief period of independence ended about a decade after his death in 1468. In 1443 Skanderbeg rebelled against his erstwhile masters and established Albania's independence with the assistance of the Italian city-state of Venice. He repulsed several Ottoman attempts to reconquer Albania until his death. The Ottoman Turks soon recaptured most of Albania, seized the Venetian coastal ports in Albania, and even crossed the Italian Alps and raided Venice. The Ottomans retook the last Venetian garrison in Albania at Shkodër in 1479, but the Venetians continued to dispute Ottoman control of Albania and its contiguous waters for at least the next four centuries. Albanian soldiers continued to serve in the military forces of the Ottoman Empire in the vicinity of the Mediterranean into the nineteenth century.

From Independence to World War II

Organized military action had a negligible effect in Albania's attaining national independence. Some revolutionary activity occurred during the rise of Albanian nationalism in the late nineteenth and early twentieth centuries. Albanian insurgents and Ottoman forces clashed as early as 1884, but although Albanians resisted Ottoman oppression against themselves, they supported the Ottoman Turks in their hostilities with the Greeks and Slavs.

By 1901 about 8,000 armed Albanians were assembled in Shkodër, but a situation resembling anarchy more than revolution prevailed in the country during the early 1900s. There were incidents of banditry and pillage, arrests, and many futile Ottoman efforts to restore order. Guerrilla activity increased after 1906, and there were several incidents that produced martyrs but were not marked by great numbers of casualties. Although it was disorganized and never assumed the proportions of a serious struggle, the resistance was, nevertheless, instrumental in maintaining the pressure that brought international attention to the aspirations of Albanian nationalists, who proclaimed Albania's independence on November 28, 1912.

Albanian forces played a minor role in the First Balkan War of 1912-13, in which Bulgaria, Serbia, and Greece attempted to eliminate the last vestiges of Ottoman control over the Balkans. At the end of 1912, however, the Ottoman Turks held only the Shkodër garrison, which they did not surrender until April 1913. After the Second Balkan War, when the Great Powers prevailed upon the Montenegrins who had laid siege to Shkodër to withdraw, independent Albania was recognized. However, less than 50 percent of the ethnic Albanians living in the Balkans were included within the boundaries of the new state. Large numbers of Albanians were left in Montenegro, Macedonia, and especially Kosovo (see Glossary), sowing the seeds for potential ethnic conflict in the future (see Evolution of National Security Policy, this ch.).

World War I began before Albania could establish a viable government, much less form, train, and equip a military establishment. It was essentially a noncombatant nation that served as a battleground for the belligerents. However, during the war, it was occupied alternately by countries of each alliance. In 1916 it was the scene of fighting between Austro-Hungarian forces and Italian, French, and Greek forces. In 1918 the Austro-Hungarians were finally driven out of Albania by the Italians and the French. Albania emerged from the war with its territorial integrity intact, although Serbia, Montenegro, Italy, and Greece had sought to partition it. Italy, in particular, had entered the war on the side of the Triple Entente with the aim of acquiring parts of northern Albania (see World War I and Its Effects on Albania, ch. 1).

Ahmed Zogu created the first armed national forces of any consequence. He served as minister of internal affairs and minister of war until 1922 and prime minister thereafter, except for a brief period of exile in 1924. Before 1925 these forces consisted of about 5,000 men, who were selected from Zogu's home district to ensure their loyalty to him. In 1925 Albania began drafting men according to a policy of universal conscription that was carried out with Italian assistance and allowed a considerable degree of Italian control. The initial drafts yielded about 5,000 to 6,000 troops per year from the approximately 10,000 men who annually reached the eligible age. The Italians equipped and provided most of the training and tactical guidance to Albanian forces and therefore exercised virtual command over them.

Under pressure from a more proximate Yugoslav threat to its territorial integrity, Albania placed its security in Italian hands in November 1927 when it signed the Second Treaty of Tiranë. The original treaty, signed one year earlier, pledged the parties to mutual respect for the territorial status quo between them. The successor document established a twenty-year alliance and a program of military cooperation between them. Thus, Albania became a virtual protectorate of Italy, with the latter receiving oil rights, permission to build an industrial and military infrastructure, and a high-profile role in Albania's military leadership and domestic political affairs.

At about the same time, the Gendarmerie was formed with British assistance. Although its director was Albanian, a British general served as its inspector general and other British officers filled its staff. It became an effective internal security and police organization. The Gendarmerie had a commandant in each of Albania's ten prefectures, a headquarters in each subprefecture (up to eight in one prefecture), and an office in each of nearly 150 communities. For many years, it had the most complete telephone system in the country. The Italians objected strenuously, but King Zog, as Zogu became in 1928, relied on the Gendarmerie as a personal safeguard against the pervasive Italian influence within his regular armed forces. He kept the force under his direct control and retained its British advisers until 1938. Zog also retained a sizable armed group from his home region as an additional precaution.

World War II

King Zog's effort to reduce Italian control over his armed forces was insufficient to save them from quick humiliation when the Italians attacked on April 7, 1939. Although annual conscription had generated a trained reserve of at least 50,000, the Albanian government lacked the time to mobilize it in defense of the country. The weak Albanian resistance, consisting of a force of 14,000 against the Italian force of 40,000, was overcome within one week, and Italy occupied and annexed the country. Later in 1939, the Italians subsumed some Albanian forces into their units. They gained little, however, from Albanian soldiers, who were unwilling to fight for the occupying power, even against their traditional Greek enemies. They deserted in large numbers.

Benito Mussolini, the Italian fascist premier, and his Axis partners viewed Albania as a strategic path through the Balkans from which to challenge British forces in Egypt and throughout North Africa. Albania served as the bridgehead for Mussolini's invasion of Greece in October 1940, and Italy committed eight of its ten divisions occupying the country.

The Albanian Communist Party and its armed resistance forces were organized by the Communist Party of Yugoslavia in 1941 and subsequently supported and dominated by it. Resistance to the Italian occupation gathered strength slowly around the party-controlled National Liberation Movement (NLM, predecessor of the NLF) and the liberal National Front. Beginning in September 1942, small armed units of the NLF initiated a guerrilla war against superior Italian forces, using the mountainous terrain to their advantage. The National Front, by contrast, avoided combat, having concluded that the Great Powers, not armed struggle, would decide Albania's fate after the war.

After March 1943, the NLM formed its first and second regular battalions, which subsequently became brigades, to operate along with existing smaller and irregular units. Resistance to the occupation grew rapidly as signs of Italian weakness became apparent. At the end of 1942, guerrilla forces numbered no more than 8,000 to 10,000. By the summer of 1943, when the Italian effort collapsed, almost all of the mountainous interior was controlled by resistance units.

The NLM formally established the National Liberation Army (NLA) in July 1943, with Spiro Moisiu as its military chief and Hoxha as its political officer. It had 20,000 regular soldiers and guerrillas in the field by that time. However, the NLA's military activities in 1943 were directed as much against the party's domestic political opponents, including prewar liberal, nationalist, and monarchist parties, as against the occupation forces.

Mussolini was overthrown in July 1943, and Italy formally withdrew from Albania in September. Seven German divisions took over the occupation from their Italian allies, however. Four of the divisions, totalling over 40,000 troops, began a winter offensive in November 1943 against the NLA in southern Albania, where most of the armed resistance to the Wehrmacht and support for the communist party was concentrated. They inflicted devastating losses on NLA forces in southern Albania in January 1944. The resistance, however, regrouped and grew as final defeat for the Axis partners appeared certain. By the end of 1944, the NLA probably totaled about 70,000 soldiers organized into several divisions. It fought in major battles for Tiranë and Shkodër and pursued German forces into Kosovo at the end of the war. By its own account, the NLA killed, wounded, or captured 80,000 Italian and German soldiers while suffering about 28,000 casualties.

The communist-controlled NLF and NLA had solidified their hold over the country by the end of October 1944. Some units, including one whose political officer, Ramiz Alia, would eventually succeed Enver Hoxha as leader of Albania, went on to fight the Germans in Albanian-populated regions of Yugoslavia, including Kosovo. Hoxha had risen rapidly from his post as political officer of the NLA to leadership of the communist party, and he headed the communist government that controlled the country at the end of World War II. Albania became the only East European state in which the communists gained power without the support of the Soviet Union's Red Army. They relied instead on advice and substantial assistance from Yugoslav communists and Allied forces in occupied Italy.

Postwar Development

Initially, Albania's postwar military forces were equipped and trained according to Yugoslavia's model. Between 1945 and 1948, Yugoslavia's control over the Albanian armed forces was tighter than Italy's control had been. Not only did the Yugoslavs have military advisers and instructors in regular units, but Yugoslav political officers also established party control over the Albanian military to ensure its reliability and loyalty.

Albania was involved in several skirmishes early in the Cold War. In 1946 Albanian coastal artillery batteries fired on British and Greek ships in the Corfu Channel. Later that year, two British destroyers were damaged by Albanian mines in the channel. Together with Bulgaria and Yugoslavia, Albania aided communist forces in the civil war in Greece between 1946 and 1948 and allowed them to establish operational bases on its territory.

Yugoslavia used its close alliance with Albania to establish a strong pro-Yugoslav faction within the Albanian Communist Party. Led by Koci Xoxe, the group served Yugoslav interests on the issue of ethnic Albanians in Yugoslavia. It also cultivated pro-Yugoslav elements within the military and security forces to enhance its influence. It sought a close alliance, a virtual union, of communist states in the Balkans, including Albania, under its leadership. However, when Yugoslavia embarked on its separate road to socialism in 1948 and was subsequently expelled from the Communist Information Bureau (Cominform—see Glossary), Albania used the opportunity to escape the overwhelming Yugoslav influence. The nation completely severed its ties with Yugoslavia and aligned itself directly with the Soviet Union.

The shift to Soviet patronage did not substantially change Albania's military organization or equipment because Yugoslav forces had followed the Soviet pattern until 1948. Albania joined the Soviet-led Warsaw Treaty Organization (see Glossary), popularly known as the Warsaw Pact, on May 14, 1955, but did not participate in joint Warsaw Pact military exercises because of its distance from other members of the alliance. Soviet aid to Albania included advisory personnel, a considerable supply of conventional weapons, surplus naval vessels from World War II, and aircraft. Albania provided the Soviet Union with a strategically located base for a submarine flotilla at Sazan Island, near Vlorë, which gave it access to the Mediterranean Sea (see fig. 1). Albania also served as a pressure point for Stalin's campaign against Yugoslavia's independent stance within the communist camp. Albania preferred the Soviet Union to Yugoslavia as an ally because its distance and lack of a common border appeared to limit the extent to which it could interfere in Albania's internal affairs.

Albania's relations with the Soviet Union were strained in 1956 when Nikita Khrushchev improved Soviet relations with Yugoslavia. Hoxha feared that, as part of the rapprochement with Yugoslavia, Khrushchev would allow Tito to reestablish Yugoslavia's earlier influence in Albania. Albanian-Soviet ties deteriorated rapidly in 1961, when Albania joined China in opposing the Soviet de-Stalinization campaign in the communist world (see Albania and the Soviet Union, ch. 1). De-Stalinization was a threat to the political survival of an unreconstructed Stalinist like Hoxha. In response, the Soviet Union cancelled its military aid program to Albania, withdrew its military advisers, and forced Albanian officers studying in Soviet military schools to return home in April 1961.

Albania in turn revoked Soviet access to Sazan Island, and Soviet submarines returned home in June 1961. Albania broke diplomatic relations with the Soviet Union on December 19, 1961; it became an inactive member of the Warsaw Pact but did not formally withdraw from the alliance until 1968.

As tensions grew between Albania and the Soviet Union, Albania sought Chinese patronage. In the 1960s, China succeeded the Soviet Union as Albania's sole patron. Albania provided China with little practical support, but its value as an international political ally was sufficient for the Chinese to continue military assistance. China provided aid in quantities required to maintain the armed forces at about the same levels of personnel and equipment that they had achieved when they were supported by the Soviet Union. The shift to Chinese training and equipment, however, probably caused some deterioration in the tactical and technical proficiency of Albanian military personnel.

Evolution of National Security Policy

Like any country, Albania's national security is largely determined by its geography and neighbors. It shares a 282-kilometer border with Greece to the south and southeast. It has a 287-kilometer border with the Yugoslav republics of Serbia and Montenegro to the north and a 151-kilometer border with the former Yugoslav Republic of Macedonia to the east. Albania's other closest neighbor and one-time invader, Italy, is located less than 100 kilometers across the Adriatic Sea to the west. Albania has had longstanding and potentially dangerous territorial and ethnic disputes with Greece and Yugoslavia. It has traditionally feared an accommodation between them in which they would agree to divide Albania. Greece has historical ties with a region of southern Albania known as Northern Epirus among the Greeks and inhabited by ethnic Greeks, with estimates of their number ranging from less than 60,000 to 400,000. Moreover, there is serious potential for conflict with Yugoslavia, or specifically the Yugoslav Republic of Serbia, over Kosovo. Nevertheless, for many years, Albania perceived a seaborne attack by a superpower from the Adriatic Sea as a greater threat than a large-scale ground assault across the rugged terrain of eastern Albania. Any attack on Albania would have proved difficult because more than three-quarters of its territory is hilly or mountainous. The country's small size, however, provides little strategic depth for conventional defensive operations.

In the early years of communist rule, Albania's national security policy emphasized the internal security of the new communist regime and only, secondarily, external threats. Evaluated against this priority, Albania's national security policy was largely successful until 1990. Because its military forces, however, were incapable of deterring or repulsing external threats, Albania sought to obtain political or military guarantees from its allies or the international community.

Initially, Albania's national security policy focused on extending the authority of the Tosk-dominated communist party from Tiranë and southern Albania into Geg-inhabited northern regions where neither the party nor the NLA enjoyed strong support from the population (see Ethnicity, ch. 2). In some places, the party and NLA faced armed opposition. The government emphasized political indoctrination within the military in an attempt to make the armed forces a pillar of support for the communist system and a unifying force for the people of Albania. In general, however, there were few serious internal or external threats to communist control. In the early years of communist rule, the communist party relied on its close alliance with Yugoslavia for its external security. This alliance was an unnatural one, however, given the history of mutual suspicion and tension between the two neighbors and Yugoslavia's effort to include Albania in an alliance of Balkan states under its control. In 1948 Yugoslavia's expulsion from the Soviet-led communist world ended the alliance.

The Soviet Union assumed the role of Albania's principal benefactor from late 1948. Albania was a founding member of the Warsaw Pact in 1955, and its security was guaranteed against Yugoslav encroachment by its participation in the Soviet-led collective security system until 1961. However, the Soviet Union suspended its military cooperation and security guarantees when Albania supported China in the Sino-Soviet split (see Albania and China, ch. 1).

Albania's military weakness and general ideological compatibility with China led it to accept Chinese sponsorship and military assistance. It did not, however, formally withdraw from the Warsaw Pact until September 13, 1968, after the Soviet-led Warsaw Pact invasion of Czechoslovakia. After the invasion, Albania drew closer to China, seeking protection against a possible attempt by the Soviet Union to retrieve Albania into the East European fold. China subsequently increased its military assistance to Albania. Despite Chinese guarantees of support, Albania apparently doubted the efficacy of a deterrent provided by a distant and relatively weak China against a proximate Soviet threat. Some knowledgeable Western observers believed that, at Chinese insistence, Albania had signed a mutual assistance agreement with Yugoslavia and Romania to be implemented in the event of a Soviet attack on any one of them.

Following China's lead, Albania accused both the United States and the Soviet Union of tacitly collaborating to divide the world into spheres of influence, becoming a vociferous international opponent of the use of military force abroad and the establishment of foreign military bases, particularly by the United States or the Soviet Union. In particular, Albania persistently called for a reduction of United States and Soviet naval forces in the Mediterranean Sea.

During the 1970s, Albania viewed improved relations between the United States and China as detrimental to its interests. This perception increased after the death of Mao Zedong in 1976. In 1978 China ceased its military and economic assistance to Albania as the Asian superpower adopted a less radical stance on the international scene and turned more attention to its domestic affairs. According to some analysts, however, China continued to supply Albania with spare parts for its Chinese-made weapons and equipment during the 1980s.

In the decade between Mao's death and Hoxha's death in 1985, Albania practiced self-reliance and international isolation. After succeeding Hoxha, President Ramiz Alia moved in a new direction, seeking improved relations with Yugoslavia, Greece, and Turkey and even participating in the Balkan Foreign Ministers Conference in 1988. He attempted to moderate the impact of the Kosovo issue on relations with Yugoslavia. Greece downplayed its historical claims to the disputed territory of Northern Epirus during the 1980s, when the two countries improved their bilateral relations. Alia also encouraged Greece and Turkey to withdraw from the North Atlantic Treaty Organization (NATO) and Bulgaria and Romania to withdraw from the Warsaw Pact. In addition, Alia improved relations with Italy and the Federal Republic of Germany (West Germany), which may have resulted in some military sales to Albania, including missile and military communications systems.

In 1986 the first deputy minister of people's defense and chief of the general staff summarized Albania's approach to national security when he stated that Albania's security depended on carefully studying the international situation and taking corresponding action. Better ties with its neighbors promised to give Albania time to generate support in the international arena and bring international opprobrium to bear on any potential aggressor while its forces mounted a conventional defense and, then, guerrilla warfare against enemy occupation forces.

In early 1992, the outlook for Albanian national security was mixed. There were important positive developments but also some negative trends. The Treaty on Conventional Armed Forces in Europe—usually referred to as the Conventional Forces in Europe, or CFE, Treaty—was signed in 1990 and promised reductions in the ground and air forces of nearby NATO members Greece and Italy and former Warsaw Pact member Bulgaria. It therefore placed predictable limits on the future size of the military threat to Albania from most of its neighbors. But the CFE Treaty did not affect nonaligned states such as Yugoslavia, and Albania remained militarily, economically, and technologically weak.

In June 1990, seeking to develop closer ties to the rest of Europe, Albania began to participate in the Conference on Security and Cooperation in Europe (CSCE—see Glossary) as an observer state. It received full membership one year later. Until joining, Albania had been the only state in Europe not a member of CSCE. Membership afforded Albania a degree of protection against external aggression that it probably had not enjoyed previously. It also committed Albania to respect existing international boundaries in Europe and basic human rights and political freedoms at home.

In the early 1990s, Albania sought a broader range of diplomatic relations, reestablishing official ties with the Soviet Union in 1990 and the United States in 1991. It also sought to join the North Atlantic Cooperation Council, a NATO-associated organization in which other former Warsaw Pact countries were already participating.

On the negative side of Albania's national security balance sheet, the improved European security environment undermined the communist regime's ability to mobilize the population by propagandizing external threats. In the early 1990s, the military press cited problems in convincing Albania's youth of the importance of military service and training, given the fact that the Soviet Union was withdrawing its forces from Eastern Europe, that the CFE Treaty promised major reductions in conventional forces, and that most conceivable threats seemed to be receding. The accounts cited instances of "individual and group excesses," unexcused absences, and the failure to perform assigned duties. These problems were ascribed to political liberalization and democratization in the People's Army, factors that supposedly weakened military order and discipline, led to breaches of regulations, and interfered with military training and readiness.

Albania's most sensitive security problem centered on ethnic Albanians living outside the country's borders, including the nearly 2 million living in Kosovo, a province of Yugoslavia's Serbian Republic. The area recognized as Albania by the Great Powers in 1913 was such that more ethnic Albanians were left outside the new state than included within it. Tension in Kosovo between ethnic Albanians, who made up 90 percent of its approximately 2 million residents, and the dwindling number of Serbs living there was a constant source of potential conflict between Albania and Serbia.

Yugoslavia's Serbian Republic ruled Kosovo harshly until the 1970s when it became an autonomous province, theoretically with almost the same rights as the Serbian Republic itself. In 1981, however, one-quarter of the Yugoslav People's Army (YPA) was deployed in Kosovo in response to unrest, which began with riots in Priština. Yugoslavia asserted more direct control over Kosovo in the late 1980s in response to alleged Albanian separatism, which aimed to push Serbians out of an area they considered to be their ancestral home. In 1989, relying on scarcely veiled threats and actual demonstrations of force, Serbia forced Kosovo to accept legislation that substantially reduced its autonomy and then suspended Kosovo's parliament and government in 1990. Sporadic skirmishes erupted between armed Albanian and Serbian civilians, who were backed by the Serb-dominated YPA. Meanwhile, the Serbs accused Albania of interference in Kosovo and of inciting its Albanian population against Yugoslav rule.

For their part, Kosovars claimed that they were the victims of Serbian nationalism, repression, and discrimination. In 1991 they voted in a referendum to become an independent republic of Yugoslavia, and Albania immediately recognized Kosovo as such. Although President Alia criticized Yugoslav policy in Kosovo, he carefully avoided making claims on its territory. Nevertheless, Serbs believed the vote for republic status was a precursor to demands for complete independence from Yugoslavia and eventual unification with Albania. As Yugoslavia collapsed into a civil war that pitted intensely nationalist Serbia against other ethnic groups of the formerly multinational state, Albania remained circumspect in its pronouncements on and relations with Kosovo in order to avoid a conflict. However, a series of border incidents, involving Serb forces killing ten Albanians along the Albanian-Yugoslav border, occurred in late 1991 and early 1992. Albanians and Europeans were seriously concerned that Serb forces would direct military operations against ethnic Albanians in Kosovo and spark an international conflict with Albania. Albania's armed forces were poorly prepared to fight the larger, better equipped, and combat-experienced Serb forces.

Defense Organization

As chief of both party and state, Enver Hoxha was commander

in chief and had direct authority over the People's Army until his death in 1985. His successor, Ramiz Alia, also had a strong connection to the People's Army through his military career, having reached the rank of lieutenant colonel and political officer in the Fifth Division of the NLA at the age of nineteen. According to the constitution adopted in 1976, the People's Assembly, a unicameral legislative body, had authority to declare mobilization, a state of emergency, or war. This authority devolved to the president when the People's Assembly was not in session, which was more often than not under communist rule, or was unable to meet because of the exigencies of a surprise attack on Albania. Albania's interim constitutional law, published in December 1990 and enacted in April 1991, made the president commander in chief of the People's Army and chairman of the relatively small Defense Council, composed of key party leaders and government officials whose ministries would be critical to directing military operations, production, and communications in wartime (see Reform Politics, ch. 4).

The People's Army encompassed ground, air and air defense, and naval forces. It reported to the minister of people's defense, who was a member of the Council of Ministers and was, by law, selected by the People's Assembly. The minister of defense had traditionally been a deputy prime minister and member of the Political Bureau (Politburo) of the party. He exercised day-to-day administrative control and, through the chief of the general staff, operational control over all elements of the military establishment. The chief of the general staff was second in command of the defense establishment. He had traditionally been a candidate member of the Politburo. Each commander of a service branch was also a deputy minister of defense and advised the minister of people's defense on issues relative to his service and coordinated its activities within the ministry. Each represented his service in national defense planning.

The major administrative divisions of the People's Army served all three services. These divisions included the political, personnel, intelligence, and counterintelligence directorates; the military prosecutor's office; and the rear and medical services. The intelligence directorate collected and reported information on foreign armies, especially those of neighboring Yugoslavia and Greece. The military prosecutor's office was responsible for military justice. It organized military courts composed of a chairman, vice chairman, and several assistant judges. The courts heard a variety of cases covered by the military section of the penal code. Military crimes included breaches of military discipline, regulations, and orders as well as political crimes against the state and the socialist order.

Military personnel, reserves, security forces, and local police were subject to the jurisdiction of military courts. The medical service had departments within each of the military branches providing hospital and pharmaceutical services. At the national level, it cooperated closely with the Ministry of Health, using military personnel, facilities, and equipment to improve sanitary and medical conditions throughout the country and to provide emergency medical assistance during natural disasters.

Political Control

The Albanian Party of Labor (APL) had an active and dominant organization within the armed forces until it lost its monopoly on political power in 1991. The postcommunist political complexion of the military was only beginning to evolve in early 1992. The great majority of officers in the armed services were still party members in early 1992 (the party was renamed in June 1991 as the Socialist Party of Albania).

The communist-dominated coalition government, which emerged from the spring 1991 elections, promised a sweeping military reform that included the depoliticization of the armed forces. The Political Directorate of the People's Army, however, continued to exist as part of the Ministry of Defense. The Political Directorate controlled political officers within all services and units of the armed forces. The communist leadership considered the directorate essential to ensure that the armed forces conformed with ideology as interpreted by the party.

The reliability of senior military leaders was assured by their membership in the party. All students over eighteen years of age in military schools were also party members. Younger students were members of the Union of Albanian Working Youth and were organized into the party's youth committee in the army. Political officers indoctrinated conscripts with communist ideology and the party line. Reinforcing the actions of officers and military courts, they helped ensure discipline in military units. They had authority to take action against soldiers whose attitudes or conduct was considered contrary to the efficiency or good order of the armed forces. Probably only a very few of the conscripts were party members, but nearly all were members of the youth organization.

In 1966 Hoxha abolished rank designations and uniforms, condemning them as unhealthy bourgeois class distinctions, in keeping with a similar Chinese move. This measure was intended to make the military more egalitarian by bringing officers closer to the soldiers under their command. It also reinforced party control over the military by reducing the prestige and independence of its leadership as well as its potential to become a political power center rivaling the party. Military professionalism became a secondary consideration to political reliability in determining promotions.

Since World War II, the abrupt shifts in Albanian foreign policy had resulted in purges of the officer corps. Those officers trained in or closely linked with Yugoslavia, the Soviet Union, or China were purged from the ranks and even executed as traitors when alliances with these countries came to an end.

Fearing a decline in his authority and party control over the People's Army, Hoxha also conducted a major purge of its senior officers during 1974. He dismissed and later executed his longtime ally and minister of defense, Beqir Balluku, as well as the chief of staff and chief of the political directorate. He replaced Balluku with his prime minister, Mehmet Shehu, another close associate of many years who had established the military and security forces in the late 1940s. Shehu was a founder of the guerrilla movement during World War II who attained the rank of lieutenant general. He was its most capable military leader, but he apparently committed suicide after he and party officials tied closely to him were purged in 1981. Prokop Murra, a relatively junior candidate member of the Politburo, succeeded Shehu as minister of defense and became a full member of the Politburo in 1986. Kico Mustaqi became chief of the general staff and first deputy minister of defense, as well as a candidate member of the Politburo, in 1986.

Military influence in politics was restored to its earlier level when Mustaqi became minister of defense and a full member of the Politburo in 1990. This closer integration of the military into the political leadership may have been an effort to ensure the military's loyalty at a time of social unrest at home and communist disintegration in Eastern Europe. In early 1991, however, President Alia replaced Mustaqi with Muhamet Karakaci, a young former officer and deputy chief of the general staff. Alia reportedly feared that Mustaqi was planning a military coup d'état.

In November 1991, the communist-dominated coalition government reintroduced military ranks and Western-style uniforms in place of plain Chinese fatigues. It pledged to emphasize military professionalism, training, and discipline and to eliminate political indoctrination from the military. The Albanian Democratic Party called for reforms in the armed forces to include reductions in military spending, military units, and conscription and the reorganization of unit structures. It proposed and initiated an effort to establish contacts and cooperation with Western military establishments, particularly Turkey's, and to send Albanian officers to study and train in foreign military academies. The chief of staff of the

Bus driver talking to soldier at the terminus near the port city of Durrës
Courtesy Charles Sudetic

People's Army attended the East-West Seminar on Military Doctrines in Vienna for the first time in 1991.

People's Army

In early 1992, the ground, air and air defense, and naval forces of the People's Army numbered about 48,000, approximately half of whom were conscripts. The ground forces were the predominant service, and ground forces commanders exercised broad authority over the air and air defense forces in providing air support to ground forces units. They also had responsibility for the defense of coastal regions and exercised considerable operational control over naval units to accomplish this mission. There was less distinction between Albania's military services than was normally the case in larger Western military establishments. The air and air defense forces and the naval forces were usually treated separately because of their distinctive missions, equipment, and training, but their personnel were frequently referred to as air or naval soldiers. Their organization and logistics differed only insofar as their missions and equipment required. The tactical missions and capabilities of each service were specialized in relation to their weapons, and organizational patterns appeared similar to most other armed forces throughout the world. During the formative years immediately after World War II, force structures for each service were adopted directly from the Soviet model, although a partial realignment according to the Chinese pattern occurred after 1961.

Ground Forces

In the early 1990s, the ground forces numbered about 35,000, or about three-quarters of all armed forces personnel. Because the strength of the ground forces was sufficient to man only about two divisions, brigades of approximately 3,000 soldiers became the largest army formation. In 1991 four infantry brigades constituted the bulk of combat units in the ground forces. During the 1980s, Albania had reduced the number of infantry brigades from eight to four. It had shifted to fully manned units from its prior reliance on the mobilization of reserve soldiers to flesh out a larger number of units manned at a lower level. Each brigade had three infantry battalions and one lightly equipped artillery battalion. Armored forces consisted of one tank brigade. Artillery forces were increased from one to three regiments during the 1980s, and six battalions of coastal artillery were maintained at strategic points along the Adriatic Sea littoral.

As of the early 1990s, most equipment used by the ground forces was old, and its effectiveness was questionable. In addition, shortages of spare parts for Soviet and Chinese equipment reduced combat readiness. The infantry brigades lacked mechanization, operating only about 130 armored personnel carriers. They included Soviet BTR-40, BTR-50, BTR-152, and BRDM-1 vehicles produced in the 1950s and Chinese Type-531 armored vehicles. Armored forces were equipped with 200 Soviet-made T-34 and T-54 tanks. The T-34 was a World War II model, and the more recent T-54 was introduced during the late 1950s. Soviet and Chinese artillery in the ground forces inventory was towed rather than self-propelled. It included Soviet M-1937 and D-1 howitzers and Chinese Type-66 152mm guns, Chinese Type-59 130mm guns, Soviet M-1931/37 and M-1938 guns of 122mm, and Chinese Type-60 guns of 122mm. The ground forces also operated Chinese Type-63 107mm multiple rocket launchers and a large number of Soviet and Chinese mortars, recoilless rifles, and antitank guns. Organic air defense equipment for protecting ground forces units consisted of several types of Soviet towed antiaircraft guns, including the 23mm ZU-23-2, 37mm M-1939, 57mm S-60, and 85mm KS-12.

The lack of modern equipment was a major deficiency in the ground forces in the early 1990s. The infantry lacked mobility and antitank guided missiles. Moreover, without mobile surface-to-air missiles or radar-controlled antiaircraft guns, army units would be vulnerable to attack by modern fighter-bombers or ground-attack aircraft. Yet the obsolescent weapons of the ground forces were suited to the relatively low technical skill of the country's soldiers as well as its rugged terrain (see fig. 3). The tactical skill of the officers might make it possible to deploy this older equipment successfully for a short period in a static defensive posture. A defensive operation that prevented an enemy from rapidly neutralizing Albanian opposition would enable Albania to seek international diplomatic or military assistance against an aggressor. Alternatively, it would gain time and retain the military equipment needed to establish a long-term guerrilla force capable of resisting a better armed conventional occupation army. The logistical support required to resupply and maintain such a defense, however, was either lacking or nearly impossible to achieve over much of the terrain.

Air and Air Defense Forces

The air and air defense forces, founded in April 1952, are the most junior of the three services. In 1991 the personnel strength of these forces was about 11,000, the majority of whom consisted of officers assigned to ground-based air defense units. The air force had nearly 100 combat aircraft supplied by China. The main air bases were located near Tiranë, Shijak, Vlorë, Sazan Island, and Kuçovë. The missions of the air force were to repel the enemy at the country's borders and to prevent violations of national airspace. However, the obsolescence of Albania's combat aircraft and probable deficiencies in readiness made it unlikely that the air force could fulfill these missions against the more modern aircraft of neighboring countries. The air force was a source of prestige for the regime, but for practical purposes it served mainly to provide the core for upgrading in the event that a new, technologically advanced foreign sponsor appeared in the future.

After 1970 the air force replaced its entire inventory of Soviet MiG-15 and MiG-17 aircraft acquired during the 1950s with Chinese-produced airplanes. It had one squadron of Chinese J-7s and two squadrons of J-6 fighter-interceptors, with ten to twelve aircraft per squadron. Ground-attack and support aircraft included two squadrons of Chinese J-4s and one squadron of J-2 fighter-bombers. The most modern of these Chinese-built aircraft, the J-7, was designed along the lines of the Soviet MiG-21, which was first introduced in the 1960s. The J-6 fighter-interceptor was the Chinese version of the MiG-19 from the 1950s. These aircraft were limited to daytime operations, lacking the sophisticated radar and avionics required to give them night and all-weather flight capabilities. Military transport aircraft and helicopters consisted of one squadron of C-5 transports, a Chinese-manufactured Soviet An-2; one squadron of Chinese Li-2 transports; and two squadrons of Chinese Z-5 helicopters. The Z-5 was basically a Soviet Mi-4.

Air defense equipment was primarily Soviet in origin. Four sites equipped with Soviet SA-2 surface-to-air missiles constituted a point air defense system for several strategic locations in Albania. The SA-2 was received initially in 1964 and became obsolete in the 1970s. The Chinese apparently did not upgrade Albania's capability. Until 1976 China supplied most of the spare parts required to maintain the air force's equipment. After 1976, however, the combat readiness of the air force declined because deliveries of spare parts were reduced. The aircraft inventory also shrank after China ceased its arms supply relationship with Albania. Increasingly, older aircraft that could not be repaired left the inventory and were not replaced.

Naval Forces

None of Albania's pre-World War II naval forces survived the occupation of Albania; the new navy was established in August 1945. The naval forces are exclusively coastal defense forces and closely coordinate their operations with the ground forces. Their mission is to provide the initial line of resistance to a seaborne invasion of Albania. Considerably weaker than their potential adversaries, the naval forces are intended to deny an aggressor uninhibited access to the waters adjacent to Albania. They would be largely sacrificed in the effort to defeat at least some of the units of a large, well-equipped opposing naval assault force. They would try to prevent submarines from approaching Albanian coasts and ports, to lay and sweep mines, and to escort convoys. The absence of a shore-based coastal defense force with surface-to-surface missiles, however, is a serious deficiency in the navy's ability to repel a seaborne attack on Albania. Naval forces, together with police patrol boats, are also responsible for preventing smuggling and controlling access to Albanian ports.

Naval forces are organized into two coastal defense brigades composed of minor surface combatants located at the Durrës and Vlorë naval bases. All combatants are assigned to one of these bases. Other naval facilities are located at Sazan Island, Pasha Liman on the strait of Otranto coast, Sarandë, and Shengjin. The Soviet Union constructed the base at Sazan Island, but it has not been used regularly since Soviet-Albanian relations ruptured in 1961. Naval personnel numbered about 2,000, with roughly one-half being conscripts.

The strength of the naval forces shrank between the mid-1970s and 1991. In particular, old Italian ships of World War II vintage and most of Albania's minesweepers left the inventory. Torpedo boats and coastal patrol craft constituted the bulk of the naval forces. In 1991 Albania had twenty-nine Chinese-built Huchwan hydrofoil torpedo boats, each of which had two 533mm torpedo tubes. Patrol craft included six Chinese-made Shanghai-II fast inshore gunboats and two older Soviet Kronshtadt-class patrol boats. Minesweeping forces consisted of old Soviet-built T-301 and PO-2 boats. The naval forces also had two obsolete Soviet Whiskey-class diesel submarines constructed during the 1950s.

Military Manpower

Traditionally most armed forces conscripts served for two years. Conscripts in the air and air defense and naval forces as well as noncommissioned officers and technical specialists in certain units served three years. In 1991, however, the freely elected, communist-controlled coalition government reduced the basic two-year term of service to eighteen months. This shorter term of service for conscripts and the small size of the People's Army would force Albania to rely on large-scale mobilization to mount a credible defense of the country. Given the small population and economy of Albania, full mobilization would seriously disrupt the civilian production and logistics necessary to sustain military operations. The military reserve training needed to support mobilization plans also imposed a burden on the country's economic activity. In the early 1990s, the population was relatively young, with fully 60 percent under the age of thirty. There were just under 500,000 males between the ages of fifteen and fifty. Of this total number, approximately 75 percent, or nearly 375,000, were physically suited to carry out military duties. More than half of them had had prior military service and participated in reserve military activities on an annual basis. Women were also trained in the reserves and available for mobilization, although in unknown numbers.

In the early 1990s, plans for expanding the existing military establishment during mobilization were unclear to Western observers. Prior to the 1980s, the ground forces maintained a peacetime structure with low personnel strength and low combat readiness. Divisions would be brought to full strength and readiness through the mobilization of reserves. The smaller brigade structure introduced in the 1980s, however, made it unlikely that newly mobilized soldiers could be integrated into existing units in the regular ground forces in wartime. Mobilized troops were more likely to be employed as light infantry, special forces, or guerrillas rather than in more technically oriented tank, artillery, air and air defense, or naval units. However, the possibility of mobilizing a substantial segment of the population for guerrilla warfare against an aggressor was evident in the large paramilitary training program. The emphasis on paramilitary training increased after the Soviet-led Warsaw Pact invasion of Czechoslovakia in 1968 demonstrated potential weaknesses in Albania's plans to meet an attack by a large, well-trained aggressor force.

In the late 1980s, even communist-controlled Albanian sources referred to serious problems with the attitudes of young people who were conscripted into the People's Army. They described social malaise, a growth in religious belief, increasing crime, and unwillingness to accept assignments to remote areas of the country. Moreover, the system of social discipline that had enforced obligatory military service under communist rule had completely disappeared by January 1992. Poor food, changing living and working conditions, and low pay led to increasing dereliction of duty, absence without leave, and desertion. More than 500 soldiers were among the thousands of Albanians who fled to Italy and Greece in 1991. The reduction in conscript service to eighteen months in 1991 exacerbated the serious and growing problem of unemployment among the male draft-age population. In early 1992, the problems of manning the People's Army continued to mount.

Conscript Training

Before 1961 military training relied on the Soviet model. Training manuals and materials were translated from Russian into Albanian. But even though China replaced the Soviet Union as Albania's foreign patron, the Chinese apparently made few basic changes in Albania's military training programs. Most conscripts received considerable physical conditioning, drill, and other basic training in school and through the communist youth organization. This foundation allowed the military to move conscripts rapidly into tactical combat training and small unit exercises. Tactical training typically involved preparation for fighting in defensive positions in the mountainous terrain characteristic of the country's interior. It emphasized physical conditioning, employment of light weapons, and the use of minimal amounts of matériel and other support. At least until 1991, the training program also devoted substantial time to political indoctrination conducted by political officers.

Service within the naval forces traditionally has been a specialty, and many conscripts from Vlorë or Durrës were assigned to the naval forces because of their familiarity with small craft and navigation. As a result, they rarely served their term in the military out of sight of their homes, and because the level of naval deployments and training was low, they remained available for part-time fishing or other work.

In general, the frequent use of conscripts as laborers on economic projects has detracted from military training. They have often been used in the construction of factories, oil refineries, and hydroelectric plants; during harvests; and for land reclamation efforts.

Paramilitary Training

The experience of the resistance to the Italian and German occupations during World War II, in which men, women, and children participated, provided the inspiration for an extensive program of paramilitary training for virtually all segments of the Albanian population. The program, which began at the end of the war, focused on young people from the early 1950s on. Paramilitary training developed to the point that many fifteen- to nineteen-year-old youths could be organized to fight as partisan forces or to operate as auxiliary units during a national emergency. Its main purpose was, however, to provide the armed forces with conscripts in good physical condition and with sufficient basic military training and knowledge to enter a military unit and perform satisfactorily with a minimum of adjustment. The academic year for secondary school and university students traditionally included one month and two months of full-time paramilitary training, respectively. Paramilitary training did not exclude older Albanians, however. Until age fifty, men were obligated to spend twelve days per year in paramilitary training. Women participated for seven days per year until age forty.

Paramilitary training included extensive physical conditioning, close-order drill, hand-to-hand combat, small arms handling, demolition, and tactical exercises applicable to guerrilla operations. It was conducted in secondary schools by military officers assigned to them and also at military units to which the schools were attached for training purposes. Paramilitary programs of the communist youth organizations were similar to those conducted in the secondary schools. Albanian youths carrying rifles and machine guns marched in May Day parades. As many as 200,000 young people participated in paramilitary training each year.

Military Schools

Specialized military schools were essentially scaled-down copies of those in the Soviet Union. Three military schools trained officers for the People's Army or provided advanced professional training for mid-career officers. The Skanderbeg Military School was a secondary school that prepared students to enter the United Higher Officers' School. Students at Skanderbeg were generally sons of party, government, and military leaders. The United Higher Officers' School, formerly named for Enver Hoxha, was the oldest military education institution in the country. According to the APL, it began operating before German occupation forces left the country in 1944 and initiated a formal curriculum in 1945. Its graduates received a university degree and became commissioned officers. The Military Academy, once named for Mehmet Shehu, was an advanced institution offering training equivalent to that of command and staff schools or war colleges in Western military establishments. It provided specialized officer courses for pilots and those serving in artillery units or aboard ship.

Military Budget and the Economy

Assessments of the impact of defense expenditures on Albania's economy traditionally have been hampered by the lack of government statistics on overall economic performance and the Albanian economy's isolation from the international economy. Albania generally appropriated 1 billion leks (for value of the lek—see Glossary) per year for the military budget, or about 5 percent of an estimated late 1980 gross domestic product (GNP—see Glossary) of 20 billion leks. This figure was a relatively modest burden on the economy compared to that borne by other communist countries. However, the absence of reliable statistics made it difficult to calculate this budget as a percentage of total government spending, a common indicator of the priority accorded defense. It likely represented approximately 10 percent of government expenditures. However, some significant costs were probably hidden in nonmilitary elements of the government budget, thus understating the defense effort as a portion of total spending. The low subsistence wages paid to conscripts also provided a downward bias. Given Albania's low standard of living, per capita military expenditures were high when compared with average family earnings, the bulk of which were required to obtain such basic necessities as food, clothing, and housing.

The Albanian Democratic Party has asserted that large defense expenditures during communist rule impoverished Albania. It cited annual drills for military reservists and live-fire exercises for infantry and artillery units as costing Albania 100 million leks, an amount equal to the yearly municipal budget for Tiranë. Moreover, the new coalition government that took office in June 1991, in a move that probably indicated that the military budget had imposed a hardship on the civilian economy, announced an immediate 20-percent reduction in defense spending.

Internal Security

During the period of uninterrupted communist rule from 1944 to 1991, the pervasiveness of repression made it difficult for information on internal developments in Albania to reach the outside world. It was the most closed and isolated society in Europe. The few Western observers who visited the country after World War II were not in a position to see or to judge its internal conditions independently, but their statements concerning the police-state atmosphere in the country indicated that public order was rigidly maintained. It was impossible for visitors to move around the country without escorts, and conversation or interaction with ordinary citizens was inhibited. Local police and internal security forces were in evidence everywhere. Albanian sources published little concerning the internal security situation, and reliable information was lacking beyond infrequent officially approved statements and data that generally covered political crimes deemed threatening to the party or state. However, this situation began to change drastically in 1991, in part because of the efforts of the Albanian Democratic Party, which advocated restructuring the security organs and purging officials who had repressed the population under Hoxha and Alia. In early 1992, officials responsible for preventing or investigating crime were disorganized as a result of political changes in the country and were unsure how to operate effectively. Organizational change in the police and security forces, initiated by the communist-dominated coalition government, also inhibited their effectiveness at least for a time.

Domestic Repression under Hoxha and Alia

Enver Hoxha was one of the last Stalinist leaders in Eastern Europe and continued to employ Stalinist techniques for controlling the population long after most other East European countries had shifted from outright terror and repression to more subtle bureaucratic-authoritarian methods. Western observers believed that no other communist country had as extensive a police and security organization relative to its size as the one that operated in Albania.

Hoxha regarded the security police as an elite group, and it underpinned the power of the ACP and then the APL during the period they dominated Albania's one-party political system. The secret police was instrumental in enabling Hoxha and the communist party to consolidate power after 1944 by conducting a campaign of intimidation and terror against prewar politicians and rival groups. Persecution of these opponents in show trials on charges of treason, conspiracy, subversion, espionage, or anti-Albanian agitation and propaganda became common. From 1948 until the early 1960s, the Ministry of Internal Affairs was involved in the search for real or alleged Yugoslav agents or Titoists in Albania, and the ministry itself was an initial battleground in the purge of Yugoslav influence. Yugoslav control of the Ministry of Internal Affairs ran deep in the years immediately following World War II. Its chief, Koci Xoxe, was part of the pro-Yugoslav faction of the party and a rival to Hoxha. In 1949, however, he was arrested, convicted in a secret trial, and executed.

Hoxha maintained a Stalinist political system even after the communist regimes in the Soviet Union and China had long since moderated their totalitarian or radical excesses. In the last years of Hoxha's life, the Directorate of State Security (Drejtorija e Sigurimit te Shtetit—Sigurimi), increased its political power, perhaps to the extent of supplanting party control. After Hoxha's death, the security forces viewed his successor, Ramiz Alia, and his modest reforms with suspicion. In the late 1980s, they reportedly supported a group of conservatives centered around Hoxha's widow, in opposition to Alia.

Under Hoxha the communist regime essentially ignored internationally recognized standards of human rights. According to a landmark Amnesty International report published in 1984, Albania's human rights record was dismal under Hoxha. The regime denied its citizens freedom of expression, religion, movement, and association although the constitution of 1976 ostensibly guaranteed each of these rights. In fact, the constitution effectively circumscribed the exercise of political liberties that the regime interpreted as contrary to the established socialist order. In addition, the regime tried to deny the population access to information other than that disseminated by the government-controlled media. The secret police routinely violated the privacy of persons, homes, and communications and made arbitrary arrests. The courts ensured that verdicts were rendered from the party's political perspective rather than affording due process to the accused, who were occasionally sentenced without even the formality of a trial.

After Hoxha's death, Alia was apparently unable or unwilling to maintain the totalitarian system of terror, coercion, and repression that Hoxha had employed to maintain his grip on the party and the country. Alia relaxed the most overt Stalinist controls over the population and instructed the internal security structure to use more subtle, bureaucratic-authoritarian mechanisms characteristic of the post-Stalin Soviet Union and East European regimes. He allowed greater contact with the outside world, including eased travel restrictions for Albanians, although the Sigurimi demanded bribes equivalent to six months' salary for the average Albanian to obtain the documents needed for a passport. More foreigners were allowed to visit Albania, and they reported a generally more relaxed atmosphere among the population as well as a less repressive political and antireligious climate. Official sources admitted that social discipline, especially among young Albanians, was breaking down in the late 1980s. The country's youth increasingly refused to accept and even openly rejected the values advanced under the official communist ideology. Moreover, small-scale rebellions were reported more frequently after Hoxha's death. Yet these developments did not alter the regime's exclusive hold on political power after the 1980s.

The dramatic collapse of communist rule in Eastern Europe in 1989 apparently had a devastating effect on the internal social and political situation in Albania despite Alia's efforts to contain it. Massive demonstrations against communist rule followed by liberalization and democratization in Eastern Europe began to affect Albania in 1990. The power of the security police was successfully challenged by massive numbers of largely unorganized demonstrators demanding reforms and democratic elections. Unrest began with demonstrations in Shkodër in January 1990 that forced authorities to declare a state of emergency to quell the protests. Berat workers staged strikes protesting low wages in May. During July 1990, approximately 5,000 Albanians sought refuge on the grounds of foreign embassies in an effort to flee Albania. The security forces reportedly killed hundreds of asylum seekers either in the streets outside foreign compounds or after they were detained, but even such extreme measures did not stanch the unrest.

In September 1990, Alia acceded to the requirements of the Conference on Security and Cooperation in Europe, committing Albania to respect the human rights and political freedoms embodied in the 1975 Helsinki Accords. When students organized demonstrations in December 1990, their demands for political pluralism received widespread support (see Further Moves Toward Democracy, ch. 4). Attempts by riot police to break up the demonstrations failed, and the party's Central Committee, in an extraordinary meeting called by Alia to discuss the growing unrest, decided not to use further force. The following year, the security forces were not in evidence at large political demonstrations and were unable to stop thousands of refugees from boarding ships bound for Italy or from crossing the border into Greece. However, the security forces attempted to maintain control by forcing the authorities to give the People's Army control over the ports of Vlorë, Durrës, Shengjin, and Sarandë. The army was ordered to clear the ports of potential refugees and to establish a blockade around them.

Penal Code

Prior to the reforms of the early 1990s, a politically and ideologically oriented penal code facilitated systematic violations of human rights and ensured the communist party control over all aspects of Albania's political, economic, and cultural life. Article 53 of the 1982 code, for example, broadly defined sabotage as "activity or inactivity to weaken or undermine the operations of the state and the Albanian Party of Labor, the socialist economy, and the organization and administration of the state and society"—a crime punishable by at least ten years' imprisonment or by death. The crime of "fascist, anti-democratic, religious, warmongering, and anti-socialist agitation and propaganda," as defined by Article 55, carried a penalty of three to ten years' imprisonment or, in wartime, not less than ten years' imprisonment or death. Article 47 stipulated a penalty of not less than ten years or death for "flight from the state" or for "refusal to return to the fatherland." The penal code listed a total of thirty-four offenses punishable by death, of which twelve were political and eleven were military. Although individuals accused of criminal behavior theoretically had the right to present a defense, they could not avail themselves of the services of a professional attorney; the private practice of law in Albania had been banned in 1967.

In 1990, following serious and widespread public unrest, steps were taken to liberalize the penal code. The number of offenses punishable by death was reduced from thirty-four to eleven, women were exempted from the death penalty, the maximum prison sentence for "anti-socialist agitation and propaganda" was reduced from twenty-five to ten years, the maximum prison sentence for attempts to leave the country illegally also was reduced from twenty-five to ten years, the legal status of lawyers was restored, and the official ban on religious activity was abolished.

Penal System

The communist regime maintained an extensive system of prisons and labor camps, including six institutions for political prisoners, nine for nonpolitical prisoners, and fourteen where political prisoners served their sentences together with regular criminals. Inmates provided the state's vital mining industry with an inexpensive source of labor. In 1985 there were an estimated 32,000 prisoners in the country.

Conditions in the prisons and labor camps were abysmal. Maltreatment as well as physical and mental torture of political prisoners and other prisoners of conscience were common. Sporadic strikes and rebellions in the labor camps, to which the Sigurimi often responded with military force, resulted in the death of more than 1,000 prisoners as well as the execution of many survivors after they were suppressed.

Many political prisoners were purged party officials and their relatives. Reflecting Hoxha's paranoia, some of them were resentenced without trial for allegedly participating in political conspiracies while in prison. Former inmates reported that they managed to survive their incarceration only through the assistance of relatives who brought them food and money.

Under Alia, several amnesties resulted in the release of nearly 20 percent of the large prison and labor-camp population, although most of those released were prisoners over the age of sixty who had already served long terms. In 1991, for example, the APL attempted to improve its popularity by pushing a sweeping amnesty law for political prisoners through the communist-dominated People's Assembly, and all such prisoners were freed by the middle of the year. The amnesty law provided for the rehabilitation of those incarcerated for political crimes, but not persons convicted of terrorist acts that resulted in deaths or other serious consequences. Specifically, it applied to persons sentenced for agitation and propaganda against the state; participation in illegal political organizations, meetings, or demonstrations; failure to report crimes against the state; slandering or insulting the state; and absence without leave or desertion from military service. It provided for material compensation, including lost wages or pensions, for time spent in prison; for preferential access to housing, education, and employment; and gave compensatory damages to the families of political prisoners who were executed or who died in detention without trial. Finally, it established a commission that included members of the new, independent Association of Former Political Prisoners to investigate atrocities carried out by the state.

Security Forces

Until April 1991, all security and police forces were responsible to the Ministry of Internal Affairs, which also exercised authority over the judicial system and the implementation and enforcement of the country's laws. In January 1991, the minister of internal affairs, Simon Stefani, held both high communist party and government posts as a member of the Politburo and as one of three deputy prime ministers.

Each security or police organization—the Sigurimi, the Frontier Guards, and the People's Police—constituted a separate directorate within the ministry; each had a larger proportion of personnel who were party members than did the armed forces because of the need for political reliability. In the Sigurimi, for example, nearly all serving personnel were believed to be party members. In the Frontier Guards and People's Police, all officers and many other personnel were party members.

The Sigurimi were the security police forces. Organized to protect the party and government system, these forces were responsible for suppressing deviation from communist ideology and for investigating serious crimes on a national scale. Frontier Guards, as their name implied, maintained the security of state borders. The People's Police were the local or municipal police.

In April 1991, shortly after the country's first free elections, the communist-dominated People's Assembly abolished the Ministry of Internal Affairs. It was replaced by a new Ministry of Public Order with authority over the People's Police. In addition, the chairman of a new National Security Committee within the Council of Ministers was given control over the Sigurimi. Both organizations, however, were headed by the same officials who had directed them within the old Ministry of Internal Affairs.

In July 1991, the communist-dominated legislature abolished the Sigurimi and established a new National Information Service (NIS) in its place. It was unclear to Western observers to what extent the new organization would be different from its much-hated predecessor because at least some of its personnel probably had served in the Sigurimi. Only former Sigurimi leaders were excluded from the new NIS. Opponents of the Sigurimi argued that former officers should not be rehired but replaced with new, untainted government employees. The officers, however, argued that the new organization needed experienced investigators who had not violated existing laws or abused their power as Sigurimi officers.

The NIS's stated mission was to enforce the constitution and laws of Albania and the civil rights of its citizens. It was forbidden to conduct unauthorized investigations, and it was required to respect the rights of citizens in every case except instances in which the constitution itself had been violated. Political activities within the NIS were banned.

In 1991 the rate of reported homicides doubled and robberies tripled over the similar period in 1990. Instances of illegal possession and use of firearms were reported. The increase in violent crime

Albanian riot police maintaining order as refuge-seekers return from Italy
Courtesy Charles Sudetic

was viewed so seriously that some citizens believed that social anarchy was overwhelming the state's ability to handle it. The end of the party's monopoly on political power and the curbing of the coercive power of the state's law enforcement mechanism gave many common criminals courage to act. The minister of public order cited a general breakdown in law enforcement and public safety in Albania in 1991. He reported that many crimes were being committed by unemployed individuals, common criminals inadvertently released from prison under political amnesties, and citizens taking revenge on officials of the former communist regime. He blamed many problems of the police on their former cooperation with the Sigurimi in its role of protecting the party and state against the citizens. According to the minister, the police would be depoliticized, and patriotic, legal, and professional training would replace members' former political indoctrination.

When the People's Assembly established the Ministry of Public Order, it placed the Frontier Guards and the Directorate of Prison Administration, both of which had been in the Ministry of Internal Affairs, in the Ministry of People's Defense and the Ministry of Justice, respectively. Shortly thereafter, in an effort to stem the flow of Albanian refugees and growing problems with drug trafficking through Albanian territory, Italy signed a cooperation agreement with Albania under which it would help train and equip the demoralized police and Frontier Guards. Albania sought similar assistance from Finland and Romania and applied to join the International Police Organization (Interpol). The head of the Directorate of Prison Administration pledged to improve physical conditions in Albania's prisons, to terminate routine detention of minors with adults, and to introduce corrective, educational, and recreational programs.

The Directorate of Law and Order, the Directorate of Criminal Police, and the Directorate of Forces for the Restoration of Order—the latter presumably being special riot control units—remained under the control of the Ministry of Public Order. In defense of his decision not to reorganize, the minister of public order cited difficulties in attempting to restructure the police force when crime was increasing rapidly. He also noted that planned cutbacks would reduce police personnel by 30 percent. Many Albanians, however, blamed years of communist dictatorship and poverty for allowing economic conditions to deteriorate to the point where the system was collapsing in a crime wave and local disorder. Some citizens believed that they needed the right to carry arms as protection against increasing violent crime and social anarchy.

Directorate of State Security

The Directorate of State Security, or Sigurimi, which was abolished in July 1991 and replaced by the NIS, celebrated March 20, 1943, as its founding day. Hoxha typically credited the Sigurimi as having been instrumental in his faction's gaining power in Albania over other partisan groups. The People's Defense Division, formed in 1945 from Hoxha's most reliable resistance fighters, was the precursor to the Sigurimi's 5,000 uniformed internal security force. In 1989 the division was organized into five regiments of mechanized infantry that could be ordered to quell domestic disturbances posing a threat to the party leadership. The Sigurimi had an estimated 10,000 officers, approximately 2,500 of whom were assigned to the People's Army. It was organized with both a national headquarters and district headquarters in each of Albania's twenty-six districts.

The mission of the Sigurimi, and presumably its successor, was to prevent revolution and to suppress opposition to the regime. Although groups of Albanian émigrés sought Western support for their efforts to overthrow the communists in the late 1940s and early 1950s, they quickly ceased to be a credible threat to the communist regime because of the effectiveness of the Sigurimi.

The activities of the Sigurimi were directed more toward political and ideological opposition than crimes against persons or property, unless the latter were sufficiently serious and widespread to threaten the regime. Its activities permeated Albanian society to the extent that every third citizen had either served time in labor camps or been interrogated by Sigurimi officers. Sigurimi personnel were generally career volunteers, recommended by loyal party members and subjected to careful political and psychological screening before they were selected to join the service. They had an elite status and enjoyed many privileges designed to maintain their reliability and dedication to the party.

The Sigurimi was organized into sections covering political control, censorship, public records, prison camps, internal security troops, physical security, counterespionage, and foreign intelligence. The political control section's primary function was monitoring the ideological correctness of party members and other citizens. It was responsible for purging the party, government, military, and its own apparatus of individuals closely associated with Yugoslavia, the Soviet Union, or China after Albania broke from successive alliances with each of those countries. One estimate indicated that at least 170 communist party Politburo or Central Committee members were executed as a result of the Sigurimi's investigations. The political control section was also involved in an extensive program of monitoring private telephone conversations. The censorship section operated within the press, radio, newspapers, and other communications media as well as within cultural societies, schools, and other organizations. The public records section administered government documents and statistics, primarily social and economic statistics that were handled as state secrets. The prison camps section was charged with the political reeducation of inmates and the evaluation of the degree to which they posed a danger to society. Local police supplied guards for fourteen prison camps throughout the country. The physical security section provided guards for important party and government officials and installations. The counterespionage section was responsible for neutralizing foreign intelligence operations in Albania as well as for monitoring domestic movements and parties opposed to Albania's communist party. Finally, the foreign intelligence section maintained personnel abroad and at home to obtain intelligence about foreign capabilities and intentions that affected Albania's national security. Its officers occupied cover positions in Albania's foreign diplomatic missions, trade offices, and cultural centers.

In early 1992, information on the organization, responsibilities, and functions of the NIS was not available in Western publications.

Some Western observers believed, however, that many of the officers and leaders of the NIS had served in the Sigurimi and that the basic structures of the two organizations were similar.

Frontier Guards

In 1989 the Frontier Guards included about 7,000 troops organized into battalion-sized formations. Although organized strictly along military lines, the Frontier Guards were subordinate to the Ministry of Internal Affairs until its abolition in April 1991 when they were subordinated to the Ministry of People's Defense. The mission of the Frontier Guards was to protect state borders and to prevent criminals, smugglers, or other infiltrators from crossing them. In the process, they were also charged with stopping Albanians from leaving the country illegally. They were effective in enforcing its closed borders, although some Albanians still managed to escape. During the period of Albania's greatest isolation from its neighbors, the lack of open border crossing points simplified border control. For example, in 1985 Albania opened its first border crossing point with Greece, fourteen years after it had reestablished diplomatic relations with Athens. In 1990, however the Frontier Guards were increasingly less able to prevent illegal crossings by well-armed citizens, who frequently sought refuge in Greece and Yugoslavia.

Personnel for the Frontier Guards generally came from the annual conscription process for military service, but the organization also had career personnel. The Frontier Guards training school was established in 1953 in Tiranë, and its students, as well as conscripted Frontier Guards, were carefully screened to ensure their political reliability.

People's Police

In 1989, the People's Police had five branches: the Police for Economic Objectives, Communications Police, Fire Police, Detention Police, and General Police. The Police for Economic Objectives served as a guard force for state buildings, factories, construction projects, and similar enterprises. The Communications Police guarded Albania's lines of communication, including bridges, railroads, and the telephone and telegraph network. Firefighting was also considered a police function and was carried out by the Fire Police. The Detention Police served as prison and labor camp guards. Finally, the General Police corresponded to the local or municipal police in other countries and attended to traffic regulation and criminal investigations.

On the outskirts of Tiranë, a shepherd uses a bunker to oversee his flock.
Courtesy Fred Conrad

Although the functions of the General Police overlapped with those of the security police to some extent, the General Police operated at the local rather than the national level. However, the headquarters of the General Police in larger towns had internal security sections that coordinated their activities with those of the security police. They maintained records on political dissidents, Albanians living outside their home districts, and foreign visitors and resident aliens. They also monitored the identification cards that Albanian citizens were required to carry. These cards, which contained family and employment information and were required for travel between cities and villages, constituted an effective control over the movement of the population.

Service in the People's Police was usually a three-year obligation, and individuals who had previously served in the armed services were preferred. After 1989, however, detailed information on the operations, staffing, and training of the People's Police was generally not known outside of Albania.

Auxiliary Police

All able-bodied men were required by a 1948 law to spend two months assisting the local police. They served with the People's Police in their localities, wearing police uniforms that were distinguished by a red armband. The Auxiliary Police provided additional manpower for the regular police and also gave a large segment of the population familiarity with, and presumably a more sympathetic understanding of, police activities and problems.

In early 1992, the police and internal security forces were losing the tight control they once held over the population. They, and the regime they supported, were beginning to yield to the impact of the popular, revolutionary forces had that toppled the other communist regimes in Eastern Europe in late 1989 and 1990. Although poorer, more isolated, and more repressed than the peoples of the other East European communist countries, Albanians were beginning to assert their civil and human rights.

* * *

Up-to-date English-language sources on Albania's armed forces and its internal security apparatus are scarce because until 1991 Albania was the most isolated and secretive state in Eastern Europe and in-depth research on these subjects was inhibited. Albania's print and broadcast media provided little information on the country's defense capabilities or policies and even less on its internal security forces. *The History of Albania, from its Origins to the Present Day,* by Stefanaq Pollo and Arben Puto, and *The Encyclopedia of Military History,* by R. Ernest Dupuy and Trevor Dupuy, present historical perspectives on Albania's national security evolution. Klaus Lange's "Albanian Security Policies: Concepts, Meaning, and Realisation," is the best, and perhaps only, scholarly article exclusively dedicated to Albania's national security. F. Stephen Larrabee and Daniel Nelson address Albania's historical and strategic relationships with its neighbors in the Balkans, and Yugoslavia in particular. Elez Biberaj's *Albania: A Socialist Maverick* provides a valuable description of the political fortunes of party officials in the national security apparatus and the impact of the party's changing foreign policies on national security.

The Foreign Broadcast Information Service (FBIS) translations of broadcasts from the official Albanian news agency as well as translations of Yugoslav and Greek broadcasts have been good sources on internal security developments, especially since 1990. FBIS translations of Yugoslav publications on the military and domestic unrest in Albania are worthwhile and probably generally accurate despite Yugoslavia's interest in portraying Albania in an unfavorable light. Louis Zanga, who writes on Albania in *Report on Eastern Europe* for Radio Free Europe/Radio Liberty, occasionally discusses internal security matters. *The Military Balance,* published annually by the International Institute for Strategic Studies, also provides information on the changing organizational structure, size, and equipment of the armed forces over time. (For further information and complete citations, see Bibliography.)

Appendix

Table

Table 1. Metric Conversion Coefficients and Factors

When you know	Multiply by	To find
Millimeters	0.04	inches
Centimeters	0.39	inches
Meters	3.3	feet
Kilometers	0.62	miles
Hectares (10,000 m^2)	2.47	acres
Square kilometers	0.39	square miles
Cubic meters	35.3	cubic feet
Liters	0.26	gallons
Kilograms	2.2	pounds
Metric tons	0.98	long tons
	1.1	short tons
	2,204	pounds
Degrees Celsius (Centigrade)	1.8 and add 32	degrees Fahrenheit

Table 2. Population of Largest Cities and Towns, 1987

City or Town	Population	City or Town	Population
Tiranë	226,000	Berat	40,500
Durrës	78,700	Fier	40,300
Elbasan	78,300	Lushnjë	26,900
Shkodër	76,300	Kavajë	24,200
Vlorë	67,700	Gjirokastër	23,800
Korçë	61,500	Kuçovë	20,600

Source: Based on information from *Vjetari Statistikor i R. P. S. Të Shqipërisë, 1988* (Statistical Yearbook of the People's Socialist Republic of Albania, 1988), Tiranë, 1988, 26–28.

Table 3. Structure of Realized Net Material Product by Sector, Selected Years, 1938–83
(in percentages, using 1981 prices) *

Sector	1938	1950	1960	1970	1980	1983
Agriculture	93.1	73.2	37.6	34.2	32.7	34.1
Industry	3.8	7.0	18.6	28.2	43.6	43.3
Construction	0.8	3.1	6.5	7.1	6.7	7.8
Services	2.3	16.7	37.3	30.5	17.0	14.8
TOTAL	100.0	100.0	100.0	100.0	100.0	100.0

* Net material product—see Glossary.

Source: Based on information from Economist Intelligence Unit, *Country Profile: Bulgaria, Albania, 1990–91,* London, 1990, 37.

Table 4. Key Economic Indicators, 1961–88
(in percentage average annual increase)

	1961–70	1971–80	1981–88
Net material product [1]	7.4	4.6	1.7 [2]
Global social product	8.3	5.4	2.2 [2]
Net material product per capita	4.4	2.2	- 0.3
Gross industrial production	9.8	7.5	2.8
Industrial labor productivity [3]	1.5	1.8	1.3
Gross agricultural production	6.0	3.8	1.5
Agricultural labor productivity [3]	1.0	- 0.2	- 2.0
Freight transportation [4]	9.0	6.7	0.8
Gross investment	8.4	4.9	1.5
Retail sales [5]	5.7	4.6	3.4

[1] Net material product—see Glossary.

[2] Estimated.

[3] Labor productivity is defined as gross production per employee.

[4] Domestic transportation by road, rail, and sea as measured in ton-kilometers.

[5] At current prices.

Sources: Based on information from Per Sandstrom and Örjan Sjöberg, "Albanian Economic Performance: Stagnation in the 1980s," *Soviet Studies* [Glasgow], 43, No. 5, 1991, 937.

Table 5. Net Material Product by Branch of Origin, 1986, 1988, and 1990
(in millions of leks) *

Branch of Origin	1986	1988	1990
Net industrial production	20,128	20,821	20,033
Net agricultural production	8,828	8,376	8,591
Construction	2,861	2,851	2,820
Transportation	971	991	904
Domestic trade	892	848	788
Foreign trade	727	720	777
Other	355	348	365
TOTAL	34,762	34,955	34,278

* For value of the lek—see Glossary.

Source: Based on information from Anders Aslund and Örjan Sjöberg, "Privatization and Transition to a Market Economy in Albania," *Communist Economics and Economic Transformation* [Abingdon, United Kingdom], 4, No. 1, 1992, 137.

Table 6. Structure of Work Force by Sector, Selected Years, 1960–87
(in percentages)

Sector	1960	1970	1980	1985	1987
Agriculture	55.6	52.2	51.4	51.3	52.0
Industry	15.1	19.2	21.8	22.3	22.9
Construction	11.4	9.9	9.1	8.0	7.1
Transportation and communications	2.0	2.3	2.5	2.9	2.9
Trade	5.9	5.9	4.8	4.8	4.6
Education and culture	3.4	4.7	4.6	4.5	4.4
Health	2.7	2.6	3.0	2.8	2.9
Other	3.9	3.2	2.8	3.4	3.2
TOTAL	100.0	100.0	100.0	100.0	100.0

Source: Based on information from *Vjetari Statistikor i R.P.S. Të Shqipërisë, 1988* (Statistical Yearbook of the People's Socialist Republic of Albania, 1988), Tiranë, 1988, 69.

Table 7. Primary Agricultural Output, Selected Years, 1979–88
(in thousands of tons)

Product	1979–81 [1]	1985	1987	1988
Wheat	492	530	565	589
Corn	318	400	320	306
All cereals	916	1,055	1,010	1,024
Potatoes	112	136	135	137
Meat [2]	52	54	55	56
Vegetables (including melons)	193	186	188	188
Tomatoes	44	47	48	48
Fruit (excluding melons)	156	193	210	216
Sugar beets	298	320	360	360
Milk	326	342	346	347
Eggs	10	13.2	13.2	14

[1] Annual averages.

[2] Beef, mutton, and pork.

Source: Based on information from Economist Intelligence Unit, *Country Profile: Bulgaria, Albania, 1990–91,* London, 1990, 40.

Table 8. Structure of Industry, Selected Years, 1950–88
(in percentages)

Product	1950	1960	1970	1980	1985	1988
Food	64.1	43.5	30.4	25.6	25.3	24.7
Oil	18.8	15.5	14.9	9.2	5.7	5.2
Light industry	7.8	21.6	19.9	15.5	16.3	16.2
Wood and paper	6.7	11.2	8.0	5.8	5.8	5.1
Building materials	3.3	4.7	5.6	7.9	6.3	5.8
Engineering	3.1	2.9	7.6	12.5	14.7	14.5
Copper	2.2	0.8	5.2	6.4	7.6	8.8
Chromite	2.1	2.0	1.3	1.7	1.7	2.0
Printing	1.6	0.8	0.9	0.8	0.7	0.7
Coal	1.4	1.6	1.5	1.3	1.7	1.7
Electric power	0.5	1.1	2.0	3.6	2.9	3.1
Chemicals	0.3	0.6	3.3	4.7	5.5	5.9
Glass and ceramies	—	0.2	0.6	0.8	0.8	0.9
Iron and metallurgy	n.a.	1.3	2.2	3.0	3.4	3.8
Other	1.5	0.2	0.3	1.1	1.2	1.5
TOTAL *	100.0	100.0	100.0	100.0	100.0	100.0

—means negligible.

n.a.—not available.

* Figures may not add to 100 percent because of rounding or because of unverified information in source.

Source: Based on information from *Vjetari Statistikor i R.P.S. Të Shqipërisë, 1988* (Statistical Yearbook of the People's Socialist Republic of Albania, 1988), Tiranë, 1988, 82.

Table 9. Output of Main Industrial Products, 1980, 1985, and 1988
(in thousands of tons unless otherwise indicated)

Product	1980	1985	1988
Electric power (in millions of kilowatt-hours)	3,717	3,147	3,984
Blister copper	9.8	11	15
Copper wire and cable	5.7	9.4	116
Carbonic ferrochrome	12.2	11.9	38.7
Metallurgical coke	173	250	291
Rolled wrought steel	96	107	96
Phosphate fertilizer	150	157	165
Ammonium nitrate	109	95	96
Urea	88	78	77
Sulfuric acid	72	73	81
Caustic soda	25	29	31
Soda ash	23	22	22
Machinery and equipment (in millions of leks) *	350	465	496
Spare parts (in millions of leks) *	327	407	493
Cement	826	642	746
Bricks and tiles (in millions of pieces)	294	295	319
Refractory bricks (in millions of pieces)	4.8	28	30
Heavy cloth (in millions of meters)	12.5	12.3	11.3
Knitwear (in millions of pieces)	9.8	11	12.1
Footwear (in thousands of pairs)	4,735	4,800	5,396
Television receivers (in thousands)	21	21.3	16.5
Radio receivers (in thousands)	8	16	25
Cigarettes (in millions of pieces)	4,950	5,348	5,310
Soap and detergent	14.7	18.2	21.5

* For value of the lek—see Glossary.

Source: Based on information from *The Europa World Year Book, 1991,* 1, London, 1991, 301.

Table 10. Production of Energy and Mineral Ores, Selected Years, 1980–88
(in thousands of tons unless otherwise indicated)

Product	1980	1984	1985	1986	1987	1988
Energy						
Coal	1,418	2,010	2,100	2,230	2,130	2,184
Crude oil	1,900 *	1,300 *	1,200 *	1,400 *	1,200	1,200 *
Electricity (in giga-watt-hours)	3,717	3,800	3,147	5,070	4,200 *	3,984
Ores						
Chromite	1,004	960	1,111	1,207	1,080	1,109
Copper	769	1,007	989	1,024	1,160	1,087
Ferronickel	597	1,080	905	n.a.	970	1,067

n.a.—not available.
* Estimated.

Sources: Based on information from Per Sandstrom and Örjan Sjöberg, "Albanian Economic Performance: Stagnation in the 1980s," *Soviet Studies* [Glasgow], 43, No. 5, 1991, 941.

Table 11. Major Trading Partners, 1982–87
(in millions of United States dollars)

Country	1982	1983	1984	1985	1986	1987
Imports						
Yugoslavia	74	50	43	42	46	37 *
Italy	42	28	27	15	9	26
Bulgaria	23	n.a.	n.a.	n.a.	n.a.	n.a.
Romania	19	27	20	22	23 *	25 *
West Germany	17	17	15	13	21	16
France	16	8	12	15	7	6
Poland	15	15	11	12 *	12 *	13 *
Greece	13	18	10	3	56	14 *
Hungary	12	9	8	10	11	13 *
China	4	7	2	6	13	19 *
United States	3	4	3	4	4	2
Britain	n.a.	n.a.	2	n.a.	n.a.	n.a.
Exports						
Yugoslavia	74	38	46	41	47	49
West Germany	36	22	14	16	18	16
Italy	32	27	22	20	21	34
Romania	27	30	25	27	28 *	31 *
Bulgaria	23	n.a.	n.a.	n.a.	n.a.	n.a.
Poland	18	18	12	13 *	14 *	15 *
United States	17	4	9	12	5	3
Greece	12	8	7	9	6	4 *
Hungary	11	10	8	10	14	13

Table 11.—Continued

Country	1982	1983	1984	1985	1986	1987
Exports (continued)						
France	9	15	28	17	6	8
Britain	8	5	6	7	4	4
China	n.a.	4	3	10	9	15

n.a.—not available.
* Estimated.

Source: Based on information from Economist Intelligence Unit, *Country Profile: Bulgaria, Albania, 1990–91,* London, 1990, 47; and International Monetary Fund, *Direction of Trade Statistics,* Washington, n.d.

Table 12. Major Imports, Selected Years, 1970–88
(in percentages)

Product	1970	1975	1980	1985	1988
Capital goods	32.8	45.2	21.7	25.1	31.5
Spare parts	7.2	3.8	2.5	5.3	4.8
Fuels and minerals	21.6	21.4	35.8	27.0	23.1
Chemicals	9.4	8.3	14.9	14.1	12.7
Building materials	1.8	0.9	2.6	1.4	0.1
Nonedible agricultural products	14.7	11.3	13.5	12.8	13.5
Foodstuffs	3.4	5.0	4.0	8.3	8.1
Consumer goods	7.7	4.1	5.0	6.0	6.2
TOTAL *	100.0	100.0	100.0	100.0	100.0

* Figures may not add to total because of rounding.

Source: Based on information from Gramoz Pashko, "The Albanian Economy at the Beginning of the 1990s," in Örjan Sjöberg and Michael L. Wyzan (eds.), *Economic Change in the Balkan States: Albania, Bulgaria, Romania, and Yugoslavia,* London, 1991, 137.

Table 13. Major Exports, Selected Years, 1970–88
(in percentages)

Product	1970	1975	1980	1985	1988
Fuels	27.4	25.7	29.0	15.1	7.9
Electric power	n.a.	2.9	9.1	7.8	7.3
Minerals and metals	31.1	26.9	24.5	31.5	39.8
Chemicals	1.2	0.3	1.2	0.7	0.8
Building materials	0.1	0.7	1.5	1.0	1.5
Nonedible agricultural products	13.1	9.4	10.4	14.6	16.1
Processed foods	15.1	15.5	8.4	10.8	8.7
Unprocessed foods	4.4	6.3	5.4	8.1	8.2
Consumer goods	7.6	12.3	10.5	10.7	9.7
TOTAL *	100.0	100.0	100.0	100.0	100.0

n.a.—not available.
* Figures may not add to total because of rounding.

Source: Based on information from Gramoz Pashko, "The Albanian Economy at the Beginning of the 1990s," in Örjan Sjöberg and Michael L. Wyzan (eds.), *Economic Change in the Balkan States: Albania, Bulgaria, Romania, and Yugoslavia*, London, 1991, 137.

Bibliography

Chapter 1

Amery, Julian. *Sons of the Eagle: A Study in Guerrilla War.* London: Macmillan, 1948.

Biberaj, Elez. *Albania: A Socialist Maverick.* Boulder, Colorado: Westview Press, 1990.

Bury, J.B. *A History of Greece to the Death of Alexander the Great.* London: Macmillan, 1956.

Djilas, Milovan. *Conversations with Stalin.* New York: Harcourt, Brace, and World, 1962.

Durham, M.E. *High Albania.* Boston: Beacon Press, 1985.

Fischer-Galati, Stephen. *Eastern Europe in the 1980s.* Boulder, Colorado: Westview Press, 1981.

Frasheri, Kristo. *The History of Albania.* Tiranë: Naim Frasheri State Publishing House, 1964.

Freedman, Robert Owen. *Economic Warfare in the Communist Bloc: A Study of Soviet Economic Pressure Against Yugoslavia, Albania, and Communist China.* New York: Praeger, 1970.

Gjecov, Shtjefen. *The Code of Leke Dukagjini.* New York: Gjonlekaj, 1989.

Glenny, Misha. *The Rebirth of History.* London: Penguin Books, 1990.

Griffith, William E. *Albania and the Sino-Soviet Rift.* Cambridge: MIT Press, 1963.

Hamm, Harry. *Albania: China's Beachhead in Europe.* New York: Praeger, 1963.

Hasluck, M. *The Unwritten Law of Albania.* Cambridge: Cambridge University Press, 1954.

Horvat, Branko. *Kosovsko pitanje.* Zagreb: Globus, 1989.

Hoxha, Enver. *The Titoites.* Tiranë: 8 Nëntori, 1982.

______. *With Stalin.* Tiranë: 8 Nëntori, 1981.

Jelavich, Barbara. *History of the Balkans.* (2 vols.) Cambridge: Cambridge University Press, 1983.

Konitza, Faik. "Albania: The Rock Garden of Southeastern Europe." Pages 8–28 in G.M. Panarity (ed.), *Albania: The Rock Garden of Southeastern Europe and Other Essays.* Boston: Pan-Albanian Federation of America, 1957.

Lampe, John R., and Marvin R. Jackson. *Balkan Economic History, 1550–1950.* Bloomington: Indiana University Press, 1982.

Lendvai, Paul. *Eagles in Cobwebs: Nationalism and Communism in the*

Balkans. Garden City, New York: Doubleday, 1969.

Logoreci, Anton. *The Albanians: Europe's Forgotten Survivors*. Boulder, Colorado: Westview Press, 1977.

Marmullaku, Ramadan. *Albania and the Albanians*. Hamden, New York: Archon Books, 1975.

Ostrogorski, Georgije. *Istorija Vizantije*. Belgrade: Prosveta, 1969.

Page, Bruce, David Leitch, and Phillip Knightley. *The Philby Conspiracy*. Garden City, New York: Doubleday, 1968.

Pano, Nicholas C. *The People's Republic of Albania*. Baltimore, Maryland: Johns Hopkins Press, 1968.

Pipa, Arshi. "The Political Culture of Hoxha's Albania." Pages 435–64 in Tariq Ali (ed.), *The Stalinist Legacy*. London: Penguin Books, 1984.

Prifti, Peter R. *Socialist Albania since 1944: Domestic and Foreign Developments*. Cambridge: MIT Press, 1978.

Rothschild, Joseph. *East Central Europe Between the Two World Wars*. Seattle: University of Washington Press, 1974.

Seton-Watson, Hugh. *The East European Revolution*. New York: Praeger, 1956.

Singleton, Fred. *A Short History of the Yugoslav Peoples*. Cambridge: Cambridge University Press, 1985.

Skendi, Stavro, et al. (eds.). *Albania*. New York: Praeger: 1956.

______. *The Albanian National Awakening*. Princeton: Princeton University Press, 1967.

Stickney, Edith Pierpont. *Southern Albania or Northern Epirus in European International Affairs, 1912–1923*. Stanford, California: Stanford University Press, 1926.

Swire, Joseph. *Albania: The Rise of a Kingdom*. London: Williams and Norgate, 1929.

Wolff, Robert Lee. *The Balkans in Our Time*. Cambridge: Harvard University Press, 1956.

Chapter 2

"Albania: Introductory Survey." Pages 284–97 in *The Europa World Year Book, 1993*. London: Europa, 1993.

Andrejevich, Milan. "Kosovo: A Precarious Balance Between Stability and Civil War," Radio Free Europe/Radio Liberty, *Report on Eastern Europe* [Munich], 2, No. 42, October 18, 1991, 23–29.

______. "Serbia Cracks Down on Kosovo," Radio Free Europe/Radio Liberty, *Report on Eastern Europe* [Munich], 1, No. 30, July 27, 1990, 48–51.

Battiata, Mary. "Albania's Post-Communist Anarchy," *Washington Post,* March 21, 1992, A1, A18.

Begeja, Ksanthipi. *The Family in the People's Socialist Republic of Albania.* Tiranë: 8 Nëntori, 1984.

Bërxholi, Arqile, and Perikli Qiriazi. *Albania: A Geographical View.* Tiranë: 8 Nëntori, 1986.

Biberaj, Elez. *Albania: A Socialist Maverick.* Boulder, Colorado: Westview Press, 1990.

Binder, David. "Albanian Exile Writer Sees Reform," *New York Times,* December 6, 1990.

______. "Albanians Expose High Living by Ex-Rulers," *New York Times,* August 25, 1991, A12.

______. "In the New Albania, a Whole New Brand of Chaos," *New York Times,* October 8, 1991, A7.

Broun, Janice A. *Conscience and Captivity: Religion in Eastern Europe.* Washington: Ethics and Public Policy Center, 1988.

______."The Status of Christianity in Albania," *Journal of Church and State,* 28, Winter 1986, 43-60.

Cikuli, Zisa. *Health Service in the PSR of Albania.* Tiranë: 8 Nëntori, 1984.

Encyclopaedia Britannica, 1. Chicago: Encyclopaedia Britannica, 1975.

______. *The Encyclopedia of Military History.* (Eds., R. Ernest Dupuy and Trevor Dupuy.) New York: Harper and Row, 1970.

Fowler, Brenda. "Albania's Economic Fall Devastates Hospitals," *New York Times,* March 8, 1992, 11.

Gjinushi, Skender. "The Educational Reform in Albania Is Connected with the New Requirements of the Time," *Albania Today* [Tiranë], 5, No. 114, 1990, 43-45.

______. "We Are Advancing Towards Compulsory Secondary Education for All," *New Albania* [Tiranë], No. 1, 1990, 2-3.

Ikonomi, Ilir. "Religion Survives 24 Years Within Hearts of Albanians," *Washington Times,* December 26, 1991, A10.

Kamm, Henry. "Albania's Clerics Lead a Rebirth," *New York Times,* March 27, 1992, A3.

Kolsti, John. "Albanianism: From the Humanists to Hoxha." Pages 15-48 in George Klein and Milan J. Reban (eds.), *The Politics of Ethnicity in Eastern Europe.* New York: Columbia University Press for East European Monographs, Boulder, Colorado, 1981.

______. "From Courtyard to Cabinet: The Political Emergence of Albanian Women." Pages 138-51 in Sharon L. Wolchik and Alfred G. Meyer (eds.), *Women, State, and Party in Eastern Europe.* Durham, North Carolina: Duke University Press, 1985.

Minnesota Lawyers International Human Rights Committee. *Human Rights in the People's Socialist Republic of Albania.* Minneapolis: 1990.

Moore, Patrick. "Noisy Neighbors in the European House: Albanian-Greek Relations," Radio Free Europe/Radio Liberty, *Report on Eastern Europe* [Munich], 1, No. 4, January 26, 1990, 1-3.

Perry, Duncan M., and Louis Zanga. "Minorities: An Overview," Radio Free Europe/Radio Liberty, *Report on Eastern Europe* [Munich], 2, No. 50, December 13, 1991, 3-4.

Pipa, Arshi. *The Politics of Language in Socialist Albania.* New York: Columbia University Press for East European Monographs, Boulder, Colorado, 1989.

Sjöberg, Örjan. *Rural Change and Development in Albania.* Boulder, Colorado: Westview Press, 1991.

Skendi, Stavro. *Balkan Cultural Studies.* New York: Columbia University Press for East European Monographs, Boulder, Colorado, 1980.

The Statesman's Year-Book, 1989-1990. (Ed., John Paxton.) New York: St. Martin's Press, 1989.

Sudetic, Charles. "The Society and Its Environment." Pages 201-87 in Glenn Curtis (ed.), *Yugoslavia: A Country Study.* Washington: GPO, 1992.

United States. Central Intelligence Agency. *The World Factbook, 1991.* Washington: 1991.

______. Department of State. *Country Report on Human Rights Practices for 1990.* (Report submitted to United States Congress, 102d, 1st Session. House of Representatives, Committee on Foreign Affairs, and Senate, Committee on Foreign Relations.) Washington: GPO, February 1991.

Vejsiu, Ylli. "On the Demographic Development of National Minorities in Albania," *New Albania* [Tiranë], No. 4, 1990, 4.

______. "The Vitality of a Population," *New Albania* [Tiranë], No. 6, 1990, 14-15.

Vichniac, Isabelle. "La grande misère des enfants albanais," *Le Monde* [Paris], No. 193, November 1991, 3.

Vjetari Statistikor i R.P.S. Të Shqipërisë, 1988 (Statistical Yearbook of the People's Socialist Republic of Albania, 1988). Tiranë: Komisioni i Planit Të Shtetit, Drejtoria e Statistikës, 1988.

"Yugoslavia: Introductory Survey." Pages 3225-46 in *The Europa World Year Book, 1993.* London: Europa, 1993.

Zanga, Louis. "Aid Stepped Up from Italy and Elsewhere," Radio Free Europe/Radio Liberty, *Report on Eastern Europe* [Munich], 2, No. 37, September 13, 1991, 1-4.

______. "Albania Moves Closer to the Islamic World," *RFE/RL Research Report* [Munich], 2, No. 7, February 12, 1993, 28-31.

______. "Albania Reduced to Total Dependence on Foreign Food Aid," *RFE/RL Research Report* [Munich], 1, No. 8, February 21, 1992, 46-48.

______. "The Defection of Ismail Kadare," Radio Free Europe/Radio Liberty, *Report on Eastern Europe* [Munich], 1, No. 47, November 23, 1990, 1-5.

______. "The Woeful State of Schools," Radio Free Europe/Radio Liberty, *Report on Eastern Europe* [Munich], 2, No. 41, October 11, 1991, 1-3.

(Various issues of the followings periodicals were also used in the preparation of this chapter: *Albania Today* [Tiranë] and *New Albania* [Tiranë].)

Chapter 3

Albania. Chamber of Commerce. *Guide to the Albanian Foreign Trade Enterprises*. Tiranë: n.d.

______. *Law on the Sanctioning and Protection of Private Property, Free Initiative on Independent Private Activities, and Privatization: Republic of Albania, People's Assembly.* (Law No. 7512.) August 10, 1991.

______. *On Development of Private Activity.* (Decision No. 138.) March 3, 1991.

______. *On Permission and Protection of Private Ownership and Private Activities.* (Decree No. 7476.) March 3, 1991.

"Albania." Pages 69-96 in *Eastern Europe and the Commonwealth of Independent States*. London: Europa, 1992.

"Albania and Its Chrome," Radio Free Europe/Radio Liberty, *RAD Background Report* [Munich], No. 178, December 8, 1986.

"Albania Moving Along, But Slowly," Radio Free Europe/Radio Liberty, *Report on Eastern Europe,* 2, No. 1, January 5, 1990, 4.

"Albanian Chrome Resources Luring Western Investment," *American Metal Market,* 98, No. 39, February 26, 1990, 4.

"Albania's New Five-Year Plan Directives," Radio Free Europe/Radio Liberty, *RAD Background Report* [Munich], No. 106, July 28, 1986.

"Albanie," *Le courrier des pays de l'est* [Paris], Nos. 309-11, August-October 1986, 5-17.

"Alia Speaks Openly about Albania's Shortage of Food and Goods," Radio Free Europe/Radio Liberty, *RAD Background Report* [Munich], No. 235, November 23, 1988.

Aslund, Anders, and Örjan Sjöberg. "Privatization and Transition to a Market Economy in Albania," *Communist Economies and Economic Transformation* [Abingdon, United Kingdom], 4, No. 1, 1992, 135–50.

Bërxholi, Arqile, and Perikli Qiriazi. *Albania: A Geographical View.* Tiranë: 8 Nëntori, 1986.

Biberaj, Elez. *Albania: A Socialist Maverick.* Boulder, Colorado: Westview Press, 1990.

Bland, William. *Albania.* Oxford: Clio Press, 1988.

Business International. *Doing Business with Eastern Europe.* (A Business International European Research Report.) Geneva: 1972.

Calmes, Albert. *The Economic and Financial Situation in Albania.* (Annex to the Report Presented to the Council by the Financial Committee on Its Eighth Session.) Geneva: Kundig, 1922.

"Capitalist Ideas Mooted," Radio Free Europe/Radio Liberty, *Report on Eastern Europe,* 2, No. 37, September 14, 1990, 1.

Deutche Bank Research. "Albania: Economic and Social Chaos Speeds up Change of Course," *Focus: Eastern Europe* [Frankfurt am Main], No, 44, April 13, 1992, 1–4.

Economic Change in the Balkan States: Albania, Bulgaria, Romania and Yugoslavia. London: Pinter, 1991.

"L' économie albanaise en 1986: le recentrage," *Le courrier des pays de l'est* [Paris], No. 320, July–August 1987, 57–64.

"L' économie albanaise en 1988: priorité à l'agriculture," *Le courrier des pays de l'est* [Paris], No. 340, May 1989, 64–70.

Economist Intelligence Unit. *Country Profile: Bulgaria, Albania, 1990–91.* London, 1990.

______. *Country Report: Albania* [London], No. 4, 1989.

______. *Country Report: Romania, Bulgaria, Albania* [London], No. 2, 1993, 39–47.

"Edge of the Abyss," *Economist* [London], December 14, 1991, 36.

The Europa World Year Book, 1991, London: Europa, 1991.

Evans, John. "Secretive Albania Going Plastic," *American Banker,* 155, No. 204, October 19, 1990, 10.

Freedman, Robert Owen. *Economic Warfare in the Communist Bloc: A Study of Soviet Economic Pressure Against Yugoslavia, Albania, and Communist China.* New York: Praeger, 1970.

Geco, Pandi. *Albania: A Physical and Economic Survey.* (Trans.) New York: CCM Information, n.d. originally published as *Shqipëria, pamje fiziko-ekonomike.* Tiranë: 1959.

Gianaris, Nicholas V. *The Economies of the Balkan Countries.* New York: Praeger, 1982.

Griffith, William E. *Albania and the Sino-Soviet Rift.* Cambridge: MIT Press, 1963.

Harrison, Joseph W. "Albania Begins the Long Road Back from Serfdom: Mineral Resources Might Pave the Road to the West, with Contributions from Tourism and Food Processing," *Business America,* 113, No. 2, January 27, 1992, 12.

"Heavy Industry in Tiny Balkan State Causing Serious Pollution, Sources Say," *International Environment Reporter,* March 1990, 106.

Hutchings, Raymond. "Albanian Industrialization: Widening Divergence from Stalinism." In Roland Schönfeld et al. (eds.), "Industrialisierung und gesellschaftlicher Wandel in Südosteuropa." (Südosteuropa-Studien, No. 42.) Munich: Südosteuropa-Gesellschaft, 1989.

International Monetary Fund. *Direction of Trade Statistics* (annuals 1981 through 1991).

Jelavich, Barbara. *History of the Balkans.* (2 vols.) Cambridge: Cambridge University Press, 1983.

Kane, Ted. "Albania: Contentment," *Third World Week,* March 23, 1990, 26–27.

Kaser, Michael. "Albania under and after Enver Hoxha." Pages 1–21 in United States Congress, 99th, 2d Session, Joint Economic Committee (ed.), *East European Economies: Slow Growth in the 1980s.* (Country Studies in Eastern Europe and Yugoslavia, 3.) Washington: GPO, 1986.

Lampe, John R., and Marvin R. Jackson. *Balkan Economic History, 1550–1950.* Bloomington: Indiana University Press, 1982.

Lange, Klaus. *Die Agrarfrage in der Politik der Partei der Arbeit Albaniens.* Munich: Trofenik, 1981.

Lhomel, Edith. "L'économie albanaise en 1990–1991: la véritable mesure d'un échec," *Le courrier des pays de l'est* [Paris], No. 362, September 1991, 62–76.

"New Economic Ideas," Radio Free Europe/Radio Liberty, *Report on Eastern Europe,* 3, No. 2, January 11, 1991, 8.

O'Donnell, Timothy S., et al. (eds.). *World Economic Data.* Santa Barbara, California: ABC–CLIO, 1991.

Pano, Nicholas C.. *The People's Republic of Albania.* Baltimore: Johns Hopkins Press, 1968.

Pashko, Gramoz. "The Albanian Economy at the Beginning of the 1990s." Pages 128–46 in Örjan Sjöberg and Michael L. Wyzan (eds.). *Economic Change in the Balkan States: Albania, Bulgaria, Romania, and Yugoslavia.* London: Pinter, 1991.

Prifti, Peter. *Socialist Albania since 1944: Domestic and Foreign Developments.* Cambridge: MIT Press, 1978.

Rabchevsky, George A. "Geology and Chromite Industry of Albania," *Earth Science,* 33, Autumn 1980, 172.

Reed, Carol. "Investors Help Albania Make Modest Steps Toward Free Enterprise," *Washington Post,* August 13, 1991, C3.

Russ, Wolfgang. *Der Entwicklungsweg Albaniens. Ein Beitrag zum Konzept autozentrierter Entwicklung.* Königstein, West Germany: Verlag Anton Hain, 1979.

Sandstrom, Per, and Örjan Sjöberg. "Albanian Economic Performance: Stagnation in the 1980s," *Soviet Studies* [Glasgow], 43, No. 5, 1991, 931–47.

Schnytzer, Adi. "Albania: The Purge of Stalinist Economic Ideology." Pages 44–61 in Ian Jeffries (ed.), *Industrial Reform in Socialist Countries: From Restructuring to Revolution.* Aldershot, United Kingdom: Elgar, 1992.

______. *Stalinist Economic Strategy in Practice: The Case of Albania.* Oxford: Oxford University Press, 1982.

Sjöberg, Örjan. "A Contribution to the Geography of Hydro-Electric Power Generation in Albania," *Osterreichische Osthefte* [Vienna], 29, No. 1, 1987, 5–27.

______. *Rural Change and Development in Albania.* Boulder, Colorado: Westview Press, 1991.

Sjöberg, Örjan, and Per Sandstrom. *The Albanian Statistical Abstract of 1988: Heralding a New Era?* (Working Papers, No. 2.) Uppsala, Sweden: Department of Soviet and East European Studies, Uppsala University, 1989.

Skendi, Stavro, et al. (eds.). *Albania.* New York: Praeger, 1956.

"Stagnation persistante de l'économie albanaise en 1987," *Le courrier des pays de l'est* [Paris], No. 330, July–August 1988, 67–71.

Steiger, Cyrill. "Albania's Unresolved National Question," *Swiss Review of World Affairs* [Zurich], No. 5, May 1992, 23–24.

______. "Albania: Up from Misery," *Swiss Review of World Affairs* [Zurich], No. 7, July 1993, 11–12.

United States. Department of State. Foreign Service Institute. *A Reader's Guide to Albania.* Washington: 1990.

Vjetari Statistikor i R.P.S. Të Shqipërisë, 1988. (Statistical Yearbook of the People's Socialist Republic of Albania, 1988.) Tiranë: Komisioni i Planit Të Shtetit, Drejtoria e Statistikës, 1988.

Vjetari Statistikor i R.P.S. Të Shqipërisë, 1989. (Statistical Yearbook of the People's Socialist Republic of Albania, 1989). Tiranë: Komisioni i Planit Të Shtetit, Drejtoria e Statistikës, 1989.

Wildermuth, Andreas. *Die Krise der albanischen Landwirtschaft. Losungsversuche der Partei- und Staatsfuhrung unter Ramiz Alia.* Neuried bei München, West Germany: Hieronymus, 1989.

Wolff, Robert Lee. *The Balkans in Our Time.* Cambridge: Harvard University Press, 1956.

(Various issues of the following periodicals were also used in the preparation of this chapter: *Business East Europe; Business International; The Christian Science Monitor;* and Foreign Broadcast Information Service, *Daily Report.*)

Chapter 4

Artisien, Patrick F.R. "Albania after Hoxha," *SAIS Review,* 6, No. 1, Winter-Spring 1986, 159-68.

Biberaj, Elez. *Albania: A Socialist Maverick.* Boulder, Colorado: Westview Press, 1990.

______. "Albania at the Crossroads," *Problems of Communism,* 40, September-October 1991, 1-16.

______. *Kosovo: The Balkan Powder Keg.* London: Research Institute for the Study of Conflict and Terrorism, 1993.

Commission on Security and Cooperation in Europe. *Report on the United States Helsinki Commission Delegation Visit to Hungary, Yugoslavia and Albania.* Washington: GPO, 1991.

Logoreci, Anton. *The Albanians: Europe's Forgotten Survivors.* Boulder, Colorado: Westview Press, 1977.

Marmullaku, Ramadan. *Albania and the Albanians.* Hamden, New York: Archon Books, 1975.

Myrdal, Jan, and Gun Kessle. *Albania Defiant.* New York: Monthly Review Press, 1976.

Prifti, Peter R. *Socialist Albania since 1944.* Cambridge: MIT Press, 1978.

Staar, Richard F. "People's Socialist Republic of Albania." Pages 1-31 in Richard F. Staar (ed.), *Communist Regimes in Eastern Europe.* Stanford, California: Hoover Institution Press, 1988.

Stavrou, Nikolaos A. "Albania: The Domino That Refuses to Fall," *Mediterranean Quarterly,* 1, No. 2, Spring 1990, 25-41.

United States. Department of State. *Country Reports on Human Rights Practices for 1990.* (Report submitted to United States Congress, 102d, 1st Session. House of Representatives, Committee on Foreign Affairs, and Senate, Committee on Foreign Relations.) Washington: GPO, February 1991.

______. Department of State. Bureau of Public Affairs. *Albania: Background Notes.* (Department of State Publication No. 8217.) Washington: GPO, 1986.

Zanga, Louis. "Albania: Democratic Revival and Social Upheaval," *RFE/RL Research Report* [Munich], 2, No. 1, January 1, 1993, 75-77.

———. "Advocates of Democracy in Albania," Radio Free Europe/Radio Liberty, *Report on Eastern Europe* [Munich], 1, No. 25, June 22, 1990, 1–4.
———. "Albania and Turkey Forge Closes Ties," *RFE/RL Research Report* [Munich], 2, No. 11, March 12, 1993, 30–33.
———. "The Albanian Democratic Party," Radio Free Europe/Radio Liberty, *Report on Eastern Europe* [Munich], 2, No. 9, March 1, 1991, 1–6.
———. "Albanian-Greek Relations Reach a Low Point," *RFE/RL Research Report* [Munich], 1, No. 14, April 10, 1992, 18–21.
———. "Albanian President Defends His First Year in Office," *RFE/RL Research Report* [Munich], 2, No. 29, July 16, 1993, 23–26.
———. "Albania's New Path," Radio Free Europe/Radio Liberty, *Report on Eastern Europe* [Munich], 1, No. 24, June 15, 1990, 1–5.
———. "Cabinet Changes in Albania," *RFE/RL Research Report* [Munich], 2, No. 19, May 7, 1993, 14–16.
———. "Central Committee Proposals for Reform," Radio Free Europe/Radio Liberty, *Report on Eastern Europe* [Munich], 1, No. 9, March 2, 1990, 1–3.
———. "The Conflict Escalates," Radio Free Europe/Radio Liberty, *Report on Eastern Europe* [Munich], 2, No. 11, March 15, 1991, 1–4.
———. "A Crisis of Confidence," Radio Free Europe/Radio Liberty, *Report on Eastern Europe* [Munich], 2, No. 16, April 19, 1991, 1–4.
———. "Daunting Tasks for Albania's New Government," *RFE/RL Research Report* [Munich], 1, No. 21, May 22, 1992, 11–17.
———. "A Progress Report on Changes in Albania," Radio Free Europe/Radio Liberty, *Report on Eastern Europe* [Munich], 1, No. 16, April 20, 1990, 1–3.
———. "Ramiz Alia under Great Pressure," Radio Free Europe/Radio Liberty, *Report on Eastern Europe* [Munich], 2, No. 8, February 22, 1991, 1–4.

Chapter 5

Amnesty International. *Albania: Political Imprisonment and the Law.* London: 1984.
Austin, Robert. "What Albania Adds to the Balkan Stew," *Orbis,* 37, No. 2, Spring 1993, 259–79.

Biberaj, Elez. *Albania: A Socialist Maverick.* Boulder, Colorado: Westview Press, 1990.

The Encyclopedia of Military History (Eds., R. Ernest Dupuy and Trevor Dupuy.) New York: Harper and Row, 1970.

Foreign Broadcast Information Service—FBIS (Washington). The following items are from the FBIS series:

Daily Report: East Europe.

"Albanians Cross Yugoslav Border Illegally." (FBIS-EEU-90-131, July 9, 1990, 24.).

"Army under Surveillance." (FBIS-EEU-90-026, February 7, 1990, 8-9.).

"ATA Carries Profiles of New Ministers." (FBIS-EEU-90-133, July 11, 1990, 3.).

"Defense Minister: Army Size Must Be Cut." (FBIS-EEU-92-082, April 28, 1992, 2.).

"Four Armed Albanians Surrender in Yugoslavia." (FBIS-EEU-90-017, January 25, 1990, 3.).

"Kico Mustaqi Speaks to Army Veterans." (FBIS-EEU-90-180, September 17, 1990, 4.).

"Massacre Allegedly Took Place in Tirana at the Beginning of July." (FBIS-EEU-90-173, September 6, 1990, 1.).

"Minister Mustaqi Speaks on Anniversary of Navy." (FBIS-EEU-90-160, August 17, 1990.).

"National Army Youth Aktiv Holds Its Proceedings." (FBIS-EEU-90-173, September 6, 1990, 1-2.).

"A Principle Turned Upside Down—On a Proposal for the Draft Constitution in the Newspaper Rilindja Demokratike." (FBIS-EEU-91-019, January 29, 1991, 4-5.).

"Revolts in Albania." (FBIS-EEU-90-010, January 16, 1990, 11-12.).

"Statement of the Council of Ministers of the PSRA on Albania's Participation in the CSCE." (FBIS-EEU-90-180, September 17, 1990, 1.).

Jane's All the World's Aircraft, 1990-91. (Ed., Mark Lambert.) Coulsdon, United Kingdom: Jane's, 1990.

Jane's Armour and Artillery, 1989-90. (Ed., Christopher F. Foss.) Coulsdon, United Kingdom: Jane's, 1989.

Jane's Fighting Ships, 1990-91. (Ed., Richard Sharpe.) Coulsdon, United Kingdom: Jane's, 1990.

Joint Publications Research Service—JPRS (Washington). The following items are from the JPRS series:

East Europe Report.

"Democracy and Public Order," *Zëri i Rinise* [Tiranë], August 3, 1991. (JPRS-EER-91-130, August 30, 1991, 1-5.).

''Eleven Years Lost in Albanian Prisons, *Svenska Dagbladet* [Stockholm], March 24, 1991. (JPRS-EER-91-060, May 6, 1991, 1-3.).

''For a Profound Restructuring of the Army,'' *Rilindja Demokratike* [Tiranë], July 20, 1991. (JPRS-EER-91-144, September 26, 1991, 3.).

''The Jails: The Hell and Shame of the Dictatorship,'' *Bashkimi* [Tiranë], July 21, 1991. (JPRS-EER-91-121, August 13, 1991, 1-4.).

''Law on Amnesty for Political Prisoners,'' *Gazeta Zyrtare* [Tiranë], October 1991. (JPRS-EER-92-024-S, March 3, 1992, 1-2.).

''Should the Sale of Arms Be Legalized or Should All Weapons Be Confiscated?'' *Bashkimi* [Tiranë], July 17, 1991. (JPRS-EER-91-113, August 1, 1991, 2-3.).

Lange, Klaus. ''Albanian Security Policies: Concepts, Meaning and Realisation.'' Pages 209-19 in Jonathan Eyal (ed.), *The Warsaw Pact and the Balkans: Moscow's Southern Flank.* New York: St. Martin's Press, 1989.

Larrabee, F. Stephen. ''Long Memories and Short Fuses: Change and Instability in the Balkans,'' *International Security,* 15, No. 3, Winter 1990-91, 58-91.

The Military Balance, 1990-1991. London: International Institute for Strategic Studies, 1990.

Nelson, Daniel N. *Balkan Imbroglio: Politics and Security in Southeastern Europe.* Boulder, Colorado: Westview Press, 1991.

Pollo, Stefanaq, and Arben Puto. *The History of Albania: From Its Origins to the Present Day.* London: Routledge and Kegan Paul, 1981.

Zanga, Louis. ''Increase in Crime and Other Social Problems,'' Radio Free Europe/Radio Liberty, *Report on Eastern Europe,* 2, No. 39, September 27, 1991, 1-4.

______. ''Military Undergoes Reforms,'' Radio Free Europe/Radio Liberty, *Report on Eastern Europe,* 2, No. 46, November 15, 1991, 1-3.

______. ''The New Government and Its Program,'' Radio Free Europe/Radio Liberty, *Report on Eastern Europe,* 2, No. 23, June 7, 1991, 1-5.

______. ''Sigurimi Dissolved and Replaced,'' Radio Free Europe/Radio Liberty, *Report on Eastern Europe,* 2, No. 35, August 30, 1991, 19-21.

Glossary

bajrak—A political union of Geg clans under a single head, the *bajraktar* (*q.v.*). Term literally means "standard" or "banner."

bajraktar—The hereditary leader of a *bajrak* (*q.v.*). Term literally means "standard bearer."

Bektashi—An order of dervishes of the Shia branch of the Muslim faith founded, according to tradition, by Hajji Bektash Wali of Khorasan, in present-day Iran, in the thirteenth century and given definitive form by Balim, a sultan of the Ottoman Empire in the sixteenth century. Bektashis continue to exist in the Balkans, primarily in Albania, where their chief monastery is at Tiranë.

bey—Ruler of a province under the Ottoman Empire.

caliph—Title of honor adopted by the Ottoman sultans in the sixteenth century, after Sultan Selim I conquered Syria and Palestine, made Egypt a satellite of the Ottoman Empire, and was recognized as guardian of the holy cities of Mecca and Medina. Term literally means "successor"; in this context, the successor of the Prophet Muhammad.

Comecon (Council for Mutual Economic Assistance)—A multilateral economic alliance headquartered in Moscow. Albania was effectively expelled from Comecon in 1962 after the rift in relations between Moscow and Tiranë. Members in 1989 were Bulgaria, Cuba, Czechoslovakia, the German Democratic Republic (East Germany), Hungary, Mongolia, Poland, Romania, the Soviet Union, and Vietnam. Comecon was created in 1949, ostensibly to promote economic development of member states through cooperation and specialization, but actually to enforce Soviet economic domination of Eastern Europe and to provide a counterweight to the Marshall Plan. Also referred to as CEMA or CMEA.

Cominform (Communist Information Bureau)—An international organization of communist parties, founded and controlled by the Soviet Union in 1947 and dissolved in 1956. The Cominform published propaganda touting international communist solidarity but was primarily a tool of Soviet foreign policy. The Communist Party of Yugoslavia was expelled in June 1948.

Conference on Security and Cooperation in Europe (CSCE)—Furthers European security through diplomacy, based on respect for human rights, and a wide variety of policies and commitments of its more than fifty Atlantic, European, and

Asian member countries. Founded in August 1975, in Helsinki, when thirty-five nations signed the Final Act, a politically binding declaratory understanding of the democratic principles governing relations among nations, which is better known as the Helsinki Accords (*q.v.*).

Constantinople—Originally a Greek city, Byzantium, it was made the capital of the Byzantine Empire by Constantine the Great and was soon renamed Constantinople in his honor. The city was captured by the Turks in 1453 and became the capital of the Ottoman Empire. The Turks called the city Istanbul, but most of the non-Muslim world knew it as Constantinople until about 1930.

cult of personality—A term coined by Nikita S. Khrushchev at the Twentieth Congress of the Communist Party of the Soviet Union in 1956 to describe the rule of Joseph V. Stalin, during which the Soviet people were compelled to deify the dictator. Other communist leaders, particularly Albania's Enver Hoxha, followed Stalin's example and established a cult of personality around themselves.

democratic centralism—A Leninist doctrine requiring discussion of issues until a decision is reached by the party. After a decision is made, discussion concerns only planning and execution. This method of decision making directed lower bodies unconditionally to implement the decisions of higher bodies.

European Community (EC)—The EC comprises three communities: the European Coal and Steel Community (ECSC), the European Economic Community (EEC, also known as the Common Market), and the European Atomic Energy Community (Euratom). Each community is a legally distinct body, but since 1967 they have shared common governing institutions. The EC forms more than a framework for free trade and economic cooperation: the signatories to the treaties governing the communities have agreed in principle to integrate their economies and ultimately to form a political union. Belgium, France, Italy, Luxembourg, the Netherlands, and the Federal Republic of Germany (then West Germany) are charter members of the EC. Britain, Denmark, and Ireland joined on January 1, 1973; Greece became a member on January 1, 1981; and Portugal and Spain entered on January 1, 1986. In late 1991, Czechoslovakia, Hungary and Poland applied for membership.

European Currency Unit (ECU)—Instituted in 1979, the ECU is the unit of account of the EC (*q.v.*). The value of the ECU is determined by the value of a basket that includes the currencies of all EC member states. In establishing the value of the basket, each member's currency receives a share that reflects the relative strength and importance of the member's economy. In 1987 one ECU was equivalent to about one United States dollar.

European Economic Community (EEC)—See European Community.

GDP (gross domestic product)—A measure of the total value of goods and services produced by the domestic economy during a given period, usually one year. Obtained by adding the value contributed by each sector of the economy in the form of profits, compensation to employees, and depreciation (consumption of capital). Only domestic production is included, not income arising from investments and possessions owned abroad, hence the use of the word *domestic* to distinguish GDP from gross national product (GNP—*q.v.*). Real GDP is the value of GDP when inflation has been taken into account.

glasnost'—Public discussion of issues; accessibility of information so that the public can become familiar with it and discuss it. The policy in the Soviet Union in the mid- to late 1980's of using the media to make information available on some controversial issues, in order to provoke public discussion, challenge government and party bureaucrats, and mobilize greater support for the policy of *perestroika (q.v.)*.

GNP—(gross national product)—GDP (*q.v.*) plus the net income or loss stemming from transactions with foreign countries. GNP is the broadest measurement of the output of goods and services by an economy. It can be calculated at market prices, which include indirect taxes and subsidies. Because indirect taxes and subsidies are only transfer payments, GNP is often calculated at a factor cost, removing indirect taxes and subsidies.

Helsinki Accords—Signed in August by all the countries of Europe (except Albania) plus Canada and the United States at the conclusion of the first meeting of the Conference on Security and Cooperation in Europe, the Helsinki Accords endorsed general principles of international behavior and measures to enhance security and addressed selected economic, environmental, and humanitarian issues. In essence, the Helsinki Accords confirmed existing, post-World War II national boundaries and obligated signatories to respect basic principles of human rights. Helsinki Watch groups were formed in 1976 to monitor compliance. The term Helsinki Accords is the short form for the Final Act of the Conference on Security and Cooperation in Europe and is also known as the Final Act.

International Monetary Fund (IMF)—Established along with the

World Bank (*q.v.*) in 1945, the IMF has regulatory surveillance, and financial functions that apply to its more than 150 member countries and is responsible for stabilizing international exchange rates and payments. Its main function is to provide loans to its members (including industrialized and developing countries) when they experience balance of payments difficulties. These loans frequently have conditions that require substantial internal economic adjustments by recipients, most of which are developing countries. Albania joined the IMF in October 1991.

janissaries—Soldiers, usually of non-Turkish origin, who belonged to an elite infantry corps of the Ottoman army. Formed a self-regulating guild, administered by a council of elected unit commanders. From the Turkish *yeniçeri;* literally, new troops.

Kosovo—A province of the Serbian Republic of Yugoslavia that shares a border with Albania and has a population that is about 90 percent Albanian. Serbian nationalists fiercely resist Albanian control of Kosovo, citing Kosovo's history as the center of a medieval Serbian Kingdom that ended in a defeat by the Ottoman Turks at the Battle of Kosovo Polje in 1389. Residents of Kosovo are known as Kosovars.

lek (L)—Albanian national currency unit consisting of 100 qintars. In early 1991, the official exchange rate was L6.75 to US$1; in September 1991, it was L25 = US$1; and in March 1993, the exchange rate was L109.62 = US$1.

machine tractor stations—State organizations that owned the major equipment needed by farmers and obtained the agricultural products from collectivized farms. First developed in the Soviet Union and adopted by Albania during the regime of Enver Hoxha.

Marxism-Leninism/Marxist-Leninist—The ideology of communism, developed by Karl Marx and refined and adapted to social and economic conditions in Russia by Lenin, which guided the communist parties of many countries including Albania and the Soviet Union. Marx talked of the establishment of the dictatorship of the proletariat after the overthrow of the bourgeoisie as a transitional socialist phase before the achievement of communism. Lenin added the idea of a communist party as the vanguard or leading force in promoting the proletarian revolution and building communism. Stalin and subsequent East European leaders, including Enver Hoxha, contributed their own interpretations of the ideology.

most-favored-nation status—Under the provisions of the General Agreement on Tariffs and Trade (GATT), when one country accords another most-favored-nation status it agrees to extend to that country the same trade concessions, e.g., lower tariffs or reduced nontariff barriers, which it grants to any other recipients having most-favored-nation status. In June 1992, Albania received most-favored-nation status from the United States.

net material product—The official measure of the value of goods and services produced in Albania, and in other countries having a planned economy, during a given period, usually a year. It approximates the term gross national product (GNP—*q.v.*) used by economists in the United States and in other countries having a market economy. The measure, developed in the Soviet Union, was based on constant prices, which do not fully account for inflation, and excluded depreciation.

Ottoman Empire—Formed in the thirteenth and fourteenth centuries when Osman I, a Muslim prince, and his successors, known in the West as Ottomans, took over the Byzantine territories of western Anatolia and southeastern Europe and conquered the eastern Anatolian Turkmen principalities. The Ottoman Empire disintegrated at the end of World War I; the center was reorganized as the Republic of Turkey, and the outlying provinces became separate states.

pasha—Title of honor held by members of the Muslim ruling class in the Ottoman Empire.

perestroika—Literally, restructuring. Mikhail S. Gorbachev's campaign in the Soviet Union in the mid- to late 1980s to revitalize the economy, party, and society by adjusting economic, political, and social mechanisms. Announced at the Twenty-Seventh Party Congress in August 1986.

Shia (from Shiat Ali, the Party of Ali)—A member of the smaller of the two great divisions of Islam. The Shia supported the claims of Ali and his line to presumptive right to the caliphate and leadership of the Muslim community, and on this issue they divided from the Sunni (*q.v.*) in the first great schism within Islam. In 1944, when the communists assumed power in Albania, about 25 percent of the country's Muslims belonged to an offshoot of the Shia branch known as Bektashi (*q.v.*).

Stalinism/Stalinist—The authoritarian practices, including mass terror, and bureaucratic applications of the principles of Marxism-Leninism (*q.v.*) in the Soviet Union under Joseph V. Stalin and in East European communist countries.

Sublime Porte (or Porte)—The palace entrance that provided access to the chief minister of the Ottoman Empire, who represented the government and the sultan (*q.v.*). Term came to mean the Ottoman government.

sultan—The supreme ruler of the Ottoman Empire. Officially called the *padishah* (Persian for high king or emperor), the sultan was at the apex of the empire's political, military, judicial, social, and religious hierarchy.

Sunni (from Sunna, meaning "custom," having connotations of orthodoxy in theory and practice)—A member of the larger of the two great divisions within Islam. The Sunnis supported the traditional (consensual) method of election to the caliphate and accepted the Umayyad line. On this issue, they divided from the Shia (*q.v.*) in the first great schism within Islam. In 1944, when the communists assumed power in Albania, about 75 percent of the country's Muslims were Sunnis.

Titoist—A follower of the political, economic, and social policies associated with Josip Broz Tito, Yugoslav prime minister from 1943 and later president until his death in 1980, whose nationalistic policies and practices were independent of and often in opposition to those of the Soviet Union.

Treaty of San Stefano—A treaty signed by Russia and the Ottoman Empire on March 3, 1878, concluding the Russo-Turkish War of 1877–78. If implemented, would have greatly reduced Ottoman holdings in Europe and created a large, independent Bulgarian state under Russian protection. Assigned Albanian-populated lands to Serbia, Montenegro, and Bulgaria. Substantially revised at Congress of Berlin, after strong opposition from Great Britain and Austria-Hungary.

Uniate Church—Any Eastern Christian church that recognizes the supremacy of the pope but preserves the Eastern Rite. Members of the Albanian Uniate Church are concentrated in Sicily and southern Italy, and are descendants of Orthodox Albanians who fled the Ottoman invasions, particularly after the death of Skanderbeg in 1468.

Warsaw Treaty Organization—Formal name for Warsaw Pact. Political-military alliance founded by the Soviet Union in 1955 as a counterweight to the North Atlantic Treaty Organization. Albania, an original member, stopped participating in Warsaw Pact activities in 1962 and withdrew in 1968. Members in 1991 included Bulgaria, Czechoslovakia, East Germany, Hungary, Poland, Romania, and the Soviet Union. Before it was formally dissolved in April 1991, the Warsaw Pact served as the Soviet Union's primary mechanism for keeping political and military control over Eastern Europe.

World Bank—Name used to designate a group of four affiliated international institutions that provide advice on long-term finance and policy issues to developing countries: the International

Bank for Reconstruction and Development (IBRD), the International Development Association (IDA), the International Finance Corporation (IFC), and the Multilateral Investment Guarantee Agency (MIGA). The IBRD, established in 1945, has the primary purpose of providing loans to developing countries for productive projects. The IDA, a legally separate loan fund administered by the staff of the IBRD, was set up in 1960 to furnish credits to the poorest developing countries on much easier terms than those of conventional IBRD loans. The IFC, founded in 1956, supplements the activities of the IBRD through loans and assistance designed specifically to encourage the growth of productive private enterprises in less developed countries. The president and certain senior officers of the IBRD hold the same positions in the IFC. The MIGA, which began operating in June 1988, insures private foreign investment in developing countries against such non-commercial risks as expropriation, civil strife, and inconvertibility. The four institutions are owned by the governments of the countries that subscribe their capital. To participate in the World Bank group, member states must first belong to the IMF (*q.v.*).

Young Turks—A Turkish revolutionary nationalist reform party, officially known as the Committee of Union and Progress (CUP), whose leaders led a rebellion against the Ottoman sultan and effectively ruled the Ottoman Empire from 1908 until shortly before World War I.

Yugoslavia—Established in 1918 as the Kingdom of the Serbs, Croats, and Slovenes. The kingdom included the territory of present-day Bosnia and Hercegovina, Macedonia, Montenegro, Serbia, Croatia, and Slovenia. Between 1929 and 1945, the country was called the kingdom of Yugoslavia (land of the South Slavs). In 1945 Yugoslavia became a federation of six republics under the leadership of Josip Broz Tito. In 1991 Yugoslavia broke apart because of long-standing internal disputes among its republics and weak central government. The secession of Croatia and Slovenia in mid-1991 led to a bloody war between Serbia and Croatia. In the fall of 1991, Bosnia and Hercegovina and Macedonia also seceded from the federation, leaving Serbia (with its provinces, Kosovo and Vojvodina) and Montenegro as the constituent parts of the federation. Under the leadership of President Slobodan Milošević, however, Serbia retained substantial territorial claims in Bosnia and Hercegovina and Croatia at the beginning of 1992.

Index

Contributors

Walter R. Iwaskiw is Senior Research Specialist in Eurasian and East European Affairs, Federal Research Division, Library of Congress, Washington, D.C.

Amy Knight is Senior Research Specialist in Eurasian and East European Affairs, Federal Research Division, Library of Congress, Washington, D.C.

Karl Wheeler Soper is Analyst of Eurasian and East European Affairs, U.S. Navy, Washington, D.C.

Charles Sudetic is Correspondent for the *New York Times,* covering Yugoslavia, Bosnia, Croatia, Albania, Bulgaria, and Romania.

Raymond E. Zickel is Head, Eurasian and East European Section, Federal Research Division, Library of Congress, Washington, D.C.

Published Country Studies

(Area Handbook Series)

550-65	Afghanistan	550-87	Greece
550-98	Albania	550-78	Guatemala
550-44	Algeria	550-174	Guinea
550-59	Angola	550-82	Guyana and Belize
550-73	Argentina	550-151	Honduras
550-169	Australia	550-165	Hungary
550-176	Austria	550-21	India
550-175	Bangladesh	550-154	Indian Ocean
550-170	Belgium	550-39	Indonesia
550-66	Bolivia	550-68	Iran
550-20	Brazil	550-31	Iraq
550-168	Bulgaria	550-25	Israel
550-61	Burma	550-182	Italy
550-50	Cambodia	550-30	Japan
550-166	Cameroon	550-34	Jordan
550-159	Chad	550-56	Kenya
550-77	Chile	550-81	Korea, North
550-60	China	550-41	Korea, South
550-26	Colombia	550-58	Laos
550-33	Commonwealth Caribbean, Islands of the	550-24	Lebanon
550-91	Congo	550-38	Liberia
550-90	Costa Rica	550-85	Libya
550-69	Côte d'Ivoire (Ivory Coast)	550-172	Malawi
550-152	Cuba	550-45	Malaysia
550-22	Cyprus	550-161	Mauritania
550-158	Czechoslovakia	550-79	Mexico
550-36	Dominican Republic and Haiti	550-76	Mongolia
550-52	Ecuador	550-49	Morocco
550-43	Egypt	550-64	Mozambique
550-150	El Salvador	550-35	Nepal and Bhutan
550-28	Ethiopia	550-88	Nicaragua
550-167	Finland	550-157	Nigeria
550-155	Germany, East	550-94	Oceania
550-173	Germany, Fed. Rep. of	550-48	Pakistan
550-153	Ghana	550-46	Panama

550–156	Paraguay
550–185	Persian Gulf States
550–42	Peru
550–72	Philippines
550–162	Poland
550–181	Portugal
550–160	Romania
550–37	Rwanda and Burundi
550–51	Saudi Arabia
550–70	Senegal
550–180	Sierra Leone
550–184	Singapore
550–86	Somalia
550–93	South Africa
550–95	Soviet Union
550–179	Spain
550–96	Sri Lanka
550–27	Sudan
550–47	Syria
550–62	Tanzania
550–53	Thailand
550–89	Tunisia
550–80	Turkey
550–74	Uganda
550–97	Uruguay
550–71	Venezuela
550–32	Vietnam
550–183	Yemens, The
550–99	Yugoslavia
550–67	Zaire
550–75	Zambia
550–171	Zimbabwe